designing with models

A Studio Guide to Making and Using Architectural Design Models, Second Edition

CRISS B. MILLS

WILEY

John Wiley & Sons, Inc.

Library of Congress Cataloging-in-Publication Data:

Mills, Criss.
  Designing with models : a studio guide to making and using architectural design models / Criss B. Mills. — 2nd ed.
        p. cm.
  Includes index.
  ISBN 0-471-64837-X (pbk.)
  1. Architectural models Handbooks, manuals, etc. I. Title.
  NA2790.M5 2005
  720'.22'8—dc22   200500684

Printed in the United States of America

10 9 8 7 6 5 4

ACKNOWLEDGMENTS

Many of the examples in this book were submitted by students, professors, and architectural offices. Their examples have imparted far greater depth to the text, and I wish to express my full appreciation for their efforts. I also would like to thank Tonya Beach, George Epolito, and Karen McNelly for their valuable contributions throughout both editions, with editing, support, and technical advice.

Cover images: *top row left:* Pittsburgh Children's Museum courtesy of Mack Scogin Merrill Elam Architects; Kimo Griggs Architects; *top row center:* Clemson University, College of Architecture Arts and Humanities courtesy of Studio Critic Keith Green; design by Steven Kendall Keutzer; *top row right:* Musée des Confluences, Lyon, France, courtesy of Coop Himmelb(l)au; *center:* Fine Arts Center, University of Connecticut at Storrs courtesy of Mack Scogin Merrill Elam Architects

FOREWORD

This book is about using the architectural model as a tool for discovery. When used as an integral part of the design process, study models are capable of generating information in time comparable to drawing and offer one of the strongest exploration methods available. The strategies and techniques presented here provide a broad range of options. However, because this book is primarily concerned with the design process, elaborate presentation models are not stressed. Instead, work is explored with quick-sketch constructions and simple finish models that can be built with materials suitable for studio or in-house construction. Although most of the projects are approached from an architectural perspective, the techniques apply equally well to three-dimensional artwork and industrial design.

There are several reasons why models should be part of every design process. Perhaps the most important one is the understanding to be gained by seeing form in physical space. This physical presence allows the designer to interact directly with the model and obtain instant feedback. Another benefit inherent to physical models, as opposed to computer drawings, is the relationship they share with buildings by existing in the world of dynamic forces. While the correspondence is not an exact analog,

physical models can be used to predict structural behavior. This role is traditional in the case of models made for wind tunnels and ship design. Finally, the communicative power of the physical model overcomes problems inherent in conveying three-dimensional computer drawings to a gathering of clients.

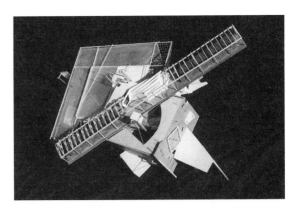

INTRODUCTION

Since the first publication of this book, several changes have taken place in the design industry that need to be addressed.

The most notable change is the use of digital information for the development of design and communication. Accordingly, the information concerning digital modeling programs has been updated, along with the interface between modeling programs and the growing use of rapid prototyping processes.

With the advent of rapid prototyping, a hybrid has emerged that bridges the limitations of computer modeling and points to a future in which it will be possible to exploit the strong points of both methods. An introductory discussion of rapid prototyping can be found in Chapter 8 as well as a number of examples in Chapter 7.

Another important shift in technology is the use of digital media to record and present design work. Cumbersome tasks such as copying, modifying, and superimposing images have become quicker and less expensive. An introduction to digital equipment and design software can be found in Chapter 8.

Other topics undergoing revision include new examples of student projects as well as urban and industrial design models.

MODEL HISTORY

During Egyptian and Greco-Roman times, architectural models were made primarily as symbols. In the Middle Ages with the advent of the cathedrals, masons would move through the countryside carrying models of their particular expertise such as arch building. During the Renaissance, models were used as a means to attract the support of patrons (as in the case of the Domo in Florence, Italy). As architectural education became dominated by Beaux Arts training, models were supplanted almost completely by drawing. Architecture was conceived in large part as elevation and plan studies, with three-dimensional media having little relevance. However, by the late 1800s, architects such as Antonio Gaudi began using models as a means to explore structural ideas and develop an architectural language. By the turn of the century, the seeds of modern architecture had begun to take root. With it came a perspective that looked at architecture as the experience of movement through space. Orthographic and perspective drawing were recognized to be limited exploration methods, giving rise to the model as a design tool. In the 1920s and 1930s, the Bauhaus and architects such as Le Corbusier elevated the use of modeling to an integral component of architectural education and practice. During the 1950s, modernism embodied form by translating highly reductive designs into one or two simple Platonic solids (cube, cylinder, etc). With this shift, beyond providing a means of apprehending scale and massing, the model's role began to wane. As the hegemony of corporate modernism was fractured in the late 1970s, spatial exploration followed a number of new branches and the model regained its position as a powerful tool for exploration. In the early 1990s, the model's role was challenged by a shift in technology. At this point, it was suggested that CAD and modeling programs could substitute digital simulations for all experiences.

While many of the advantages offered by digital media did prove to offer positive benefits, the condition of removal inherent to the virtual experience could not be easily overcome. In reaction to the problem of removal, Ben Damon, an architect with Morphosis (a pioneering office in rapid prototyping), responds to the idea of a completely digital modeling environment by stating, "Physical models will never go away." He goes on to add that the immediacy and direct relationship offered by the physical model play a vital role in design development. Similar sentiments are echoed by James Glymph with Frank Gehry Partners LLP. In regard to digital modeling, Mr. Glymph points out that "it would be a serious mistake to think it could replace models and drawing entirely." With these realizations has come a resurgence of interest in traditional physical models and the introduction of rapid prototype models aimed at reconnecting digital and physical design methods.

CONTENTS

START
Equipment, Materials, and Model Types

This chapter includes the basic equipment and model definitions needed to prepare for modeling. Although an effort has been made to employ common terms, in the absence of industrywide standardization, alternate or overlapping definitions may be encountered in different studio settings.

The equipment and materials presented in this chapter are appropriate to basic study models. For additional information on materials and equipment, see Chapters 5 and 8.

Equipment

The equipment used for the majority of modeling needs is divided into two sets.

Basic Equipment

This equipment can be very simple and is adequate for most modeling tasks.

Expanded Equipment

This equipment can make the job easier and help with specialized tasks. For additional equipment, see Chapters 5 and 8.

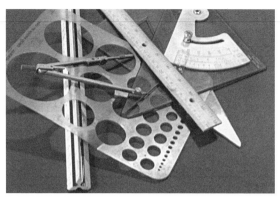

Drafting Tools
A set of common drawing tools used to lay out the model parts.

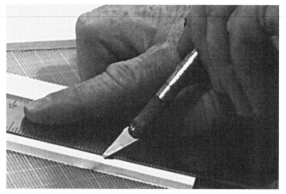

X-Acto Knife and No. 11 Blades
The primary knife. Keep knife sharp with frequent blade changes. Blades are most economically purchased in packs of 100.

Steel Ruler
The primary cutting edge. The ruler should have a nonslip cork backing. For economy, a wooden ruler with a metal edge can be used. Avoid aluminum rulers, as they will dull knife blades very quickly.

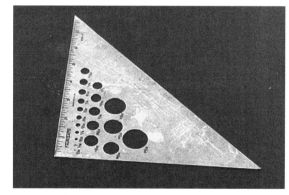

Metal Triangle
Used for right-angle cuts and drafting with the knife. Unfortunately, most metal triangles are made of aluminum, but plastic triangles with steel edges can be found at some suppliers.

Scissors

For quick study models and editing cuts.

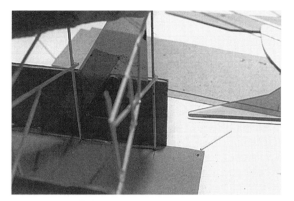

Small Plastic Triangle

Used to square and level model parts for accurate assembly.

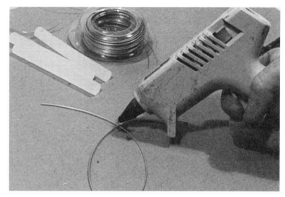

Hot Glue Gun

For quick assembly and hard-to-glue materials like metal. Can be very messy and is not well suited for finish work.

White Glue

The primary adhesive. Keep in a pool on scrap board to air-dry for working thickness. Apply sparingly with a cardboard strip to material edge.

Acetate Adhesive

Used for Plexiglas. A drop on the end of a knife blade can be applied by dragging the blade along the edge of the Plexiglas.

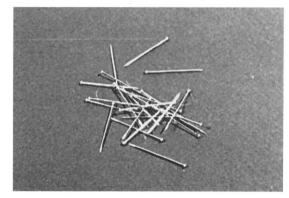

Straight Pins

Used to attach parts while glue is setting. Pins can be pulled, set for reinforcement, or cut off with side cutters.

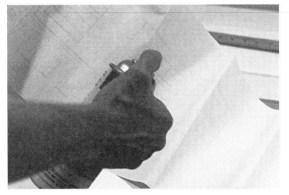

Artist Spray Adhesive
Used for attaching paper surfaces that will buckle with white glue. A very light coat on plans allows them to be used as templates. Avoid hardware store adhesive sprays, as they are too strong for this use.

Matte Knife
For cutting very thick materials. The blade thickness on this tool is not suited for fine work.

Small Metal and Plastic Triangles
Can be used to align model parts for gluing and for making accurate modification cuts directly on the model.

Drafting Tape
Used to attach parts while glue is setting. Avoid masking tape, as it will tear paper surfaces.

Small-Scale rule with End Cut Off
Used for taking measurements directly from the model. A scale can be drawn on a wooden stick to serve the same purpose.

Needle-Nose Pliers
Used for delicate work and as an inexpensive third hand.

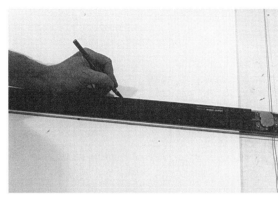

Steel-Edge Parallel Bar

Makes cutting parts much faster. Useful for manufacturing multiple pieces of the same pattern.

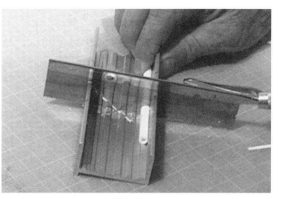

Modeling Saw and Miter Box

Used for clean cuts on small blocks and rods as well as angle cuts.

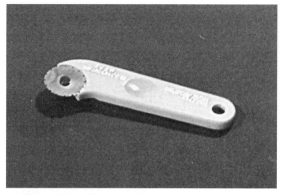

Rolling-Style Pizza Cutter

Used for transferring drawing lines to modeling surfaces. Roll cutter along lines to leave traces in modeling material. Cutters with pointed edges work best.

Sandpaper

Sandpaper can be used to level and remove the burrs from cuts.

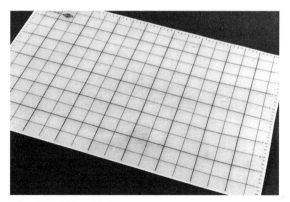

Vinyl Cutting Matte

Used to save drawing-board surfaces.

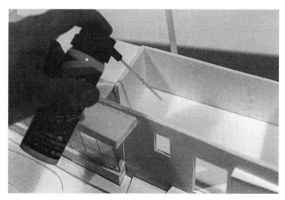

Canned Compressed-Air Cleaner

For cleaning dust off models. Works well for hard-to-reach inside corners.

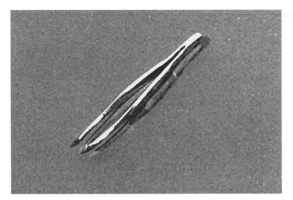

Tweezers
Used to handle delicate parts.

Electric Drill and Small Bits
Used for gang-drilling multistory column holes in floor plates and other special holes.

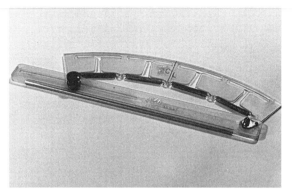

Acu-Arc
Used for drafting smooth, scaled curves.

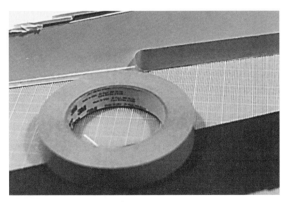

Double-Face Transfer Tape
Used to attach paper without the buckling tendencies of white glue.

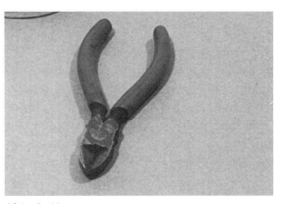

Side Cutters
For cutting pins and wire.

Soldering Gun
For soldering copper and steel wire. *Note:* Use rosin-core solder.

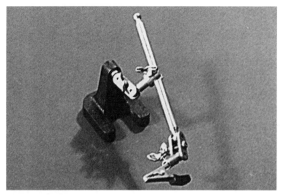

Third Hand
Helps hold parts for gluing, drying, and other tasks.

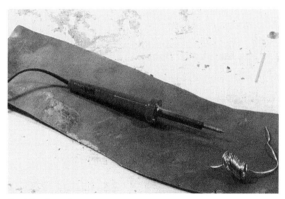

Soldering Iron
An inexpensive alternative to a soldering gun. Small irons like this produce comparatively little heat. They can be used by waiting longer for materials to heat up.

Materials

The following section describes the basic materials used for the majority of modeling tasks. Many choices are available; however, for the purpose of this book, the primary focus is on inexpensive, easily manipulated paperboard materials. See Chapters 5 and 8 for additional materials.

Material Considerations

- The speed with which the model is to be built
- The degree of modification and experimenting desired
- The ability of a material to hold its shape or span at scale modeling distances
- The thickness of the scaled component the model is intended to reflect

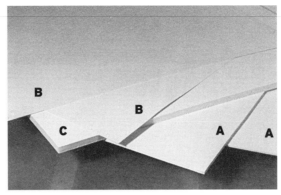

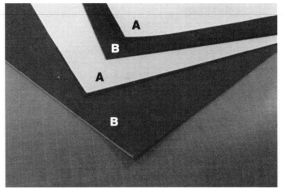

A–Gray Chipboard

- Available in two- or four-ply
- Inexpensive
- Cuts easily
- Spans moderately
- Thicker plys hard to cut
- Rougher finish
- Interesting alternative to whiteboards

B–Corrugated Cardboard

- Sheets are usually ⅛ in. thick
- Rough finish provide
- Interesting alternative
- Inexpensive and cuts easily
- Spans larger spaces well
- Reflects material thickness of midsize to larger models
- Can mock textured surface if top layer is removed

A–Foam Core

- Available in 1/16-, ⅛-, 3/16-, ½-in. thicknesses
- Finished in appearance
- Cuts easily
- Suitable for large scales
- Can be matched to scale thickness

B–White Museum Board (Strathmore)

- Available in two-, four-, five-, and six-ply thicknesses
- Finished in appearance
- Relatively expensive
- Easy to cut
- Thinner plys not suitable for large spans

C–Gatorboard

- A thick, tough board similar to foam core
- Used primarily for model bases
- Finished in appearance
- Very difficult to cut

A–Poster Paper

- Similar to thin museum board
- Inexpensive
- Available at drugstores and office supply stores
- Reasonably finished in appearance
- Suitable for small models
- Easy to cut
- Spans poorly

B–Colored Matte Board

- Similar to four-ply chipboard
- Takes several passes to cut
- Spans well
- Used for coding and contrast
- Edges should be mitered at 45 degrees on nonintegral color board

Note: Integral color board, with color going all the way through, should be used if possible. The exposed white edges of nonintegral color board severely degrades model appearance.

Plastic and Wood Modeling Sticks
Available in square and rectangular balsa or basswood shapes.

Plastic and Wood Dowels
Available in a variety of sizes and lengths.

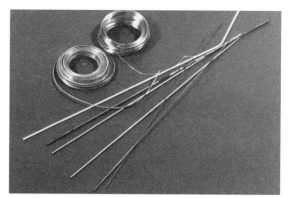

Wire
- White, plastic-coated wire
- Copper, steel, and aluminum rolls
- Straight modeling wire

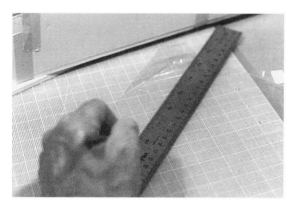

Clear Plastic and Plexiglas Sheets
- Used for glass simulation
- Available as thin Plexiglas from suppliers and hobby shops and as inexpensive picture-framing sheets; avoid thin acetate sheets.

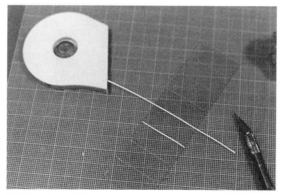

White Graphic Art Tape
- Used for mullion simulation
- $\frac{1}{32}$ in. wide and smaller

Sewing Thread
Can be used to simulate cable lines or thin rods in tension.

Plastic Mylar

Mylar drafting sheets can be easily cut and used for curved translucent panels.

Enamel Spray Paint

- This can be used to paint models and wood rods.
- Automobile primer should be used as an undercoat on cardboard to prevent buckling.

Cloth and Trace

Drawing trace or light cloth can be used to fill in planes and simulate translucent membranes. These materials can be curved and warped as needed.

Metal Sheets

Thin metal sheets can be used to make planes and curving forms (see Chapter 5).

Model Types

Models are referred to in a variety of ways, and terms may be used interchangeably in different settings. Although there is no standard, the following definitions in the following lists are commonly used.

All of the model types discussed (sketch, massing, development, etc.) are considered to be study models, including those used for formal presentations. As such, their purpose is to generate design ideas and serve as vehicles for refinement. They can range from quick, rough constructions to resolved models. Whatever state they are in, the term *study model* implies that they are always open to investigation and refinement.

Study models can be considered to belong to two different groups: *primary models* and *secondary models*. The primary set has to do with the level or stage of design evolution, and the secondary set refers to particular sections or aspects of the project under focus. A secondary model may be built as a primary model type, depending on the level of focus. For example, a model used to develop interior spaces would be thought of as an interior model but would also be a sketch model, development model, or presentation model, depending on its level of focus.

Primary Models

Primary models are abstract in concept and are employed to explore different stages of focus.

Sketch

Diagram

Concept

Massing

Solid void

Development

Presentation/finish

Secondary Models

Secondary models are used to look at particular building or site components.

Site contour

Site context/urban

Entourage/site foliage

Interior

Section

Facade

Framing/structure

Detail/connections

Sketch Models

Sketch models constitute the initial phase of study models. They are like three-dimensional drawing and sketching—a medium for speed and spontaneity.

Sketch models generally are not overly concerned with craft but provide a quick way to visualize space. They are intended to be cut into and modified as exploration proceeds. These models may also be produced as a quick series to explore variations on a general design direction.

Although many of the models shown throughout the book are produced as expressive explorations, sketch models are also valuable when built with greater precision and used to explore qualities of alignment, proportion, and spatial definition.

Sketch models are generally built at relatively small scales from inexpensive materials such as chipboard or poster board.

Several examples of sketch models are shown, ranging from small building propositions to ideas of space and site relationships.

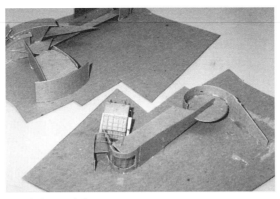

Sketch model
Small alternative sketches can be made early in the design phase to explore basic building organizations and reflect general relationships of program circulation and architectural concerns (actual size, 4 in.).

Sketch model
Sketch models can explore basic relationships between a number of program components (actual size, 11 in.).

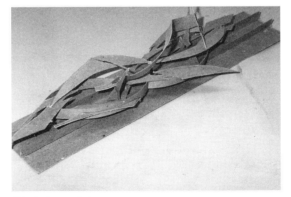

Sketch model
Sketch models can carry genetic information about the way building spaces will flow and read. In this case, the model was a translation of drawing exercises that began incorporating the program (actual size, 6 in.).

Sketch model
Sketch models can explore sectional relationships and act as schematic three-dimensional diagrams (actual size, 6 in.).

Diagram Models

Diagram models are related to sketch models and conceptual models; however, like their two-dimensional counterparts, they map out abstract issues of program, structure, circulation, and site relationships.

Although they are similar to drawn forms, the three-dimensional quality of diagram models can begin to describe space as it relates to architectural issues and suggest ideas for further exploration.

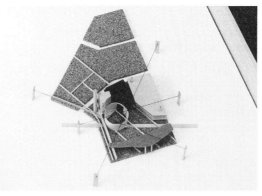

Diagram model
A small model used to map out abstract site relationships and establish initial tectonic elements such as the circular element.

Diagram model
Three alternative spatial organizations diagram relationships between overall circulation and program issues.

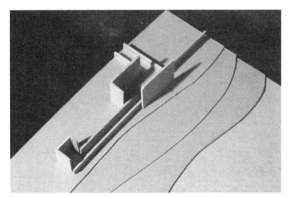

Diagram model
Diagrams can be used to explore the basic organization of site schemes.

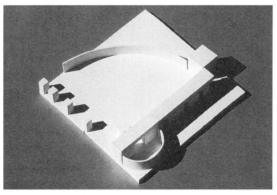

Diagram model
Diagrams can be used to explore basic organizational schemes such as a datum wall to set up overall relationships.

Diagram model
Another simple diagram used to describe contrasting relationship between the indirect processional element and axial the component.

Concept Models

Concept models are built at the initial stages of a project to explore abstract qualities such as materiality, site relationships, and interpretive themes. These models can be thought of as a specialized form of the sketch models and are used as the "genetic coding" to inform architectural directions.

Translations can be made by a variety of means, such as dissecting the model with drawings, using suggested geometries, producing readings based on formal qualities, or interpreting literary themes.

The following concept models were established at the outset of several different projects. Although their use as genetic information is similar, their conceptual bases are quite different and illustrate the degree to which conceptual approaches can vary. Several other examples of concept models and architectural interpretations have been derived from these models. See "Interpreting" in Chapter 3.

Concept model
A model made to explore ideas about shade, light, and shadow.

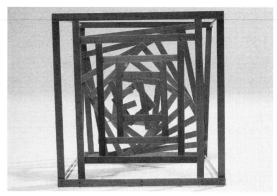

Concept model
A model used to make interpretations of compartments and empty space, based on Andy Warhol's book *From A to B and Back Again.*

Concept model
A model exploring abstract qualities of light and material relationships.

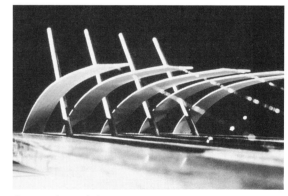

Concept model
A spatial response to interpret passages from the book *Everglades: River of Grass* by Marjory Douglas.

Massing Models

Massing models are simple models that depict volume and are typically devoid of openings. These models can be constructed at small scales due to their lack of detail and will quickly reflect a building's size and proportion at an early stage.

Massing models are used in a similar manner to sketch models and solid/void models. At times they may be built as partial solid/void models.

Massing model
Small massing models are typical of the building representations used for site plans.

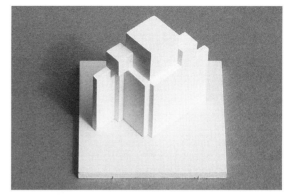

Massing model
The kind of block massing typical of models that reflect only the solid form of the building.

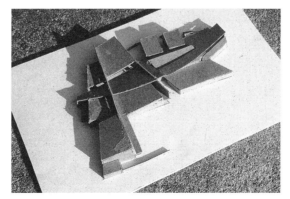

Massing model
Very small models lend themselves to simple massing interpretations, as all but the largest of voids will have little meaning at this scale.

Massing model
Massing models can be made in any number of forms, but their defining characteristic is the absence of openings.

Solid/Void Models

Solid/void models can be built as development or sketch models, but unlike massing models, they display the relationship between the open and closed areas of the building. Generally, these models are more useful for understanding a building's character than simple massing models. A comparison with massing models reveals the potential misreading of character conveyed by massing models, particularly in less conventional designs.

The examples primarily reflect models that have reached the stage of development models; however, any of these studies could have been made at very small sizes and still have displayed the differences between open space and solid mass. The main difference imposed by size is that smaller openings can be omitted as the model is decreased in size.

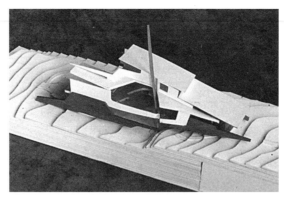

Solid/void model
The central void and linear nature of wall and roof planes is easily read in this solid/void study.

Solid/void model
This model type is somewhere between a development model and a refined sketch model. *Note:* All major voids have been incorporated to reflect the light and open quality of the building.

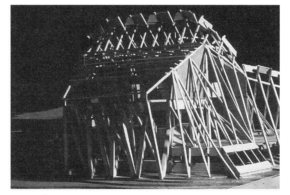

Solid/void model
This model represents an extreme case where the voids are all important and use of pure massing would offer very little comprehension of the space.

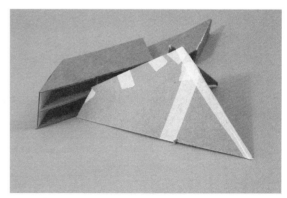

Solid/void model
A simple model that can be visualized as a massing model and then compared with the effect of cutting out primary openings.

Development Models

Use of development models implies that some initial decisions have been made and a second or third level of exploration is being conducted. It also implies that the overall geometry remains fixed, and at least one intermediate stage of exploration will be executed before proceeding to the presentation model. This stage may involve looking at alternate wall treatments, refining proportions, or developing alternate elements.

Development models are typically increased in scale from the previous sketch studies to allow the designer to focus on the next level of design.

The examples can, in some instances, be considered to be finish models. The main difference is that they are essentially abstract representations of building relationships and are still open to modification and refinement. Moreover, they have not been detailed to reflect such aspects as material thickness and glazing.

In a number of cases, after further exploration, the building design may end with a development model or with drawing as a means to communicate the final level of details.

For more on development models and their place in the progression of building design, see "Development" in Chapter 3.

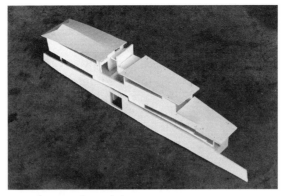

Development model
After several studies, the model was built to reflect basic decisions accurately. At this stage, relationships in the middle section of the building were refined, as were wall and roof configurations.

Development model
A typical level of design resolution at the development model stage. General building relationships have been established, but window openings and other details are undergoing design development consideration.

Development model
Complex geometric patterns have been established at this stage, but the model has not been taken to the level of defining glass planes and material hierarchies.

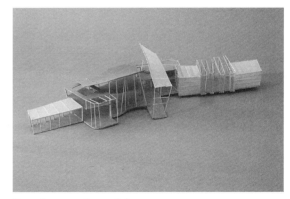

Development model
This is a refined study in which relationships and proportions have been adjusted. At this stage, the designer is ready to begin overlaying a second layer of architectural detail.

Presentation/Finish Models

The terms *presentation model* and *finish model* are used interchangeably to describe models that represent a completed design and are built with attention to craftsmanship.

They are used to confirm design decisions and communicate with clients who may not fully appreciate the implications of rougher studies.

Finish models are typically built as monochromatic constructions made from one material, such as foam core or museum board. This blank, abstract treatment allows the model to be read in many ways without the potential distractions of material simulations. White or light-colored materials such as balsa wood are also used because shadow lines, voids, and planes are well articulated by light.

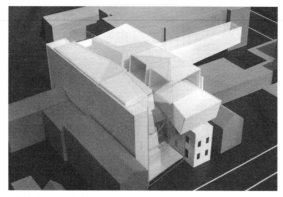

Finish model
A wood finish model is shown in the space of a site context model. *Note:* The context model is treated as a massing model to focus attention on the new building.

Finish model
A well-detailed finish model at this scale of study. It can be compared to the development model for the same project on the preceding page (lower right).

Finish model
This finish model delineates the structure and glass mullions. With this definition of enclosure, it is not necessary to provide glazing. *Note:* The different material elements of the building have been color coded.

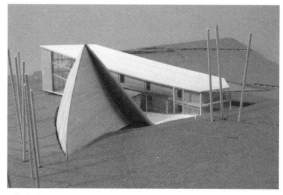

Finish model
A small-scale basswood model cut into the grades of the site model. The model is simple but conveys all the basic characteristics of the architecture.

Site Contour Models

Site models, or contour models, are built to study topography and the building's relationship to the site. They typically reproduce the slope of the land, or *grade,* by employing a series of scaled layers that represent increments of rise and fall in the landscape.

As study constructions, they can be modified to fit the building to the site, control water, and implement landscape design.

Site contour
A typical contour model displays site grades at regular intervals. Grade increments may represent anywhere from 6 in. to 5 ft, depending on the size of the site and the size of the model.

Site contour
A steeply sloped site is modeled with faceted, corrugated-cardboard planes.

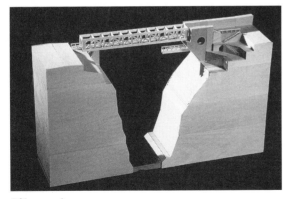

Site contour
Steep site contours may be modeled as a section of property limited to the area of focus.

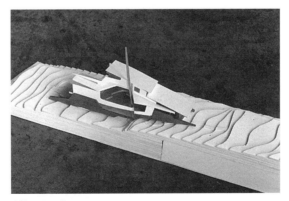

Site contour
A site model is often limited to the property lines and appears as a section of the landscape.

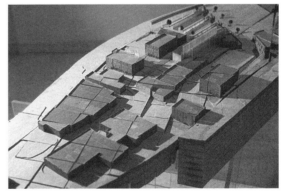

Site contour
In modeling relatively large, flat areas such as urban blocks, contours may reflect only the character of the urban street grid.

Context Models and Urban Models

Context models are models that show the surrounding buildings. They are built to study the building's relationship to the mass and character of existing architecture. Context models can be used to show an existing building on the property or the neighboring area, or expand to include an entire urban section.

Context models are incorporated into contour models and allow issues of grading and landscape design to be explored in relation to the building.

It is typical to treat the existing buildings of a context model as mass models, using neutral coloring to allow the new work to read as contrasting construction.

Context models can be built to accommodate different projects by leaving a blank hole to fit various buildings into the site. In the example on the bottom right, the ground plane has been built over a hollow void. Context buildings are then inserted into the hole left in the surface material.

Urban models look at an entire urban condition from sectors of the city to the entire urban settlement. They are used like other study models to explore relationships, only on a much larger scale. They usually depict all built elements as massing blocks.

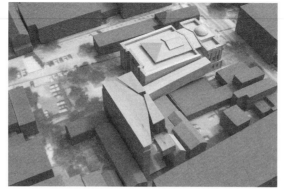

Site context

This project uses an existing building as the site for a building addition. The context building is needed as a basis for reaction and scaling the addition. The completed project is shown with finish models (top left).

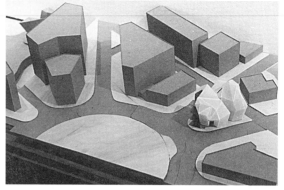

Site context

The immediate context has been expanded to include buildings in a portion of an urban area. Although the buildings do not directly touch the site, they set the overall scale relationships between the existing and new.

Site context/urban model

An example of a context model with a large area of study. The scale relationships between new and existing buildings is critical. The model also functions as an urban model, looking at issues concerning the development of several city blocks.

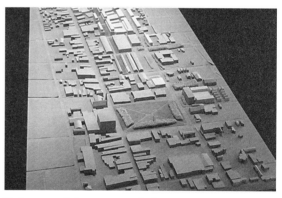

Urban model: green axis/access

This massing study has been built to look at schemes for developing a linear park along an abandoned railroad right-of-way in the north part of Charleston, SC. For more examples of urban study models, see Chapter 8.

Entourage/Site Foliage

Entourage refers to the modeling of people, trees, and site furnishings. Scaled figures are modeled during the investigative stages, to give a sense of the scale of the building. Trees are included at the presentation stage (usually without people). Site furnishings, such as benches, lamps, and so forth, are typically reserved for elaborate model simulations.

For design studies and simple finish models, it is best to treat foliage and entourage simply and abstractly. Elaborate simulations can easily overshadow the building both in terms of its psychological importance and by physically obscuring the project itself.

The examples offer several simple but effective methods used to provide unobtrusive site foliage. For more information on site foliage, see Chapter 2.

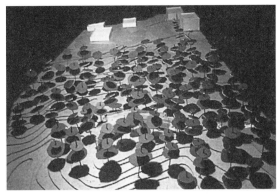

Entourage
Trees have been made by stacking layers of cut paper on wooden sticks. This method lends itself to larger-scale foliage.

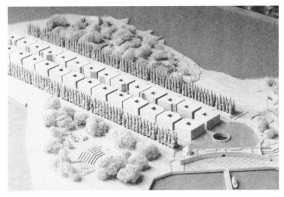

Entourage
Lichen and rolled paper trees have been used for small-scale foliage.

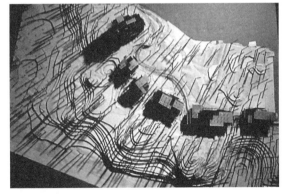

Entourage
Trees have been treated abstractly by using bare plastic rods. This gives a sense of wooded density without interfering with the perception of the building.

Entourage
Yarrow trees or dried plants can be used for larger-scale models.

Interior Models

Interior models generally function as development models and are constructed to study interior architectural spaces and furnishings. They are built at scales starting at ¼″ = 1′0″ but are more useful at ½″ = 1′0″ and larger. These models need to define the borders of the space but remain open for viewing and accessibility.

The design of interior spaces is approached much the same as the building itself. A designer should realize that a building contains internal space worthy of the same consideration given to the exterior form. By opening up the building and "walking through" the space, observing it in three dimensions, many ideas can be generated.

Interior models typically employ various means to gain visual access to internal space. Rooftops can be removed to look down into the model, sides may be removed to gain horizontal access (as in section models), and holes can be cut into the underside to allow the viewer to look up into the space. In large models, very large openings in the bottom can permit total visual access.

½″ scale house interiors study
This ½″ = 1′ 0″ scale foam core model employs a removable roof for viewing. The scale is large enough to permit reading of details as small as 1 in. and allows components to be developed inside the model.

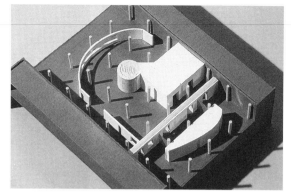

Interior model
This is a case where the entire design is an interior project, and the architecture is worked out in much the same way as external building design.

¼″ scale house interiors study
Existing ¼″ = 1′ 0″ scale models such as this are often large enough to develop interior partitions and circulation elements.

Interior facade
In certain cases, elevations exist inside buildings. If a section is cut through the building to reveal internal elevations, interior and facade models become quite similar.

Section Models

Section models are built to study relationships between vertical spaces. They are produced by slicing the building at a revealing location. The cut is usually made at the point where a number of complex relationships interact and can be jogged or sliced on an angle if needed. The use of section models as study models can be most effective in working out the complexities of relationships, which are often difficult to visualize in two dimensions.

Section models are related to interior models in that they reveal interior spaces. One of the key differences lies in their vertical orientation, in contrast to the plan or top view typically offered by interior models.

Section models are also closely related to facade models and are sometimes referred to as *cutaway elevations* or *section/elevations*.

Section model
A section of a longer building reveals the play of elements and spaces between floor plates, balconies, and the roof form.

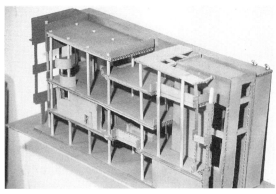

Section model
This section model was built to explore relationships between internal floors and vertical spaces. It can be thought of as an interior model as well.

Section elevation
This model looks at internal sections and allows study of three-dimensional relationships between separate systems and elements.

Section model
Section models can provide another way of looking at interior spaces while maintaining the relationships of the room in a way models with removed roofs cannot easily do.

Facade Models

Facade models are built when isolated elevations are needed for study and refinement. This situation typically occurs with infill buildings where the street elevation is the primary building image. In other cases, facades may be created to serve as context for additions to exterior elevations.

In the context of the urban street fabric, the manipulation of relatively shallow depths is used to create the illusion of greater spatial volumes. This can be taken further to look at the negative space produced by the facade and generate new readings.

Although facade models are ideal study vehicles for flat, orthogonal elevations, they may not prove very useful in determining the character of nonorthogonal geometries.

As noted earlier, facade models and section/elevations can appear very similar to each other. Similarly, interior models also can include internal elevations.

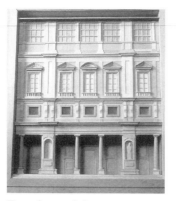

Facade model
A classic example of a facade as it might occur in an infill situation. Relatively flat elevations like this are well suited to facade model exploration.

Facade model
The facade was built to serve as a background to develop the deck and entry canopies. *Note:* The windows have been drawn on rather than cut out as in a solid/void study.

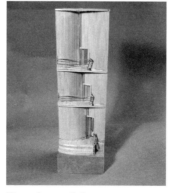

Facade model
A facade model built to work out the design for an infill project.

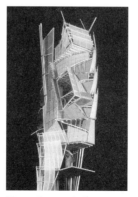

Facade model
Although facade models are typically thought of as articulated flat elevations, isolated studies may also be conducted to focus on sculptural development of the exterior building face.

Framing/Structural Models

A framing/structural model is related to a detail model in that its primary use is in visualizing the relationship between framing and structural systems in space. The exact location of beams, load transfers, and other technical considerations can be determined. When built to large scales, framing models can be used to study the detailing of complex connections.

This model type can also be used to explore creative designs for structures such as bridges and trusses, to convey details to builders, and to test loading characteristics.

Framing models are built at relatively large scales (¼″ = 1′0″ minimum) in order to show the relationship between members.

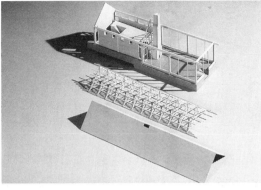

Framing model
Framing models are used to work out the design and location of all structural members and can be extremely useful in working with complex geometries.

Structural model
The lower section of Frank Gehry's Experience Music Project has been modeled to understand the structural system used to support undulating exterior panels.

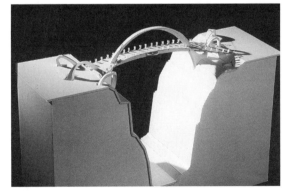

Bridge model
The usefulness of the model in designing structural elements should be apparent when working out innovative solutions to architecturally designed structures such as this bridge.

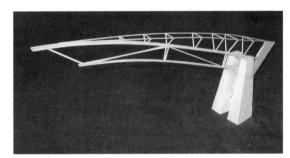

Structural test
A single cantilever truss is made at ¼″ scale to refine the design and test its structural integrity. A simple application of pressure at its end can quickly determine weak points.

Connection/Detail Models

Connection and detail models are built to develop interior and exterior details such as structural joints, window treatments, railings, and fascias.

These models are treated in a similar manner as models of complete buildings but are built at much larger scales to allow the finer readings of form articulation and connections. Connection models are closely related to structural and framing models, as they provide a closer look at critical joints and intersections.

Scales typically range from ½″ = 1′0″ to 3″ = 1′0″. Detail models can be helpful in resolving design ideas and construction details and in facilitating client communication.

The examples demonstrate various ways models can be used to develop building details or furnishings.

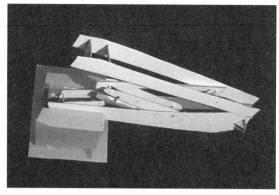

Connection model

This study of ramp supports used modeled components to explore the joint action of members as they were folded together.

Building detail model

This window surround was built at 3″ = 1′ 0″ (a relatively large scale) to study relationships between corner connections and wall depth. This is typical of the way models can be used to develop and refine building details.

Connection model

This model has been built to focus on the design of a specific connection. The way in which the joint is expressed and the mechanical action have been worked out on the model.

Furnishing model

This small study for a movable book carrel was built to explore the effect of shades and adjustable racks.

CONNECT

Basic Techniques for Assembling Model Components

This chapter presents a catalog of basic modeling techniques. Many of the same examples are presented throughout the course of the book in the context of step-by-step models; see Chapter 4. This dual presentation is intended to convey an understanding of where and how the techniques may be used.

Cutting Materials

Cutting Sheets

Cutting sheet material such as chipboard and foam core is accomplished by applying light pressure on a knife and making multiple passes as required for material thickness. A sharp blade is needed, as well as a steel edge with nonslip backing or steel-edged parallel bar. *Note:* Sheets should be cut on a cutting mat or other protective surface such as heavy cardboard.

Foam Core

Foam core is cut using multiple passes, similar to chipboard. Foam core will dull blades very quickly, which means they must be changed often to avoid rough edges. The blade can be angled for mitered joints.

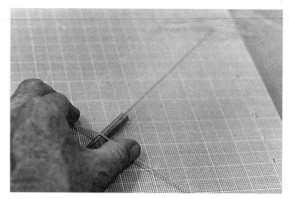

Plastic and Acetate

Plastic sheets are not cut through but must be scored with a sharp blade. This requires a little more pressure, and the score should be made in one accurate pass. After scoring, the score line should be placed over a hard edge such as the knife handle and broken by pushing down on both sides. To help cuts break cleanly, the raised edge may have to run continuously under the cut.

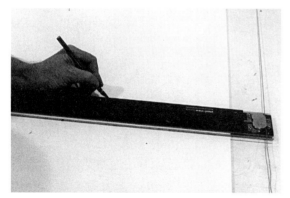

Paper and Cardboard

These materials are cut by pulling the knife in several passes, depending on thickness. A steel-edged parallel bar can be useful for making multiple components such as a series of parallel strips.

Balsa Wood Sheets

Balsa sheets can be treated similarly to heavy cardboard and foam core. Like foam core, balsa sheets are prone to rough edges if knife blades are not changed regularly.

Cutting Sticks and Wire

Sticks employed in model making are primarily made from wood, plastic, or wire. Most of these can be cut with a modeling knife, but if they are large or harder, such as wire, saws and snips will be needed.

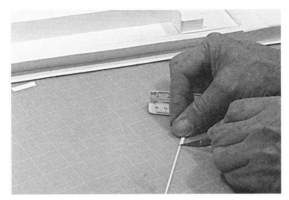

Plastic Sticks

Small rectangular sticks are cut similarly to wood sticks. The ends can be squared with sandpaper.

Large Wood and Plastic Sticks

For larger shapes, the modeling saw and miter box are needed. For difficult cuts, place the raised edge on the bottom of the box over a table edge and saw forward. Chipboard in the box bottom will protect the saw edge.

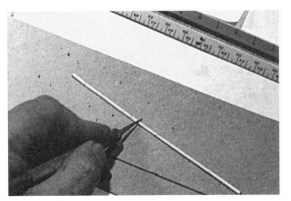

Wood Sticks

Small sticks can be cut by pressing down with the knife. Basswood sticks require more pressure and a slight sawing action. Rough edges can be squared with sandpaper. *Note:* Dull knife blades will crush the wood.

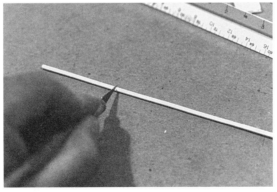

Round Wood and Plastic Sticks

Round sticks should be cut by rolling the knife. Small sticks can be cut completely through, but large ones should be scored and broken on the cut line. Rough ends can be dressed with sandpaper.

Wire and Metal Rods

Small wire snips can be used to cut rolls of copper and steel wire. Heavy electrical dykes are needed for harder rods. A small hacksaw and miter box will be needed to saw bronze and copper tubes.

Cutting and Drilling Holes

There are a number of uses for cutting holes in modeling sheets. Holes can serve as simple notches or sockets to receive other parts, they can provide a positive connection in the modeling base for a series of columns, or they can penetrate a number of common parts to create multiple floor plates.

Holes can be made by cutting or punching with a knife or using a small electric drill. If a knife is used, the No. 11 blade with its thin, tapered point provides the best results.

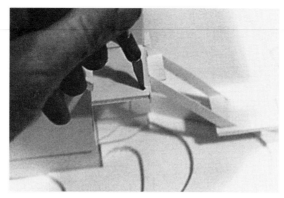

Creating Sockets
Holes cut into the partial depth of foam core create a positive seat to insert columns. To excavate, insert the knife to the desired depth and rotate the blade. Make a tight fit, trying not to overcut the hole diameter.

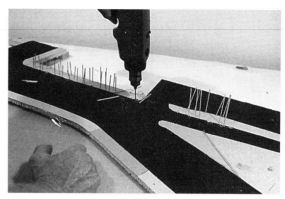

Drilling Column holes
For speed and greater accuracy, an electric drill is useful. An added advantage is that holes can be excavated to greater depths without widening the entry point, as a tapered knife blade tends to do.

Punching Column Lines
For quick studies, holes can be punched with the knife. The material will need some thickness such as corrugated cardboard. Holes can almost be simple slits that sticks are pushed into.

Gang-Drilling Holes
For multiple layers such as floor plates with column penetrations, the plates can be stacked using pins to keep them aligned and drilled through their entire depth. *Note:* A base sheet is used to protect the cutting board.

Trimming and Clipping

In the course of model building, it is often useful and necessary to make cuts directly on the model.

They can be used to make modifications to a study model, to refine a model, to fit parts, or to clean up connections.

Most trimming and clipping can be accomplished with a knife, scissors, and a small triangle.

Cutting New Openings

Openings can be cut with relative accuracy directly on the model using the triangle as a guide and a very sharp knife. Rather than making several passes, push through the material and cut or saw in one pass.

Trimming and Modifying

Scissors can be effectively used on study models for quick cuts. They are less disruptive to lightly glued joints and are capable of making clean, straight cuts over small distances.

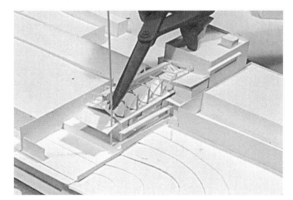

Trimming and Fitting

Small sticks can be trimmed in place with scissors, as their pincer action is less disruptive to delicate joints. This method also provides accuracy for fitting new parts to existing ones.

Cleaning Up Connections

Edges and other protrusions can be modified with the knife by cutting or carefully shaving overlapping connections.

Attaching Parts
Attaching Planes

Model building for study purposes should be an ongoing process with as little time as possible spent waiting for parts to dry. To this end, most materials are assembled with white glue.

When applied properly, white glue will dry quickly; however, cuts must be very straight for this method to work. In instances where drying time is not fast enough, a number of aids, such as the use of pins or tapes, can be employed to allow the designer to continue working. It is important not to overglue model components, as this tends to make them tear and deform when disassembled for experimentation.

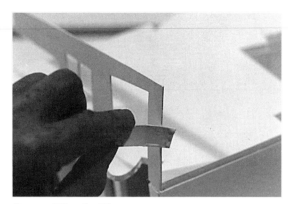

Assembling in Place
Glue can be applied to the material edge of assembled pieces directly on the model.

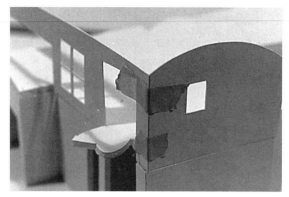

Temporary Joint Connections
For edges that do not dry immediately, use drafting tape for temporary connections. After 10 or 15 minutes, the tape can be removed. *Note:* Avoid masking tape or Scotch tape, as they will tear paper surfaces.

Placing Glue
Keep glue in a pool to work out of. This helps it to become thicker and reduces drying time. Using a small cardboard stick, very lightly coat the edge of material. Too much glue will cause joints to dry much more slowly.

Joining Parts
Press edges together and ensure that they are flush. After several seconds, the connection should be dry enough to hold on its own. Further drying will take place, but the part can be worked with right away.

Pin Connections
Joints can be temporarily held together with straight pins, which can be removed when glue is dry. In cases where joints will be hidden, pins can be pushed in all the way. The end of the knife handle is useful for setting and sinking pins.

Alternative Attachment Methods

There are several adhesives other than white glue that are appropriate to paper constructions, each with advantages and limitations. In applications where face gluing is encountered, such as in site models or paper coverings, the water content in white glue tends to buckle the paper. In these instances, adhesives such as Spray Mount, hot glue, or double-face tape are better choices.

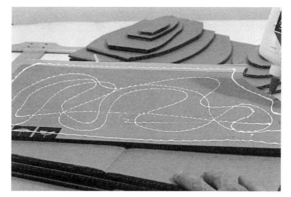

Face-Gluing Contour Models

White glue is effective for thick materials such as corrugated cardboard. For site models that are to be experimented on, glue should be distributed in lines to allow alterations to the layers.

Nonbuckling Spray Adhesives

Apply a light, even coat of adhesive to attach cover materials and paper site contours. Site model contours can be modified as desired; however, holding power is limited.

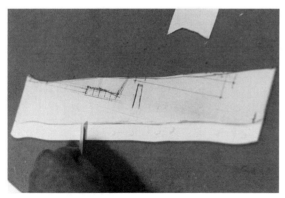

Face-Gluing Sheets

White glue can be used on thick materials such as foam core and corrugated cardboard. For permanent, well-jointed connections, the glue should be spread evenly over the entire surface interface.

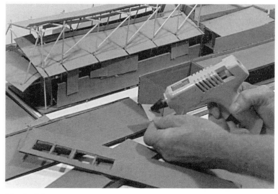

Hot Glue

Due to quick setting time, hot glue is useful for quick sketch and study models where finished appearance is not demanding. Hot glue is also strong and can be used for reinforcing, but it tends to vibrate apart when moved.

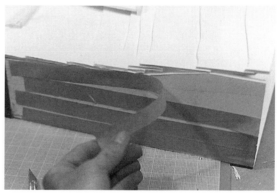

Covering with Transfer Tape

Fill in area with strips, pull away paper backing, and attach cover sheet. Although this is an effective nonbuckling method, the cover sheet must be correctly aligned, as there is no chance for further adjustment.

Integrating Forms

One of the key exercises in exploring readings between elements is to engage the parts in various relationships.

The rough study model makes this exercise quick and effective. Rather than avoiding difficult connections where model parts must share the same space, parts can be held in relative attitudes and quickly cut away, allowing the designer to visualize adjustments.

After final arrangements have been selected, the rough cuts can be recut or refaced; see "Converting" in Chapter 3.

1. After building separate forms, the two parts are placed in approximate plan relationship and traced at the point of intersection. *Note:* For angled relationships, the plan location of entry and exit can be different sizes to reflect the diminishing penetration.

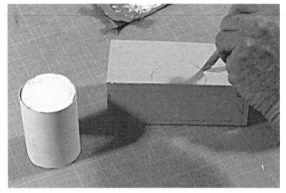

2. The point of penetration is cut out on the box top. *Note:* Material could have been removed from the cylinder instead of the box to achieve the intersection, but the cylinder would have been prone to come apart when removing this much material.

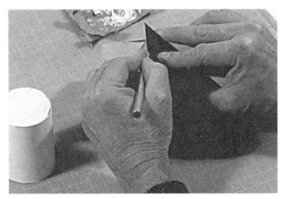

3. Lines from the point of intersection are cut down the face of the box with the aid of the small triangle. *Note:* Blades must be sharp to do this without damaging the box. Scissors are sometimes better employed and create less disruption.

4. Material is removed from the box, and the parts are engaged by sliding the cylinder into the cut.

Attaching Sticks

Attachment methods appropriate to wood, plastic, and metal differ depending on the material and the level of finish desired.

Wood sticks typically use white glue. Hot glue can be used in applicators where more speed is desired.

Plastic sticks are attached with specially designed acetate adhesive, although model airplane glue can be used with some success. It is possible to glue plastic sticks with hot glue for quick studies, but the plastic surface can reject the glue. When attaching plastic sticks to paper, white glue or hot glue must be used in place of the acetate.

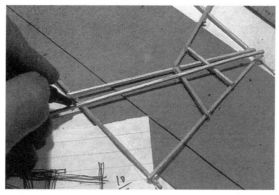

Wood Sticks
Apply a touch of white or hot glue to the end connections and joints. To keep glue from sticking to working surfaces, place construction on top of plastic food wrap or other non-stick surface.

Attaching in Place
Apply a drop of acetate to end of stick and place it in contact with existing framework. Light sticks can be released within a few seconds and remain in place to dry.

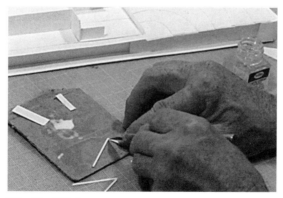

Plastic Sticks
Place a drop of acetate on end of knife blade and transfer it to the joint. The material should be ready to use in less than a minute.

Attaching Dissimilar Materials
Plastic components must be interfaced with paper using white glue, as acetate adhesive will not work with paper or cardboard.

Attaching Plastic Sheets and Wire

Relatively standard methods using acetate adhesive are employed for plastic sheet connections and offer predictable results.

Wire and metal connections in model applications present several problems, and no one solution is ideal. Since white glue does not adhere well to metal, the most practical and effective alternatives are hot glue, superglue, Zap-A-Gap, and solder. Of these, only hot glue and Zap-A-Gap will interface with paper with relative success. Even then results are mixed and a combination of drilled sockets and white glue may be necessary to achieve the desired connection.

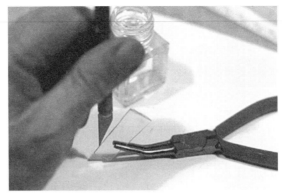

Attaching Plastic Sheets
Spread a thin line of acetate adhesive along the edge of the material. *Note:* A third hand is provided by the needle-nose pliers.

Attaching Wire and Metal
Hot glue can be used; however, joints will not hold if rotated. Superglue and delicate handling is another alternative. White glue can hold to a degree but must be dried for several hours.

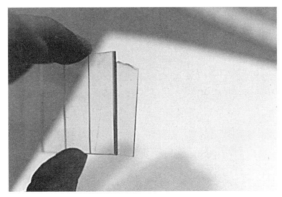

Attaching Plastic Sheets
After applying the acetate adhesive, hold the edges together and wait a minute or more before testing. Joints will be fragile and attaching them can be time-consuming. *Note:* Cuts must be straight or it will be difficult for the glue to adhere.

Acid-Core Solder Connections
Heat wire with soldering gun near connection point. Test wire temperature with the end of solder. When the solder melts, apply it to connection point and allow to cool. Do not melt solder directly with soldering gun.

Fitting Components
Aligning Edges

Once a model is partially constructed, irregularities such as minor misalignments, offsets because of material thickness, and stretched blueline drawings are inevitable despite attention to accuracy. To help ensure tight connections, model components cut from plan and elevation drawings should be checked with the emerging model dimensions before assuming blueline templates will produce parts that fit.

To keep component edges plumb and square, a small triangle can be used. The triangle is particularly important for vertical alignment inasmuch as no drawing lines will be available to follow.

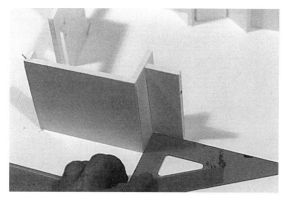

Aligning Plan Components
Place a small triangle at wall intersections and align the parts with triangle edges. For angled intersections, use an adjustable triangle. If walls are short, template the angle off the triangle, cut out shape, and use to align the model parts.

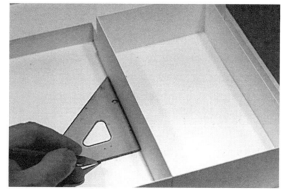

Drafting on the Model
Small triangles can be used to draft guidelines on the model. This is useful when a model is being made without drawings or when new components are added.

Vertical Alignment
For vertical alignment, hold part directly against the triangle, or mark guidelines on the adjoining wall face.

Detailing Connections

As models become larger and more refined, joints reflect greater levels of detail. Edges should read clearly and be accurately scaled. Thicker materials should be dovetailed to conceal interior layers, particularly with the use of colored boards with nonintegral interior layers.

Several conventions are used to code building parts. One of the most commonly employed is the use of standing edges to simulate parapet walls at the perimeter of low-slope roofs.

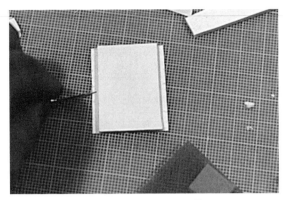

90-Degree Foam Core Intersections

Cut a line into the foam filler equal to the thickness of the intersecting wall and scrape away all the foam down to the paper backing. The remaining paper face can then fit neatly over the edges of intersecting walls.

Corner Detailing

Another method of achieving tight-fitting corners is to cut the material on an angle, as shown. The cuts must be accurate for a good fit, but the angle can vary on the tight side if only one side is exposed.

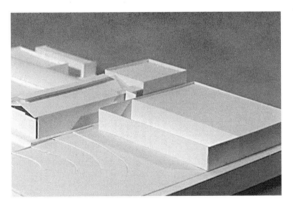

Roof Detailing Conventions

The plane of the low-slope roofs on this context model have been set slightly below the perimeter walls to create a parapet wall. This convention helps code the roof plane as being visually different from the ground plane.

90-Degree Intersection

The wall is placed in relation to its adjoining parts. As the wall is fit together, the edges will meet without any of the core material being revealed.

Compound Joint Detailing

Joints that angle in more than one direction, or *compound joints,* such as shown in the upper right corner of the illustration, can be made by cutting and adjusting test fits, then templating the two ends onto a single piece the full width of the opening.

Handling Small Parts

As model parts become more delicate and refined, it may not be possible to place them by hand. A few simple tools can be employed to help make clean connections.

In the illustrations to the right, tweezers, needle-nose pliers, and a modeling knife are used in various applications. Although their uses can overlap, certain tools are better suited to particular situations than others.

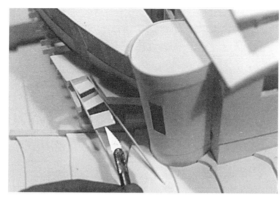

Knife Edge Placement
By inserting the tip of the modeling knife into the paper edge, components can be guided into place. Care must be taken to lightly engage the knife, or else parts can be pulled free when extracting the blade.

Knife Face Placement
Parts can be placed with the knife by gently inserting the knife in the face of the material. Too much blade engagement may leave visible marks in the surface.

Tweezers for Delicate Members
The automatic-release spring action of tweezers allows placement without disturbance, and tweezers can handle parts, such as plastic, that a knife cannot easily penetrate.

Plier Grips
Although it's not as easy to release objects from pliers as from tweezers, needle-nose pliers offer a steady grip for positive placement. By keeping one finger inside the handle, they can be gently opened to release components.

Shaping and Reinforcing

Making curvilinear shapes from various materials can be accomplished in a number of ways. Many specialized techniques are covered in Chapter 5; however, two very common techniques for curving and warping planes are useful at even the basic levels of model building. Planes can be rolled or applied to a series of curved frames.

After pieces have been curved, they can be cut along bias lines to form a number of derivative shapes. Planes also can be made to fit curved armatures and warped in an infinite variety of ways.

For larger components, holding an accurate radius on curved pieces requires some type of reinforcing members. These can usually be hidden inside wall lines or disguised in some way, as they are not really part of the building. This is not to say that they may not become part of the building, because these components may generate ideas for holding the actual building radii and be incorporated into the design.

Reinforcements are also useful under long spans of thin board and at wall edges to support planes and roofs inserted into perimeter walls.

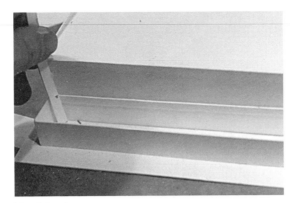

Roof Ledger
A ledger strip has been attached to the wall slightly below the top so that the roof can be dropped in and carried on an even line. The cardboard stick is being used to press the strip against the wall until it sets.

Curving Cardboard
Board can be curved by rolling it over cylindrical objects. It can be pulled across small cylinders for a tight radius or molded on larger objects for gentler curves. Forms should be slightly overrolled, then relaxed to fit.

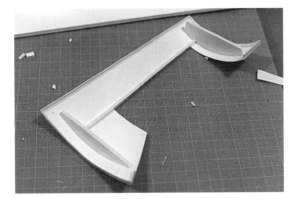

Reinforcing Curves
To maintain large radii, curved reinforcing sections of foam core have been glued into place. *Note:* Edge fascia detailing using scaled curved pieces.

Warped Surfaces
Thin plastic Mylar sheets and tracing paper can be glued to wire or cardboard frames and made to conform to various compound curves. Mylar tends to simulate the qualities of glass but is less pliable than paper.

Templating

Transferring Drawings

One of the quickest methods for transferring drawn information to modeling components is to template them. This is done by cutting through the drawings to score the material below. The drawing is then removed and parts are attached using the score lines as a layout guide.

Alternately, the plans can remain mounted to the model surface and built directly on top. Aside from the visual distraction, this sometimes causes problems, as the walls are glued to the drawing and the drawing is attached only with spray adhesive.

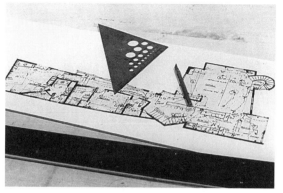

Plan Readied for Transfer

In a typical operation, the plan is secured to the modeling sheet with spray adhesive, then traced lightly with a knife using steel drafting edges. The plan is then removed, and the lightly cut lines are followed when placing components.

Cutting In Elevations

The drawing is cut through to create the fenestration pattern. To avoid overcutting the corners, finish cuts from the opposite side. *Note:* Only the larger window mullions have been reproduced. See "Scale" in Chapter 3.

Spray Adhesive

Apply a light, even coat of adhesive in a well-ventilated area, then spread out the plan smoothly on the material surface by attaching corners and smoothing it down from one end. For large plans, a third hand may be needed.

Drafting with the Knife

Even without plans, a layout can be drafted onto the modeling material with a knife, just as one might draft on paper with a pencil.

A Cut Elevation

A finished elevation is attached to a model. This can be done a number of times to study different opening schemes in the context of the building.

Templating Parts

Parts can be templated, that is, traced directly from the outline of another component, or measured directly from drawings without the use of a ruler.

For complex connections, the process may have to be repeated several times while adjusting the new part each time to fit into the desired form.

Typical Templating Application
A form can be cut to the model shape by tracing around the form and cutting out the desired piece. In the illustration, a top for an irregularly curved conical tower is made quickly using this method.

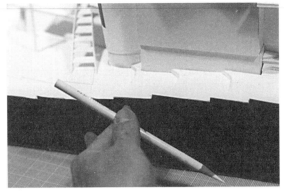

Templating Contours
In a manner similar to projecting contour lines in a section drawing, a side cover is made by placing the modeling material next to the existing model contours and tracing the profile.

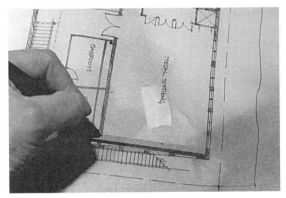

Measuring from Drawings
As the model proceeds, parts such as ledgers and other components can be marked directly from the drawings.

Templating Complex Forms
For complex forms, a rough version can be cut or approximated from several spliced pieces, then transferred to another sheet with adjustments. This can be done several times until the final piece fits accurately.

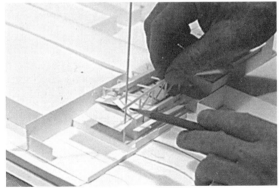

Projecting Lines
Accurate cuts on the model may be located by extending a line with a straightedge to find the intersection point with another component.

Templating Multiples

A template also can be a device that is used repeatedly to reproduce a single item. Templates can be made and used for model building. A very practical application is using a template to make a series of repetitive roof trusses.

This technique can employ a range of approaches from drawing a simple template to building a model jig for mass assembly.

Drawn Template
A simple template can be made by tracing the design on paper and laying each new component over the drawing.

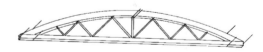

Block-Type Jig Template
Pin-type jigs can be improved by cutting blocks and gluing them to a base to form the boundary edges for truss members. Block-type jigs are stronger and may be needed when making curved trusses.

Cast Multiples
Multiple elements also can be cast from a single mold using plaster or anchoring cement (see Chapters 5 and 8).

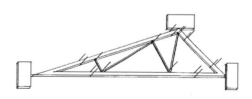

Pin-Type Jig Templating
Pin templates can be made by inserting straight wire pins in a base and laying members inside the defining points.

Braced Curve Template
Curved members can be made by pinning the two ends and using restraining pins in the middle. Once web members are installed and end connections made sound, the truss should hold its shape without the pins.

Finishes

Fenestration

Fenestration, or the act of creating windows and glazed openings, can be accomplished in a variety of ways.

Guidelines for denoting openings should be to keep them simple and to detail only what can be accurately depicted at scale. *Note:* It is usually better to avoid drawing openings on surfaces.

For alternate glazing simulations, overlays can be used as well as plastic sheets with applied mullion patterns.

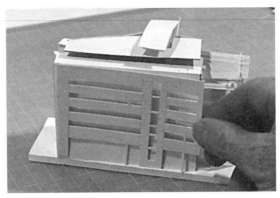

Fenestration Overlay
A simple overlay can be cut and placed on top of a base sheet to provide a subtle reading of openings.

Art Tape on Plastic Sheet
Art tape can be stretched across plastic to create mullions, using score lines as guides. Trim the tape ends after they have been pressed down.

Curtain Wall Glazing
Even small models can use plastic glazing sheets to create glass walls. For small areas and curved pieces, thick acetate can be used. As size increases, sheets of thin plastic will be needed to maintain rigidity.

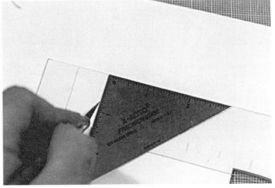

Scoring Mullion Lines
Lines can be scored in plastic with the knife to serve as the actual mullion pattern or as guidelines for applying art tape.

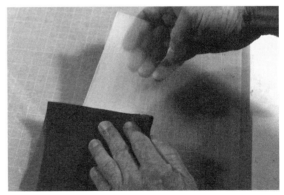

Translucent Glazing
Translucent glass can be made from plastic or thin Plexiglas sheets by sanding one side with very fine paper.

Surfacing

For simple presentation models, final detailing and finishing can be accomplished through clean construction and a few simple techniques.

Surfaces can be covered with additional layers of paperboard to clean up exposed joints and create opening patterns. Edges can be detailed to convey correctly scaled depths.

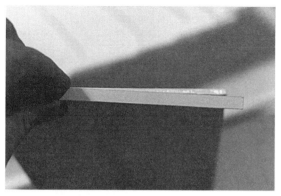

Edging Detailing
Museum board strips, cut to the scale of fascia details, are adhered to the edge of ⅛-in. foam core roof panels. The factory edges of foam core and cardboard sheets are too thin to convey the correct reading for ¼″ scale.

Painting
Models can be cleaned up and finished by light spray painting. Flat automotive primer is recommended as an undercoat for heavy spray painting to prevent paper buckling.

Covering
The model is in the process of being covered with colored construction paper. This is applied by coating paper with spray adhesive, but the paper will eventually separate from the model. For more permanent applications, transfer tape should be used.

Sanding
Rods and sticks can be sanded by rubbing them back and forth across a sheet of sandpaper placed on a flat surface; 100-grit paper will serve for most purposes.

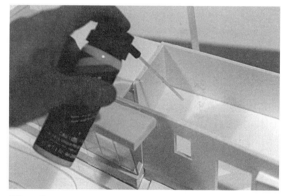

Cleaning
Models littered with postconstruction debris can benefit from cleaning with blasts of compressed air.

Site Work

Solid Contour Model

Select a material thickness that will scale to the desired grade steps. In the example, the scale is ⅛″ = 1′0″ and the corrugated cardboard is ⅛ in. thick, representing 1 ft. grade steps.

Adhesive Guide

Spray Mount (Spray-Type Adhesives)

Paper and chipboard models work best with spray adhesives, inasmuch as the water in white glue tends to buckle the material. Foam core can work with either spray adhesive or white glue. For study models, spray-mounted model layers are much easier to modify.

White Glue

For heavy materials such as corrugated cardboard, white glue may be needed for strength. It can be spread evenly for permanent construction or applied in lines to allow for removal of the layers. White glue can take up to 12 hours to dry when applied to the face of the material.

Hot Glue

Hot glue can be used but can be difficult to disassemble for modifications. Moreover, as the model is moved around, hot glue tends to lose its grip.

1. Use a copy of the contour map to template cuts (apply with spray adhesive to keep it from shifting). The copy can be cut to score the surface of the cardboard, or a pizza cutter can be rolled over the lines to transfer marks to the material.

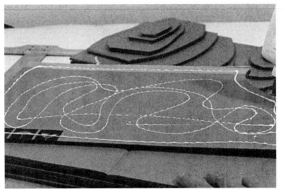

2. Starting with a full sheet the size of the site, cut away the first contour line. Glue this sheet to a base sheet the size of the entire site.

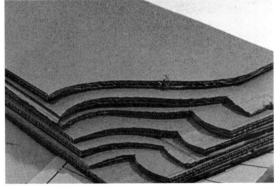

3. Cut away the next contour from another full sheet and place this one on top of the first contour. All layers can be stacked first without gluing. When prestacking layers, splice lines should be marked and grades labeled to help guide reassembly.

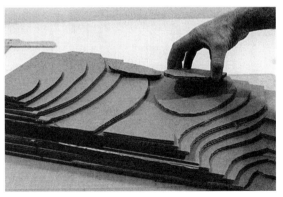

4. Continue stacking contours until they are small enough to use partial sheets, as for hilltops and other small sections. Grades can be lightly labeled on each contour to aid in counting elevations and controlling site work.

Drying

After gluing, the model is weighed down with books or magazines to press layers tight until dry.

Hollow Contour Model

Hollow models are built in a similar manner to solid ones, but only partial sheets are needed.

Contours can be either cut away to insert building volumes or built up around buildings. *Note:* Be careful not to cut along each contour without providing extra material for overlap between the sheets.

See Chapter 4, "Case Study A," for an example built directly on the model.

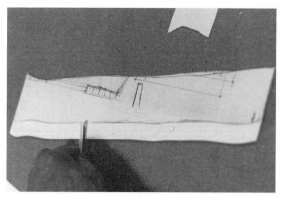

1. Cut sheets with enough area behind the contour line to supply adequate gluing surface (about ½ to 1½ in., depending on the size of the exposed piece and the weight of the material). Mark edges to keep glue out of areas that will be exposed.

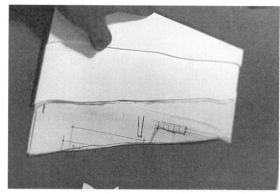

2. Splice the successive contour layers to each other and provide support from below to hold the construction at the proper slope. This can be done by building a series of columns or templating a section with graded steps that follow the rise of each contour.

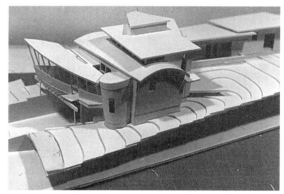

3. With the majority of contours in place, the cavity below is clearly evident, as well as the overlapping splices between partial pieces.

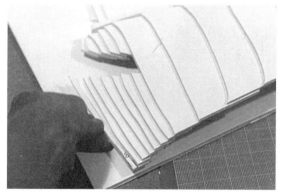

4. Small-grade sections can be completed off to the side and installed as a unit.

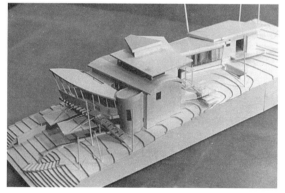

5. The finished construction has side walls added to support the edges at the proper rate of rise. To cut support walls, lay the model on its side and template the pieces. Side pieces can also be drafted as a section projection of the contour map.

Site Foliage

For design studies and simple finish models, it is best to treat foliage and entourage simply and abstractly. Elaborate simulations can easily overshadow the building, both in terms of its psychological importance and in the way they visually obscure the project.

Illustration

The examples offer simple but effective methods commonly used to provide unobtrusive site foliage.

Foliage
Trees have been created using lichen placed on small sticks. The lichen does not interfere with the ability to see the project and works well at small scales.

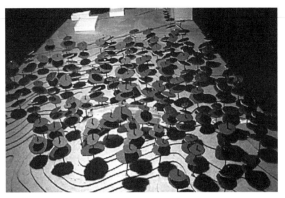

Foliage
Simple trees have been made by stacking layers of cut paper on wooden sticks. This method works better for larger-scale foliage.

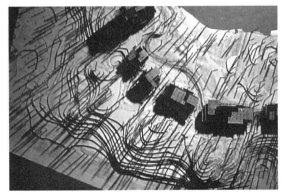

Foliage
The trees have been treated very abstractly by using bare plastic rods to give a sense of wooded density without interfering with the perception of the building.

Foliage
Dense foam can be sanded and shaped to create massing trees and plantings.

Tree Material
Round Styrofoam balls.

Tree Material
Small, dried flowering plants or yarrow trees.

Tree Material
Lichen sold as modeling material or found in sandy areas.

Tree Material
Paper and Styrofoam layers.

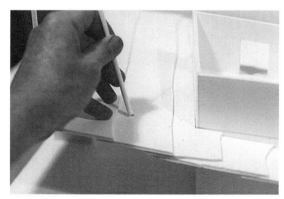

Tree Material
Wood or plastic dowels.

Tree Material
Dense foam sold to make flower-arranging bases and at model supply shops.

Model Base Construction

A number of bases are shown throughout the chapters of this book, and the discussion on contour models in Chapter 2 provides the basic information for base construction. However, some general guidelines are given here.

The main objective of a base is to support the model without warping or sagging. This is easily accomplished on small models but requires reinforcement and heavier material as models gain weight and size. Deep reinforced bases, Gatorboard, and plywood offer solutions in such cases.

Sketch Model Base

Small sketch models can be built on pieces of corrugated cardboard or foam core. Layers can be stacked in rough simulation of sloped sites.

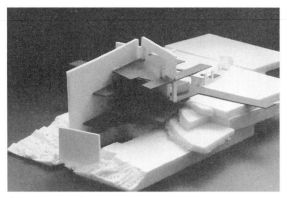

Study Model Base

Foam can be used to create quick grade simulations and provide instant rigidity.

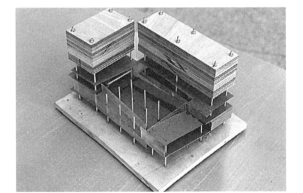

Flat Base

For heavy models such as this solid wood construction, plywood or Gatorboard can be used to make flat bases.

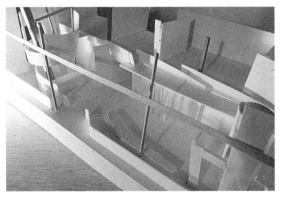

Reinforced Bases

For large models with flat bases, boxes with top and bottom surfaces can be built and reinforced with internal strips running at 90 degrees inside the box. Increased box depth will add strength.

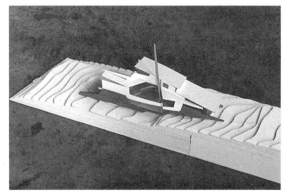

Hollow Contour Bases

Although solid contour models tend to become rigid of their own accord, it is necessary to reinforce the internal spaces of hollow bases with cardboard uprights and horizontal strips.

EXPLORE

A Skeletal Framework for Conceiving and Using Models

The design process is an evolutionary event that involves establishing a direction and developing it through experimentation and refinement. At each stage, a range of studies should be conducted to explore the direction and strength of various design moves.

An Overview of Section Concepts

The following outline presents an overview of the typical stages in the design process for models. The considerations are similar to those of drawn projects, but most of the required information is derived directly from the model. *Note:* The linear form of the outline is one of convention, as many of the steps may be combined or used interactively.

SCALE

Determining appropriate scale based on:

Project Size
Fitting the building and site to the available work space.

Type of Study
Adjusting for the stage of development.

Level of Detail
Scaling for the size of details being explored.

Assigned Scale
Determining scale, after making concept and sketch models without using a fixed scale.

IDEAS

Generating initial information through:

Drawing with the Model
Sketching ideas exclusively with the model using expressive and carefully proportioned approaches.

Working with Two-Dimensional Drawings
Working back and forth between drawn and modeled information.

ALTERNATIVES

Exploring design directions by:

Multiple Approaches
Building multiple solutions or testing multiple treatments on a single model.

Adjustable Models
Using movable parts to explore alternative relationships.

SITE

Integrating site concerns with other design information.

Contour Models
Including site information as an integral part of the initial driving forces for design direction.

Context Models
Responding to environment as it affects initial design direction.

MANIPULATION

Working with models to visualize options:

Modifying and Editing
Cutting and adding parts to design directly on the model.

Modifying Site Contours
Integrating the building with the site.

Digression
Using the unexpected and unintentional to inform design ideas.

Interpreting
Making a fundamental shift in the physical form or perception of the model.

DEVELOPMENT

Developing the project by:

Project Development
Exploring an evolutionary path from initial concepts to a complete project.

Increasing Scale
Building larger models as the investigation moves from general concerns of site and scheme to focused concerns of elevations, interior space, and detailing.

Coding and Hierarchy
Establishing hierarchy and coding to define a range of contrasting elements and code conceptual layers.

Converting
Renovation of existing models versus entirely rebuilding.

Focusing
Moving studies through successive stages of refinement.

Scale
Key Scaling Issues

Models can be built at various scales. The size of the model may not be indicative of the scale, as physically large models may be built at small scales and vice versa. Determining the appropriate scale depends on several considerations, as discussed in the following paragraphs.

Project Size

The size of the model depends on how large the actual building and/or site will be, and is governed by the availability of work space.

Level of Study

The scale and size of the model depend on the level of detail that is needed, such as sketch, development, presentation, interior, or detail.

Level of Detail

The scale of the model depends on the level of detail that is needed. A prime reason to increase a model's scale is to include more detail. A scaled-up model without additional detail may appear ungainly.

Accordingly, it can be more convincing and practical to imagine fine details on smaller models rather than to construct large models with insufficient detail.

Assigned Scale

By maintaining the relative proportions between components, models may be initiated without using a particular scale. A scale can be assigned to a model after it is built. This technique is useful on small sketch studies. In this case, a small model of a human figure can then be made to a size that is correctly proportioned to the building model in relation to how the designer envisions the actual size of the building. The full-scale height of the figure (assumed to be approximately 6 ft.), can then be compared

to various scales on a scale ruler to find the one that matches the 6-ft. dimension of the model figure. This scale can then be assigned to the building model and used to determine its actual, "full scale" dimensions. This can also be done by assuming a typical floor-to-floor height of 12 to 14 ft. on a multistory building (or as appropriate to the project such as 9 to 11 ft. for a typical residential model). The designer then can compare various scales on the ruler to find the one that matches the floor-to-floor heights on the model at the assumed "full scale" dimension. For small models, it will probably be necessary to use an engineering scale rule, where scales between 1″ = 20′ and 1″ = 200′ are available. For an example of this technique at work, see Chapter 4, "Case Study B."

EXAMPLES: SCALE DECISIONS
AND CONSIDERATIONS

- A typical model of a house might be scaled at a maximum of ¼″ = 1′0″ so that an actual length of 96 ft. would occupy 2 ft. of desk space.

- For a larger building involving several hundred feet, a scale of ⅛″ = 1′0″ might be used effectively.

- Large sites usually use engineering scales of 1″ = 50′, 100′, or 200′ to make the model manageable.

- Sketch models typically start at very small scales such as ½″, ⅛″, or ⅛″ = 1′0″, and focus on general relationships. As the design direction is further developed,

models can be increased in scale to study detailed issues.

- Models needed for context only may be scaled at smaller sizes such as 1″ = 20′ or ⅛″ = 1′0″.

- Presentation models are generally effective if they are built large enough to be detailed. For a house, this could be ¼″ = 1′0″ or larger. For a large building, ⅛″ = 1′0″ might be an appropriate size.

- Modeling details must be constructed to scale. This consideration makes it very difficult to simulate dimensions such as 2 or 3 in. at a scale of ⅛″ = 1′0″ or smaller.

- For studies such as window mullions, roof fascia, and connections, larger scales such as ½″ or 1″ = 1′0″ are needed.

- For smaller scales, fine details should be implied.

Scale Relationships

Another aspect of scale that is important to consider is the scale relationship between different elements. This can range from very small things, such as a detail or a connection, to very large things, such as a city or a landscape. In all cases, it is important to understand and control the scale of the space and its elements by placing them in direct context with scale human figures and context buildings.

Understanding scale does not mean that every judgment revolves around the body. Spatial experience may be unaccommodating and completely outside this perspective. However, space should still be understood in terms of human perception when exploring it.

Examples encountered include:

- The scale of the human body to the scale of a room
- The scale of an element of a building to the entire building
- The scale of a building to a city block

Scale figures
Scale figures can be cut as model parts or inserted with montage techniques. They should be included at every stage of development.

Scale of entry
The entry to the Chrysler Building is typical of an opening scaled to fit the building. The actual entry door is one small element inserted into the opening.

The body in space
The scale of a room should be explored in relation to its inhabitants. Large public spaces are particularly instructive.

Scale of context
All scale issues do not center on the human body. Buildings should be considered in context with other buildings and at an urban scale.

Ideas
Expressive Model Drawing
Strategy

Models assembled with the speed of two-dimensional sketching can be effectively used as the prime generator of information without the aid of drawings or exact scales. To facilitate this, begin by becoming familiar with the basic program, site requirements, and structural options until they become part of the designer's internal knowledge of the project parameters. These can then be put aside to approach the model from another perspective. It may be difficult at first to reconcile practical concerns with your discoveries; however, with experience, they can be intuitively approximated and later used to inform design moves.

Although the model need not be built to a predetermined scale, it should employ relatively proportioned relationships between its parts, such as floor-to-floor heights. These heights can be measured later and assigned a scale to fit the project. For more information on assigning scale, see "Scale" in Chapter 4.

Illustration

Abridged steps are shown from the beginning phases of two different projects. Although specific project requirements were in mind, sketch models were constructed without exact scales or drawings to generate initial ideas.

Sketch model residence
A small frame is erected and used to visualize successive moves.

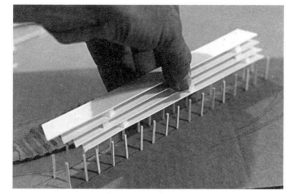

Sketch model office building
Columns are installed and a stack of floor plates is mounted on top. *Note:* Floor plates have been separated by small pieces of foam core to establish equal floor-to-floor heights.

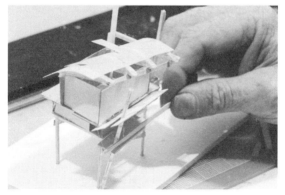

Sketch model residence
The basic form is established and pieces are added as they contribute to the expression of the model.

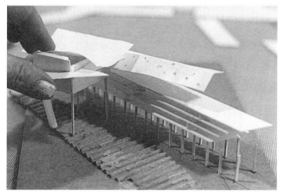

Sketch model office building
The unit is tested for design fit by holding it up to various locations on the framework until an optimum relationship is determined.

Additive/Subtractive Drawing

Strategy

One way of approaching three-dimensional forms is in terms of additive and subtractive operations. In additive operations, individual components are joined together to form a construction. In subtractive operations, models are initiated with a block of material, and pieces are subtracted to arrive at the design. Additive processes are more often associated with solid/void models, and subtractive models and mass models are closer in conception. In practice, a combination of additive and subtractive approaches is employed.

Illustration

The two projects on the immediate right employ additive and subtractive processes respectively.

Formal Proportioning

Strategy

Another important approach is to use the model as a device for refining proportions and making exacting spatial alignments. This approach requires tighter control and greater attention to crafting the model and focuses on placement and adjustment as its primary concerns.

Illustration

The example on the far right illustrates space developed through rational alignment.

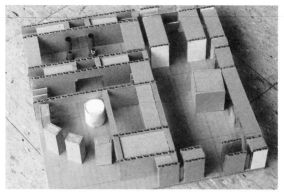

Additive space
Individual planes and sticks have been joined together in an additive process to define space. The reverse perception of the cube might see it as a solid, carved away to leave the voids.

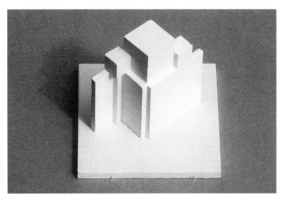

Subtractive space
The massing model can be perceived as having been carved away from a solid block. Although typically thought of as a subtractive procedure, the reverse perception might see the model as an additive construction.

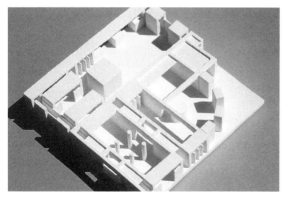

Alignment sketch model
The model is used as a drawing tool in this instance to develop controlled relationships between elements. Although its focus is more rational, it serves as a sketch model similar to those used for other types of approaches.

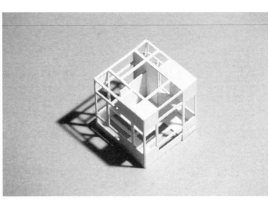

Alignment development model
Modeling precision is increased as the study is refined. The idea of drawing as an exercise in fine-tuning proportion and alignment becomes well defined with this model.

Working with Plan and Elevation Drawings

Strategy

The sketch model can be used in concert with simple scaled drawings to set a general direction. Once the building begins to emerge, the model can be used as a focal point to help visualize additional design decisions. Conversely, design elements carried out on the model can be used to refine drawings such as elevation studies, which in turn can be used to inform the model. The key to using each effectively is to decide which medium offers more efficiency and at the same time provides useful information in relation to the investigation at hand. For example, at the development stage, elevation drawings of flat walls can be more effective in refining compositions than a model. Conversely, elevations of a sculptural building geometry may offer little useful information about the building as compared with a model. This type of dialogue between drawn information and modeled information can be one of the most efficient means for project development.

Illustration

The projects to the right were initially generated from scaled schematic plans and sketches.

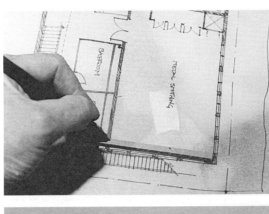

Schematic drawings

Relatively large-scaled drawings (⅛″ = 1′0″) were used to establish this development model. In this instance, there was no sketch model, as the orthogonal geometries were worked out in two-dimensional drawings. A large model was needed to develop the external frame and wall details. *Note:* Parts were cut directly from the drawings. For step-by-step illustration of the model assembly, see Case Study C in Chapter 4.

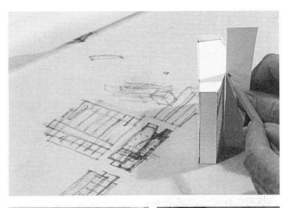

Schematic drawings

Small-scaled plan and section studies were used to produce initial model information. Curved pieces are measured directly off the actual model radii. *Note:* For step-by-step illustration of the model assembly, see Case Study D in Chapter 4.

Working with Concept Drawings

Strategy

Another way of approaching the relationship between two-dimensional drawings and three-dimensional constructions is to exploit the conceptual dialogue between the two media. In this process, drawings such as collages and paintings can be interpreted to produce three-dimensional forms, and conversely, models can be interpreted as drawings to set up orthogonal plan and section relationships.

This process is usually carried out in the early stages of a project, and the constructions typically require further interpretation to move them forward into architectural propositions.

Once the basic operation is understood, this relationship can be transferred back and forth a number of times to develop an evolving process. For related examples, see "Interpreting" later in this chapter.

Illustration

The following five projects show examples of drawing and model strategies used to work with drawings in this way. In the first three projects, the model preceded the drawing and was interpreted to generate it. In the last two projects, the two-dimensional drawing was interpreted to generate the three-dimensional forms.

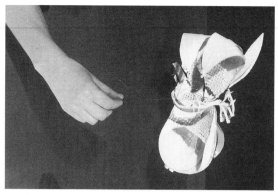

Project 1 pattern model
The model was developed using pattern pieces through the process described under "Manipulation" in the section called "Interpreting" in this chapter.

Project 2 transformer model
This model explored the idea of change and transformation. The potential unfolding of its components was analyzed in the accompanying drawings.

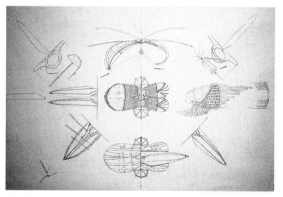

Project 1 pattern drawing
The object was carefully dissected with elevations and section drawing studies and reduced to a set of two-dimensional diagrams.

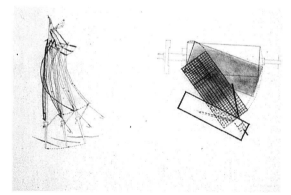

Project 2 transformer drawing
Drawings of the model in motion were subsequently used as abstract generative information to begin plan and section studies.

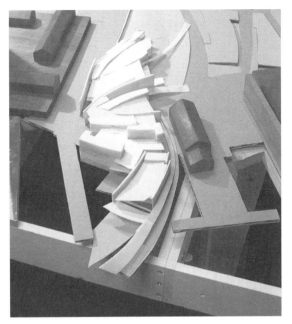

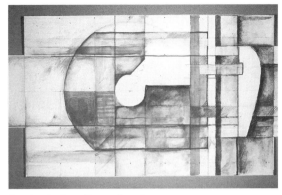

Project 4 collage drawing
The collage was designed as an abstract composition from a series of overlays. Once experience is gained with the process, elements can be controlled to help facilitate specific program needs.

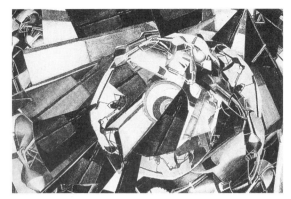

Project 5 Duchamp collage drawing
A collage drawing created from Marcel Duchamp's *Nude Descending a Staircase* served as the initial design move.

Project 3 site overlay
The model was extracted from overlay drawings developed as integral studies of site geometries, histories, and traces. Although not a two-dimensional drawing in the conventional sense, at this scale the model reads like one and makes clear the interwoven plan geometries used to form it.

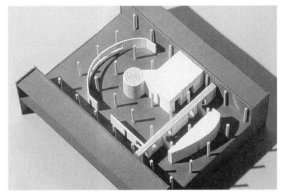

Project 4 collage space
The model was interpreted as space for a gallery from the collage drawing above. This particular translation moved the project directly into the articulation of programmed spaces.

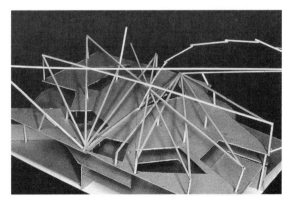

Project 5 Duchamp collage space
An interpretive concept model was made from the collage.

Alternatives

Multiple Approaches

Strategy

Whatever stage of development the project is investigating, distinctly different approaches should be explored to generate ideas and potential directions. In studies, this implies the construction of multiple sketch models. Models can in turn be selected from the alternative approaches and used for further study. As the project develops, alternatives might include ways to handle certain sections or building details. Composite models can also be made that incorporate ideas from different explorations.

Illustrations

In the first project, multiple sketch models were constructed to explore several directions.

In the following four projects, various approaches were taken to produce multiples. While Projects 2 and 3 are similar to the project in exploring three different approaches, Projects 4 and 5 look at alternative refinements to a single scheme.

Project 1—first alternative
The model approaches the project as a formal assemblage.

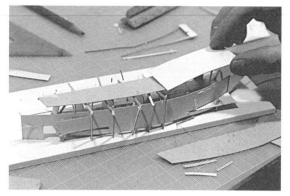

Project 1—second alternative
A linear organizational element in the form of a curved wall is used.

Project 1—third alternative
The project is explored as an elevated solution.

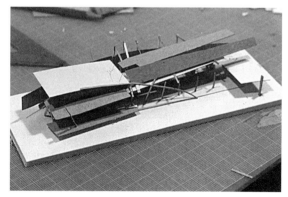

Project 1—fourth alternative
Uses the second alternative as a basis to mutate the design in another direction.

Project 2-three schemes

The models illustrate three different but related studies, produced to explore formal proportioning and alignment of space.

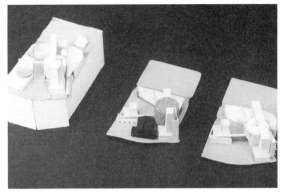

Project 3-three schemes

Three different schemes have been generated to explore possible directions for a project. The project is illustrated through all its phases under "Focusing: Mixed-Use Complex" in this chapter.

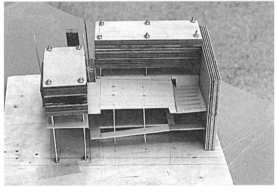

Project 5-alternative variations

These two alternatives are similar in approach and represent refinements to the design as opposed to completely different directions.

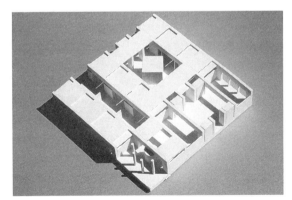

Project 2-development model

The model is a refinement of the preceding models, but rather than selecting one model for further study, it combines aspects of all three models.

Project 4-development model alternative

These development models explore closely related variations to a single scheme. As such, this study represents the kind of alternatives that might be explored after an initial direction is set.

Project 5-alternative variations

Although the project is strong at this level of finish, it may be more efficient to record changes with photography rather than to completely rebuild the model.

Adjustable Models

Strategy

Another method for exploring alternative approaches is to construct models with components that can be adjusted to test various arrangements. Changes to the models may be recorded with a camera. This method of recording alternatives can also work well when making significant changes to a conventional sketch or development model.

Adjustable models are set up so that each component can be repositioned. This model type is built with a deep, open base to allow columns to be pushed or pulled through the base. The holes for columns should be cut tightly so that friction will arrest the movement at the desired points. By moving the columns up and down, it is possible to examine the elements in a variety of different attitudes.

Illustration

The models depict an alternative exploration method that allows components such as roof planes to be varied in relationship to each other without the designer's having to build multiple models.

Roof relationships

This ⅛" = 1′0″ scale model was built to study and fine-tune the relationship between a series of intersecting roof planes.

The model is turned up to expose the tails of controlling sticks beneath. Pulling or pushing on the sticks changes the attitude of the roof and can be set and considered in an infinite number of increments. *Note:* It can be helpful when fine-tuning roof attitudes to include perimeter walls, but in some cases this may inhibit the ability to alter relationships.

Roof relationships

The initial setting of roof planes. *Note:* Straight pins have been used to attach museum board to the balsa sticks. If pins interfere with adjustments, they can be trimmed with side-cutting pliers or electrical dykes.

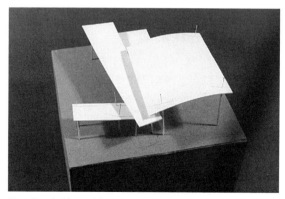

Roof relationships

This setting displays the roof planes in a new attitude. *Note:* It is also possible to remove the sticks and change heights and/or stacking order.

Site
Contour Models
Strategy

Exploration should include the impact of the site on design decisions from the earliest stages. The construction of a contour model is an effective way to consider alternative site relationships.

Sketch contour models can be built out of chipboard, scrap corrugated cardboard, and other inexpensive materials and should be assembled with the idea that their reason for existence is to be cut into and modified in a number of ways. Presentation contour models are constructed with the use of similar methods but differ in their use of materials.

Typical studies employing the contour model include exploring:

- The building's scale in relation to the land mass
- How the building will knit into the site through devices such as grade changes and retaining walls
- Landscaping issues such as drives, walks, and other outdoor spaces

Illustration

The examples show two common types of contour models employed. For building demonstrations and discussion, see Chapter 2, "Solid Contour Model" and "Hollow Contour Model."

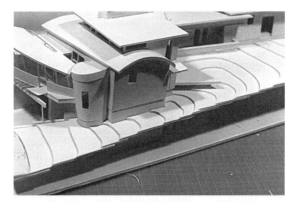

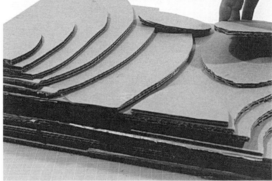

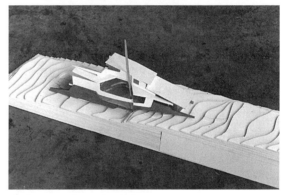

Solid contour Models

Solid constructions are versatile and stable. One of their main advantages is that they can be easily cut and patched. This makes them ideal for experimenting with grades and site designs as the project evolves.

Because the layers go all the way across their grade level, any cut into the grades will pass through the layers below. This makes it very easy to keep track of the effects of changes by counting contours.

Hollow contour Models

Hollow models use less material and can be added to existing models. They can be difficult to modify, as any cut through the contours reveals the space below and must be patched. They are also less durable than solid models.

The lower model has been built as a partial solid/hollow model. As the site gets progressively steeper, solid sections can be stepped up to include only those areas where alterations are likely to occur. *Note:* Panels at rear of model reveal the hollow section.

Context Models

Strategy

For all projects, especially sites in urban environments, it is necessary to construct at least the neighboring context buildings early on in the investigation. By representing them in some form, the scale of the project and relation between buildings can begin to be understood.

Illustration

Models ranging from a large urban area to the immediate site are shown. *Note:* The context is treated as an abstract mass to allow the new work to be easily apprehended.

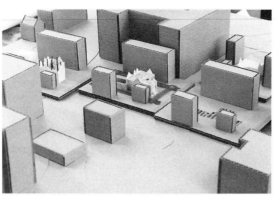

Immediate-building context
The adjacent buildings on this site are critical to understanding the nature of the project, as they actually define the space of the site.

Large urban context
Buildings have been cut from laminated layers of particle board and painted flat gray as a noncompeting background.

Neighboring context
Neighboring structures have been built from neutral corrugated cardboard as simple mass models in order to understand the new building's relationship with the existing fabric.

Immediate-building context
Adjacent buildings have been built with less detail to serve as context for the new addition (light wood), and gray paint helps code and downplay them.

Context model in progress
An urban context model in the process of construction is shown. Massing models of surrounding buildings have been cut from wood blocks and placed on the topographic map over their respective footprints.

Manipulation
Modifying and Editing

Strategy

Equally important to creating the model is the act of operating on it to discover and refine ideas. Modifications are most effective if the model is cut into and explored without the designer's becoming unduly concerned about its appearance or original configuration. If design operations appear to be difficult to implement, rough cutting will help establish the initial idea, and the resulting jagged surfaces can then be "cleaned up" once the idea is developed.

This type of investigation is important since many of the design decisions cannot be visualized until the model is established. A number of ideas will be suggested by the model itself, and the new readings may prove more interesting than the original construction.

Illustration

Two projects have been modified and illustrate the kind of investigations that might be carried out at two different stages of model evolution. The sketch model is still in the process of formation and can undergo radical transformations before moving on to the development model stage. The development model has reached the point where major relationships have been established and individual sections of the model can be modified and reformed.

Modifying sketch models

A sketch model has been used as a working site and is radically altered to discover other relationships. The process was initiated by cutting completely through the model along a selected bias.

Modifying a sketch model

The resultant halves were reassembled in a new relationship. This assemblage was used to visualize new components that were then quickly cut and tested for successful integration.

Modifying development models

One of the development models shown in Chapter 1, "Model Types/Development Models," was used to refine the exterior wall relationship. At this point, the previous wall components have been taken off and new cuts have been made directly on the model.

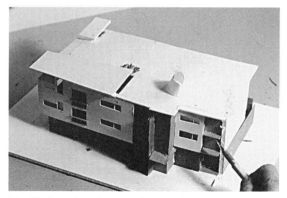

Modifying development models

The wall area has been rebuilt in a new but related configuration to refine this section of the design.

Modifying Site Contours

Strategy

Experimentations should be carried out on the site in a manner similar to that used for the building. Solid contour models made from inexpensive materials such as chipboard or corrugated cardboard are ideal for these studies. Grades can be cut out or added to accommodate a variety of conditions. As you experiment with various landscape treatments, it is helpful to save removed contour material so it can be replaced for alternative solutions.

Modifications also can be made to hollow models, but new contours must be attached to fill the holes left by cutting into the model.

TYPICAL MODIFICATIONS

- Creating a level grade for the building

- Creating drives and walks that cut into or rise above existing grades

- Creating cuts through several grades where soil must be retained (this typically occurs along property lines where changes are made)

- Creating terraces, berms, and drainage swales

Illustration

The images on the right show cardboard study models used to explore grade changes for drives, walks, and buildings. The images on the far right are of sites made from malleable materials that can be molded as desired.

Contour model changes
Contours are cut for an entry drive in the model. Slopes can be calculated by counting contours and the distance to the next level. The model is ⅛″ scale. Each contour = 1′0″, so 10 ft forward produces a 1 in 10 slope.

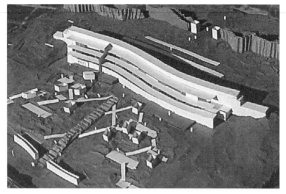

Plasticine site model
Grades and leveled areas for building footprints can easily be molded from this claylike material. Grades have the advantage of smooth appearance, but it is difficult to transfer the contours to drawings.

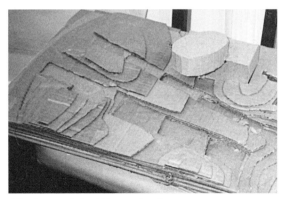

Study model with grade changes
Areas with two or more contours cut down will require retaining walls. *Note:* Bad cuts can be reversed simply by replacing material. Rough splice lines will not matter for this experimental phase.

Plastic clay study for a park
This material can be quickly formed and is conducive to exploring alternatives. *Note:* As in the preceding example, it can be difficult to transfer grades accurately to drawings, and achieving crisp edge definition is challenging.

Digression

Strategy

Many times in the course of exploration, new directions emerge that do not follow the original intention. Instead of ignoring these and steering the design along preconceived paths, it can be profitable to let go of earlier ideas and follow implications suggested by the model. This may involve following the design through a strong shift in direction or even returning to an earlier generation in favor of later versions. Readings that emerge from rough modeling craft, such as warped, off-center, or overlapping materials, can be adopted as a discovered event and are many times more interesting than the intended readings.

Illustration

The sketch model and second-stage interpretations on the right demonstrate the tendency to regularize anomalies in the model in keeping with intended readings. This is a case where it can be argued that the earlier exploration was potentially more interesting than the "tightened-up" finish model and interpretation of the sketch model.

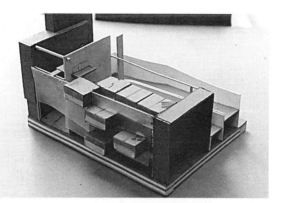

Using accidents

The thin acetate wall on the front of this sketch model displays a degree of unintentional warping and curvature that is potentially interesting. Although not the actual second stage for the project, the lower model is typical of the regularization applied to make the model conform to preconceptions. The results can be less interesting than the "accidents" suggested by the rough sketch. For this reason, it can be useful to let the project evolve on its own and take advantage of unintended discoveries.

Maintaining discovery

A form of reverse digression can occur in which model discoveries are lost in the translation to a higher level of refinement. In this example, many ideas developed in earlier stages have been "normalized" when moving to the refined version. The loss of discovery is similar in effect to a failure to use accidents. In both cases, regularizing tendencies and an unwillingness to let the model guide the evolution of the project have displaced some interesting ideas.

Interpreting

Strategy

Sometimes manipulation can be a matter of making a fundamental shift in either the model or the designer's perception of the model. This can be accomplished by using a number of processes. Processes can be combined or modified to generate other approaches based on your own exploration.

Illustration

The examples represent several typical strategies. They are similar in nature to concept models and are offered as experimental approaches to stimulate ideas.

The study models typically used to explore various strategies employ quick assembly techniques and offer the designer freedom to experiment without becoming unduly attached to the product.

The final set of projects consists of concept models paired with models made to extract a reading from which to create an architectural space. These models provide a link between the abstract, conceptual nature of models used to generate ideas and models that begin translating ideas into integrated building designs.

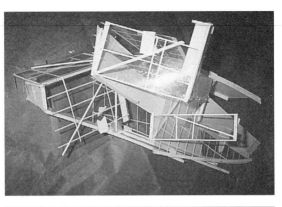

Fragment

A section of a large model has been severed from its original context and placed in a new attitude. This fragment is then reinterpreted as a complete building. By exploring new attitudes, several different solutions to the project are suggested.

Recycling

Another example that expands on the idea of fragments is to treat parts from previous models as found objects. By building a large inventory of cast-off project pieces, you can rethink and cross-assemble them. With modifications and the introduction of new elements, a number of ideas can be produced in short order.

Distortion

The models have been intentionally crushed and distorted by applying pressure from one location with a flat surface. The resulting geometry offers a number of new readings that carry the internal logic of their initial relationships.

Sectioning

The model is transformed by cutting it into two parts along a carefully selected bias line. The resulting parts are then realigned along a new axis and stitched together. The resulting formation is used to generate ideas based on the implications of space, form, and structural demands. The model can also be sectioned and used to discover new relationships based on the internal order revealed by the cut.

Scale shift

A section of the ⅛″ = 1′0″ scale model (lower model) has been identified with particularly interesting relationships. This section was isolated and reinterpreted at four times its original size.

The new model is now taken to represent the same square footage as the original project, and the program is reinserted into it.

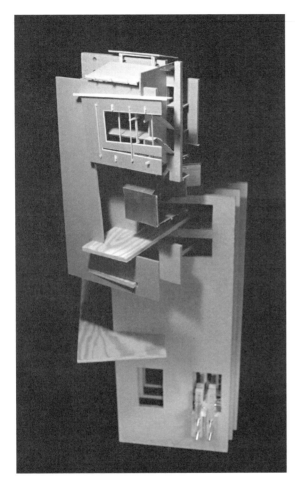

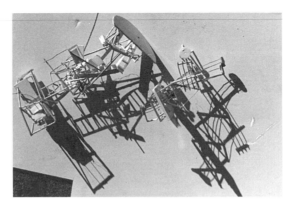

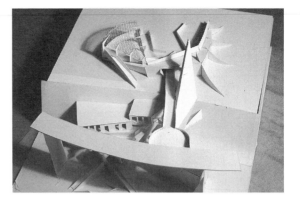

Fragment

This project derived an intricate acoustic universe by analyzing the structure of Giorgio de Chirico's paintings and making a number of machine studies. A fragment of the proposed building was constructed to examine the physical structure, building systems, and spatial and auditory environments.

Projecting

An interesting exercise for generating new ideas involves the use of three-dimensional forms to produce two-dimensional images. The shadows thrown off by the objects are best experimented with at lower angles of sunlight or artificial light. The models can be turned in many directions to explore various types of shadow patterns. The patterns can be interpreted to create new models, and models can in turn generate successive two-dimensional patterns through a reflexive interchange of information.

Axonometric

The process involves a dialogue between drawing and the model and is related to the topics discussed in "Working with Drawings" in this chapter. It is initiated by overlaying several outline drawings and extruding selected elements upward at varying heights to create a three-dimensional axonometric drawing. The drawing is then interpreted as a building and invested with program, site considerations, and structure to produce the model. The process becomes more controllable after experimenting several times.

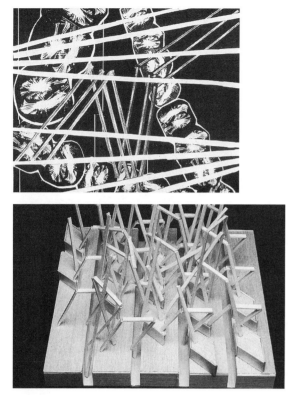

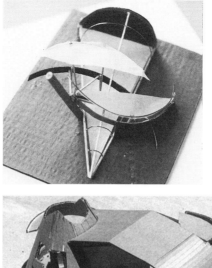

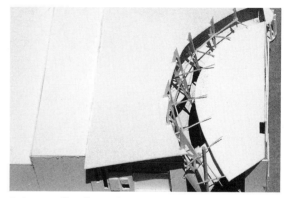

Collage

To begin, a collage is created by manipulating a set of base images from any number of sources. A model is then made based on the collage. The models will most likely become a concept model, but interpretations can convert the ideas directly into a building scheme. Part of this is controlled by the nature of the drawing. Repetitive images are less likely to lend themselves to the hierarchy of programmatic issues. For possible variations on the collage approach, see "Working with Concept Drawings" earlier in the chapter.

Collision

Two strategies employing the idea of collision are shown. Both are initiated in model form. The model above was started by building two open "wire frame" forms of contrasting size and shapes and engaging the two parts. The resultant collision can be used to make decisions about what is solid and open and how programming might be accommodated.

The model below uses a similar approach, but the three forms used for collision were solid masses carved away to create the voids. Intersections offer the most potential.

Intervention/rotation

Intervention is similar in concept to collision. A regular field such as a grid or other repetitive pattern is established as the ground or regular field. An "alien" in size and shape is then imposed in the body of the pattern at some disruptive or rotated angle. The resultant space is interpreted to accommodate architectural considerations. The diagram above illustrates the basic idea. The lower model is a building developed from imposing a curved gesture on an existing grid structure.

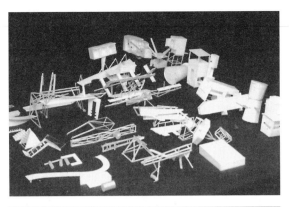

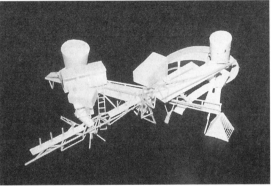

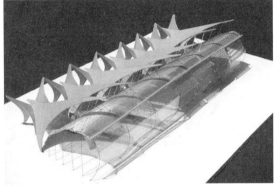

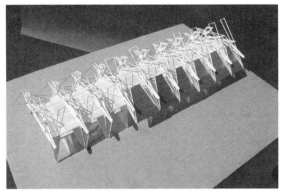

Lexicon

This process is related to recycling elements; however, rather than using existing elements, a vocabulary (or lexicon) of new parts is generated. The elements can be created as a number of platonic forms with variations. The parts for this example were generated by designing seven kiosks, then disassembling them. Many elements were used to create critical mass capable of producing unpredictable combinations. The model below was one of dozens made from combining the various elements.

Repetitive frames

This process involves the use of a repeated element to form an architecturally designed armature. To begin, a single frame is designed with a height and span in mind. The frame is stressed by pressing on key points, and ideas for modifications are incorporated to reinforce structural weak points. The frame is repeated to enclose a generic volume of space and becomes the structural frame for a building. In the example, the frames have been roofed and glazed to develop a small airport terminal.

Repetitive frames

Like the previous example, schematic models and development studies can be seen with the single frame. In the first example, the material is intended to be concrete shell construction, and for this one, steel members are employed. Designs were developed by looking at the body, tectonic structures such as bridges and cranes, and work by other architects.

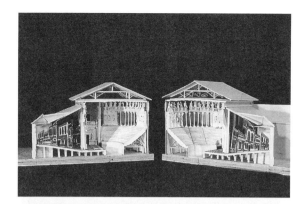

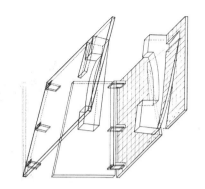

Precedent interpretation

This strategy is shown in four frames and is initiated by using an existing architecture as a ground for study and interpretation. In this example, the Teatro Olimpico in Vicenza, Italy, was built in model form and then cut into two sections with a band saw. The sections were carefully studied with drawings (not shown) and translated into interpretive ideas about space using the study models shown in the lower frame. The process then proceeded to a fifth and sixth stage shown in the following frames.

Precedent interpretation

Ideas from the study models in the previous frames were selected and combined to produce a spatial interpretation with the Hydrocal (plaster) model shown above. The space discovered in this model was then studied in drawing form on an experiential level, that is, as a projection of what the experience might be like when moving through the space. For related topics, see "Working with Concept Drawings" in Chapter 3 and "Casting Plaster Molds" in Chapter 5.

Cartesian transformation

Transformation, or the manipulation of existing orders, can be carried out in many ways. One method is to establish a gridded cube in drawing form. The faces of the cube are then rotated at various angles and decisions are made for pushing and pulling forms from them. Once under way, a three-dimensional interpretation is established and suggests moves that can be pursued on the model. See "Working with Concept Drawings" earlier in this chapter.

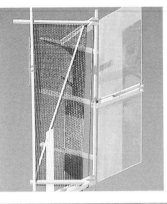

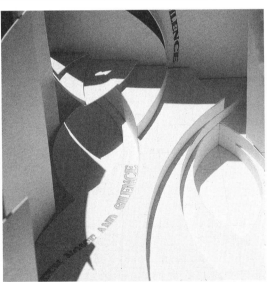

Concept model and interior space

The proportion and movement study is translated into the space shown in the lower model, using the flowing lines of the concept model to inform elevations and sections.

Concept model and building

The shade, light, and shadow device shown above has been translated into ideas that inform the shading elements and geometry of the beach pavilion shown in the lower model.

Diagram model and building

The geometry of the building follows the basic direction set by the diagram model in orchestrating the play between a strong central axis and the wandering quality of the intersecting wall as it moves across the site.

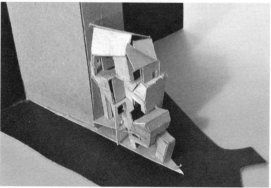

Mechanical apparatus

A mechanical set of tectonic components was explored as a means to translate the internal dynamics of contextual collage. The machine was stressed by a crank and flew apart in a controlled collapse to reassemble itself as a means of combating the exhaustive effects of familiarity. The lessons learned from this apparatus were translated into a car lift for a parking deck project in an urban park.

Frame violation

A frame is made (in this case) by winding a dense layer of wire and sticks. This frame is intersected by other elements. The frame is cut away to establish a dialogue between the space and frame.

A building interpretation is made of the frame model that includes the program. The piling of spaces attempts to be true to the implications of the frame model.

Superimposition of shifted geometry

The project was conceived by overlaying shifted geometry drawings. The two primary geometries are expressed in layers of transparent structure against the solid program elements.

Oblique Folding

This process explores space on the oblique, or angle. Initial moves were developed in three dimensions by means of folding and cutting a single 12 in. × 12 in. sheet of chipboard to produce spaces in relation to a site. The spaces responded to three abstract program elements: spaces of enclosure, sight, and movement. The sheet had to remain one continuous plane. Parts were not to be cut away or moved around. The flowing sheet created an internal logic that carried through the components.

The site model was derived from sections taken through anything that exhibited elements of the oblique as part of its space, such as stairs, ramps, and roofs. Models were made of these isolated elements and reconceived in scale to become large architectural sites. The models show the various stages, from the initial folding to development and final renderings in wood.

Folding–study model stage 1
The initial fold made from the 12 in. × 12 in. sheet.

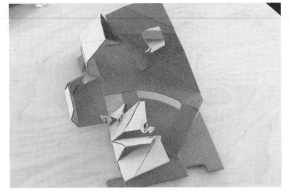

Folding–study model stage 2
The sheet is folded on itself to create layers and define spatial enclosure.

Folding–study model stage 3
The study model is developed in context with the site model. The site model consists of two walls and a fragment of a bike rack.

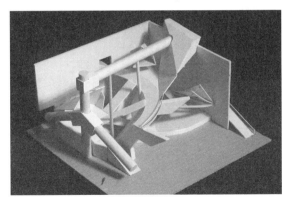

Folding–final model stage 4
The final development model translated into wood.

Exquisite Corps Form Z Tower

This process works with the computer-modeling program Form Z to generate spaces. A radicalized program is established to inform decisions on each floor. Project limits are set at 24 ft × 24 ft grid space with 8-ft levels. Each level can overlap the others by 4 ft.

The project proceeds by designing one floor at a time to create a 10-story tower. Each floor focuses on a different tool to create the forms. A reciprocal process between digital modeling and physical modeling is the goal. Work is started in the computer and each level is built physically. Reaction to the physical model level is then transferred to the digital model. The physical model provides a means to apprehend what the space is like and contributes to the process as a design model.

The most productive focus is found in designing spaces from the inside out rather than trying to define an exterior envelope. A natural disjunction occurs at each level due to the myopic focus on individual floors. The most successful projects create unclear divisions between levels and elements that relate sections of the overall tower.

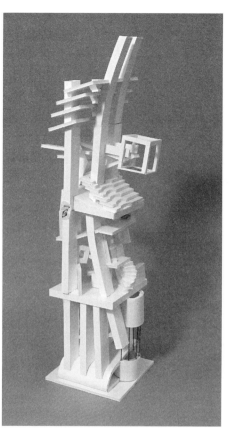

½-in. detail model

The first three levels of the Form Z tower to the right have been increased in scale to make a more detailed study of connections and relationships between forms.

Spaces for a "collector"

The two projects on the left are based on the idea of collecting: to design a set of spaces for a "collector" in the city. In opposition to linear processes, the architectural inquiry consisted of a "collection" of inquiries and related tasks involving words, graphic images, and related material. Students define what their collectors collect and how they exchange the collections. The architecture accommodates an exhibition and storage space and a living space, as well as a gallery space for display and barter. The models represent proposed buildings and the collection of spaces they contain, following the collectors' particular manner of collecting.

Curio cabinet
Building for a collector of architectural artifacts translated as a curio cabinet of architectural collectibles.

Ironing board
Project for a collector becomes an ironing board that frames the tight urban void filled with various building elements.

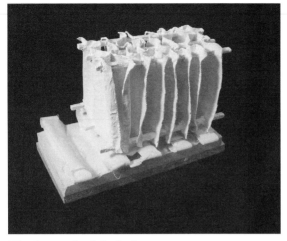

Plaster material study
The studio investigation involves exploration of material behavior as a rethinking of architectural formation. Studies include reaction to planar materials such as cloth and metal deformation, draping, and folding. Section studies look at repetitive relationships to form a dialogue between layers of space. The language established by the investigation is developed to translate into building propositions. In this example, sheets of gauze have been dipped in plaster and compressed into folds on a framework. The plastic quality of the space is a direct result of the coalition of material constraints. This approach is in contrast to conventional methods that conceive of form as skin or cladding supported by framework.

Development
Project Development

The development process is central to use of the model as a design tool. The approaches discussed in the sections "Ideas" and "Manipulation" are applied using study models in a chain of evolutionary stages. This process is similar to two-dimensional design evolution in that concepts are used to develop schemes and are integrated with structure, site, and programming issues to produce a complete architecture. The process relies on the interrelated concepts of increasing scale and focusing (discussed later in this chapter) as methods for advancement and is reinforced by coding and hierarchy of materials and the converting techniques also discussed later in the chapter.

Illustration

An abbreviated model progression with four stages of refinement bridges the gap between the single-stage interpretations of concept models (shown previously) and the expanded set of model stages in "Focusing," presented later in this chapter.

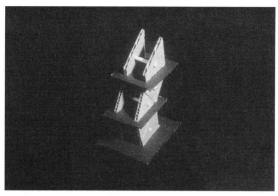

Retreat Stage 1
The project explores themes from the play *Eleemosynary* to design a retreat for Echo, a primary character in the play. The study employs a simple harmonica as its initial design generator.

Retreat Stage 2
A sketch model is used to develop spatial organizations and site engagement using the conceptual tectonic system as a basis for decisions.

Retreat Stage 3
The concept model is used to develop basic tectonic systems.

Retreat Stage 4
The study is increased in scale and focus to develop the ideas into the retreat for Echo. The final project can be seen to effectively integrate ideas from the isolated study models.

Increasing Scale: Sketch-Development-Finish Models

Strategy

As a model evolves, it is typical to increase its size, moving from general relationships to greater levels of detail. This process of starting small and moving up in scale is analogous to focusing a lens. At low powers, the lens sees only general shapes and gestures. As greater focal powers are applied, elements become increasingly defined until details are clearly apprehended. See "Scale" in Chapter 3.

Illustration

In the examples to the right, the initial sketch models were established at small scales. As the direction became more focused, the scale was increased to develop more detailed readings.

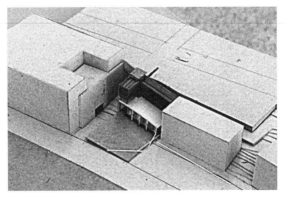

Project A—initial ¹⁄₃₂″ scale model
Project investigation looking at overall issues of scale, massing, and mechanics of the scheme with a small ¹⁄₃₂″ = 1′0″ sketch model.

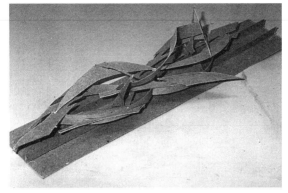

Project B—initial 1″ = 50′ scale model
Project investigation looking at overall issues of gesture, flow, and spatial layering.

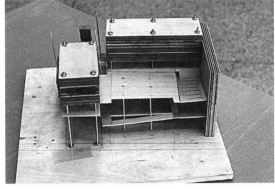

Project A—¹⁄₈″ scale development model
With the direction of overall issues established, the model is enlarged by a factor of 4 to ¹⁄₈″ = 1′0″ to facilitate a higher level of focus.

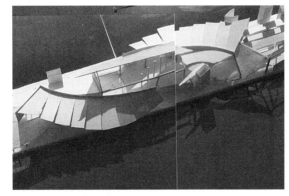

Project B—1″ = 1′ development model
An increase in scale to 1″ = 10′, which considers looks at the articulation of components, refines relationships and further develops the play between program and structure.

Increasing Scale:
Sketch-Development-Finish Models

Illustration

The two development models to the right take the idea of scaling to the next level of focus. By increasing the scale of isolated sections, exploration and refinement continue to evolve.

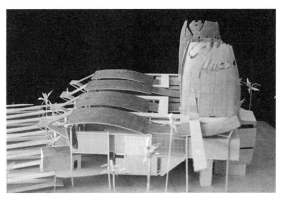
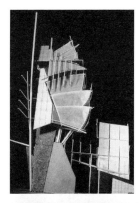

U.S./Cuba customshouse
Development model
The building is articulated to a certain level of resolution that is convincing at this scale of study. However, it cannot show a lot of detail and requires a larger model if another layer of information is to be provided.

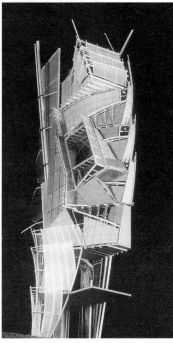

U.S./Cuba customshouse
Larger development detail
A section of the smaller development model above has been increased in scale and shows more detail.

Finish and development model
A section from the finish model above has been isolated and scaled up (lower model) to develop the facade elements. See "Focusing" later in this chapter.

Increasing Scale: Building Interior Models

Strategy

Part of the process of increasing scale involves enlarging the model to be able to focus and develop interior components. Such models typically function as development models and are constructed to study interior architectural spaces and millwork.

Interior models are typically built at scales starting at ¼″ = 1′0″ and larger if possible. These models must define the borders of the space but remain open for viewing and working room.

Illustration

The models to the right demonstrate typical scales and treatments for interior models.

½″ scale house interiors study

This ½″ = 1′0″ scale foam core model employs a removable roof for viewing. Components were developed directly inside the model. *Note:* The scale is large enough to read details as small as 1 in.

¼″ scale house interiors study

Many times, existing ¼″ = 1′0″ scale models such as this are large enough to develop interior partitions and circulation elements.

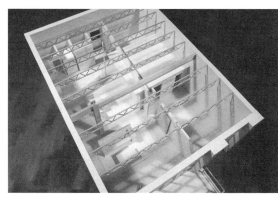

½″ scale interior unit model

This model was built to convey the interior space of a typical loft unit. At this scale, it carries all the detailing of every truss member and includes furnishings for scale comparison.

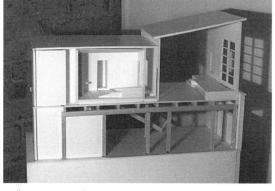

½″ scale section study

An interior development model of a unit in a condominium building has been built at a ½″ = 1′0″ scale to develop interior components.

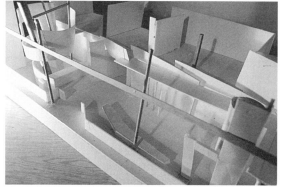

½″ scale atrium/lobby study

This ½″ scale development model was used to add, remove, and refine various elements for an atrium space. Portions of the rough model were recut after alterations were made.

Increasing Scale: Detail Models

Strategy

As project development proceeds, models are built at even larger scales to develop details such as window treatments, railings, fascias, and so forth.

These models are treated in a manner similar to building models but are built at much larger scales to study the finer readings of form articulation and connections.

Scales typically range from ½″ = 1′0″ to 3″ = 1′0″. Detail models can be helpful in resolving design ideas and construction details and in facilitating client communication.

Illustration

The detail models on the right demonstrate ways in which the models can be used to develop details or special furnishings.

A window surround
This museum board and foam core model was built at relatively large 3″ = 1′0″ scale to study relationships between corner connections and wall depth. *Note:* Test angles have been cut to fit the curved corners together.

Table
This 1″ = 1′0″ scale, foam core model was used to develop a small table. Detail models are also useful for the study of interior elements such as cabinets and built-in shelving.

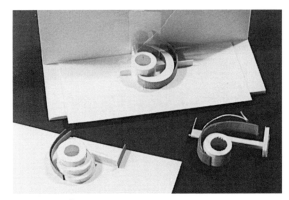

Fireplace/waterfall
These relatively small ¼″ = 1′0″ scale sketch models were used to develop designs for a fireplace/fountain. *Note:* As is typical of developing designs, three alternative solutions were constructed.

Library kiosk
This small study for a movable book carrel was built at ½″ = 1′0″ scale, and its parts could be turned to explore the effect of shades and adjustable racks.

Coding and Hierarchy of Materials

Strategy

It is effective to use different materials based on classifications of building elements such as exterior walls and interior partitions. This type of coding reinforces the ability to "read," or understand, the project's defining elements and geometries. It also begins to convey the sense of weight the various elements will project in terms of both their relative importance and their physical heaviness.

As projects become more resolved, components should reflect the actual scale thickness of walls, roofs, slabs, beams, and so on. This hierarchical range imparts a level of contrasting elements to make the model convincing as an architectural representation.

Illustration

The following projects use a range of scales and color to reflect different component types.

The two illustrations at the bottom of the page demonstrate the practice of detailing edges to reflect their true scaled thickness. *Note:* As a model is scaled up, it will not present a contrasting range of elements and can appear unconvincing if the thicknesses of modeling sheets do not accurately reflect the true scale of the elements.

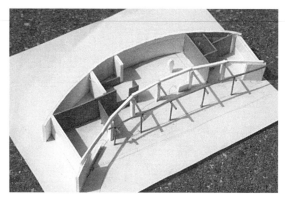

Coded structure
The structure of this ⅛" = 1'0" scale house model is made up of 8-in. concrete masonry units and is internally divided with wood-framed walls. All members representing the masonry elements have been constructed from 3⁄16-in. foam core. Interior partition walls and exterior trellis components are cut from chipboard. Beams over front wall openings have been cut to scale.

Coded materials and concept
The coding of this model can be read in two ways. The material of the central datum wall, dark box behind it, and translucent screen wall in front all convey a sense of contrast in color, weight, and material. Alternatively, the conceptual organization anchored by the central wall with adjoining components is clearly delineated.

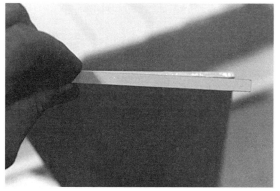

¼" Scale fascia detail
A ⅛-in. foam core roof plane is edged with a 10-in. scaled strip of museum board.

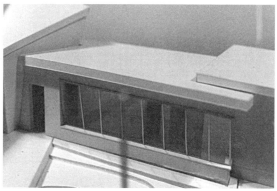

¼" Scale fascia detail
The edge of the roof now reflects the true 10-in. depth of the fascia.

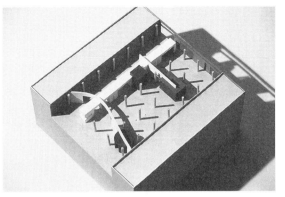

Coded program components

A clear delineation is made between the program components by coding the interior of the space gray, circulation elements in white, and program spaces in dark board.

Coded buildings and addition

The model components for an addition use coding to differentiate between the dark-colored existing building and the new elements.

Coding planning elements

In this model, buildings, site elements, and tectonic constructions such as the unifying trellis work have all been coded with a range of materials to clearly differentiate the complex.

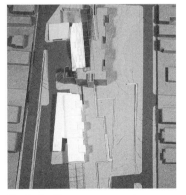

Coded site components

The site is coded to differentiate the ground plane, roads, existing buildings, and new structures (in white). *Note:* The site and existing buildings are in darker neutral tones and allow the new work to stand out.

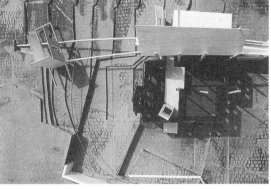

Coded addition elements

The variation between the dark walls of the existing building and the new components intervening through its space can be clearly read because of the contrasting materials.

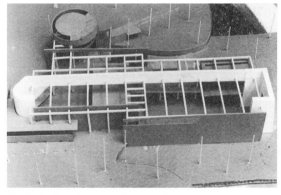

Coded structure and organization

White anchor and circulation elements, gray board walls, and wood structural gridding have been used to reinforce structural systems and program organization.

Converting: Renovating Models

Strategy

Although there is a point when many decisions have been made and a model has to be recrafted, models are often needlessly rebuilt every time a few elements are changed. This can consume a lot of time. Instead, renovation techniques can be used to effectively clean up the model. In many cases, the results of these techniques are entirely adequate for more formal presentations.

Illustration

The sketch model on the right is refaced to upgrade its level of finish. For complete step-by-step illustration of this project, see "Case Study B" in Chapter 4.

Models on the far right have been covered in paper to code and upgrade their level of finish.

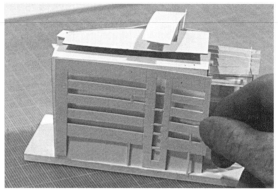

Project A—Renovation

A typical refacing begins by cutting openings in an overlay sheet. This method is more practical than cutting holes through the model. Transfer tape is used for large surfaces likely to warp if glue is applied.

Project B—Covering with paper

Colored paper can be used to renovate or code the model's surface. Paper can be attached with Spray Mount or double-face transfer tape. Glue sticks can be used on the edges.

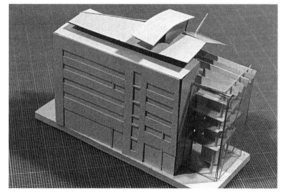

Project A—Renovation

The resultant understated shadow lines generally read better on small models as visual layers. Additional facings can be cut and applied over all the original cuts to continue elevating the model's finish.

Project C—Site renovation

Site surfaces can be covered with paper to smooth out contours on rough models. The paper helps visually reduce the large change in contours on the initial model and serves to elevate the level of finish.

Focusing

Strategy

Focusing refers to the application of evolutionary stages of development. It draws on all the ideas presented in this chapter and is central to the process of moving a project from a germ of an idea through successive stages of refinement. The process may begin with alternatives and digression, but as it evolves, each new model builds on the generalized relationships of the previous stage to arrive at an integrated building design.

Typical Evolutionary Stages

Proceeding from initial information:

- To alternate concept and sketch studies
- To fixed geometry and relationships
- To exploring alternative treatments
- To looking at alternative detailing
- To a resolved project design

Illustration

The models on this page show an array of development stages typical of a project designed with the model as a primary study tool.

The projects on the following pages illustrate a variety of methods used in the evolutionary chain of model progression.

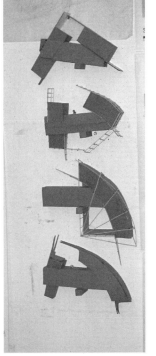

Model stages—Newry Mill intervention

Model stages—mixed use tower

Model stages—folk art museum

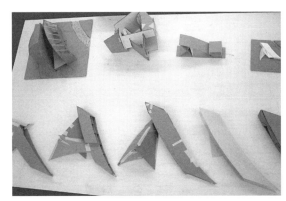

Model stages—music hall annex

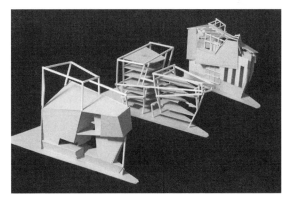

Model stages—folk art museum

COLLEGE COMPLEX

This project presents several strong aspects of modeling. They include development of conceptual ideas through successive stages and the use of the model to develop the facade and elevations. See "Increasing Scale" earlier in the chapter.

College complex stage 1
The development of dormitories, galleries, and art studios is initiated with a concept/gesture model to interpret the dichotomy between the suburban and urban landscapes.

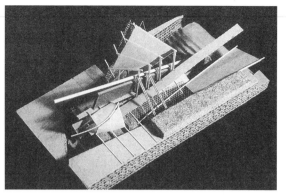

College complex stage 2
The relationship suggested by the concept model is engaged with the site. This sketch model serves to translate gestures into a building construct.

College complex stage 3
Growing out of the earlier discoveries, the program and other organizational issues are engaged for possible occupations on the site.

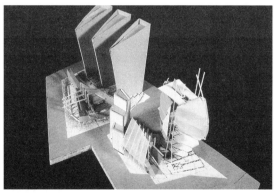

College complex stage 4
The overall organization and general form of the complex has been developed, and attention turns to refining individual elements.

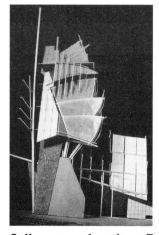

College complex stage 5
The tower is developed as a finish model. A section of the tower is then scaled up for more study. See Chapter 3, "Increasing Scale Development/Finish Models."

BRANCH BANK

This project is a small, 2,000-sq.-ft. branch bank in a suburban outparcel. It represents a design methodology that uses the model to envision subsequent development stages. As such, it relies heavily on the direction set by the diagram model for plan and sectional relationships. As it proceeds, a careful exploration of each level of development is carried out. In this case, the program space becomes a layer of information that is fed into the model after conceptual and movement relationships have been set. There is a basic implication of space and movement that is adhered to and advanced as a result of the exploration.

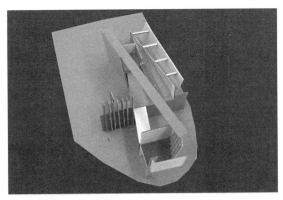

Branch Bank stage 1
The project is initiated with a diagrammatic study of key spatial relationships.

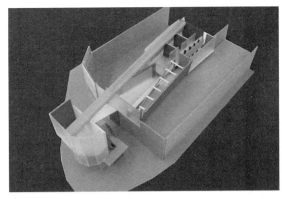

Branch Bank stage 2
The skeletal relationships are reacted to and developed as architectural program spaces.

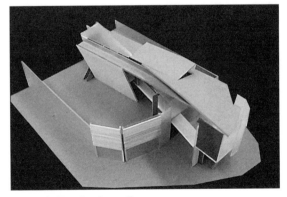

Branch Bank stage 3
The geometry and interpenetration of layers inherent in the diagram are developed into a resolved system of enclosure.

COURTHOUSE

This project is for a new courthouse in Charlotte, NC. The courthouse proposal includes a plaza on the north side of the site. An overarching concern for the development of the architectural forms is to respond to daylight in ways that would not block the sun in the plaza. The unconventional form is determined using physical and computer models to carve away mass in response to a pragmatic set of criteria and tests.

The process works back and forth between physical and computer models. The physical models are used to simulate light projections and shadows on the plaza at different sun angles.

The studies clearly illustrate the movement from early sketch models to a developed and crafted final version.

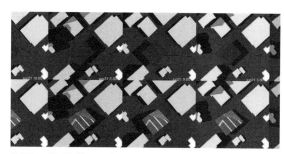

Office Building stage 1–concept drawing
The initial project information is derived from a two-dimensional pattern drawing. Although a lot of interpretive space is left by the drawing, it provides direction and is fully exploited by the three-dimensional studies.

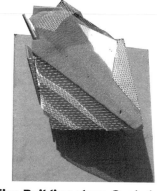

Office Building stage 2–sketch model
The drawing is interpreted as a three-dimensional construction that begins to respond to the shadows cast on the plaza.

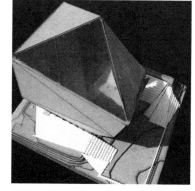

Office Building stage 3–development model
The conceptual model is developed into a spatial proposition that reacts to program and site response.

Office Building stage 4–finish model
The final model has developed readings of skin, structure, and layering as a refinement of the development study. Although the glazed structure transmits maximum light, it would have been instructive to take photographs with the light source behind the building.

VERTICAL MALL

The project consists of a large, multilevel shopping mall on an urban corner lot. The mall covers some 150,000 sq. ft., including parking. The project begins with the idea of a plant unfolding and moving upward. The proposition is pushed to extremes to conceive of the mall as a collection of vertical towers with sectional relationships.

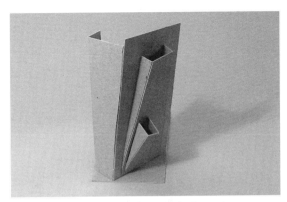

Vertical Mall—Concept model stage 1
The initial growth model sets the direction for the project.

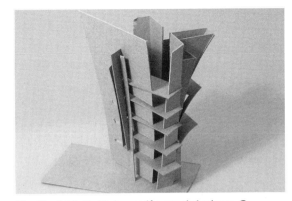

Vertical Mall—Schematic model stage 2
A genetic section applies building tectonics to the concept model and establishes layers to initiate development.

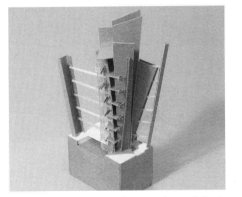

Vertical Mall—Development model stage 3
The section is developed into an ordered set of relationships matched to the scale and program of the project.

Vertical Mall—Final model stage 4
The final model develops a hierarchy of components that place the structure in context with the city.

VERTICAL MALL

The project is another version of the mall shown on the previous page. This particular project begins by looking at two-dimensional overlay drawings of cartoons and interpreting them as a section model. The mall is conceived as a multilevel experience that flows through a box surrounded by parking ramps. The street is fronted by the presence of cars. Parking access to the interior mall space penetrates the box at a number of locations.

Vertical Mall—Concept model stage 1
The initial concept section model taken from *The Simpsons* cartoons. At this point, interpretations are primarily sectional extrusions and require further study.

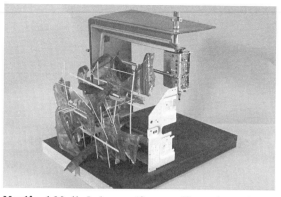

Vertical Mall—Interpretive section stage 2
The model is interpreted as an abstract section with glass fragments. The television fragment provides a frame and a connection to the media culture.

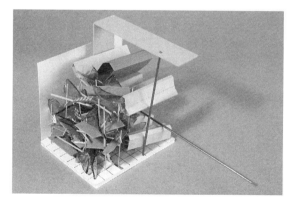

Vertical Mall—Combined section stage 3
The glass model is translated with scale and program in an attempt to find relationships. *Note:* The extruded pieces have been included as well as the translated television.

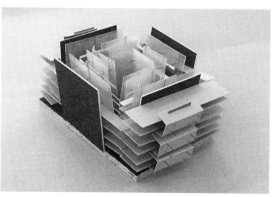

Vertical Mall—Section development stage 4
On a parallel track, the idea of wrapping the mall space with parking ramps is being explored.

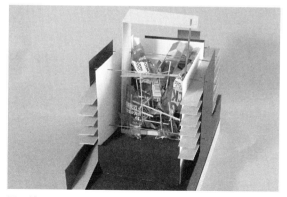

Vertical Mall—Development model stage 5
A sectional model is made to examine the interior relationship between internal studies and parking models.

MIXED-USE COMPLEX

Several strategies have been used in evolving this project. A concept/diagram model and context study are used to generate initial information, then three sketch models are used to translate the raw concepts into alternative building propositions. By beginning with the three small sketches, then moving to a development model, increasing scale for a finish model, and finally scaling up the structure of the circular building, four levels of scaled models can be observed at work.

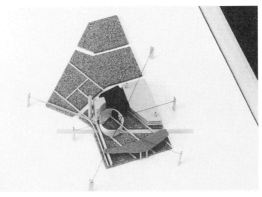

Mixed-use complex stage 1

The project is initiated with a conceptual diagram of the site to generate physical ideas based on relationships between the overlaying forces and existing structures.

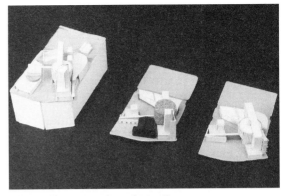

Mixed-use complex stage 2

Ideas from the initial investigation are used to explore three different organizational schemes.

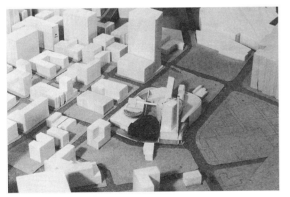

Mixed-use complex stage 3

Schemes are tested in the context of the site as they are developed.

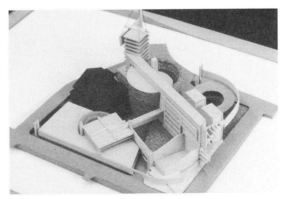

Mixed-use complex stage 4

A scheme is selected and refined at a larger scale with a development model.

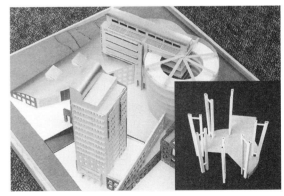

Mixed-use complex stage 5 and 6

The study is increased in scale and detailed to produce the finish model. The circular structural system is also scaled up to develop details.

NEWRY MILL INTERVENTION

The project explores the insertion of an alien intervention within the body of an existing structure. The architecture is developed as a negotiation between the historical context and new overlay of program and geometries. The body is provided by an abandoned nineteenth-century textile mill in need of a new life. The intervention is conceived as an initial plan overlay based on analysis and diagramming of an architect's work. The moves are initiated in three dimensions at smaller scales and developed in stages into large finished models.

Newry Mill—mill existing
A nineteenth-century mill building is the site of the intervention. As such, it provided a body for grafting, reaction, and invasion.

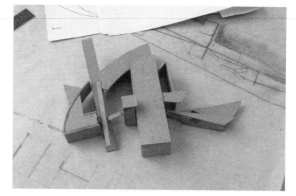

Newry Mill—Schematic model stage 1
Overlay drawings were produced based on a Daniel Libeskind project and translated into small massing/program studies.

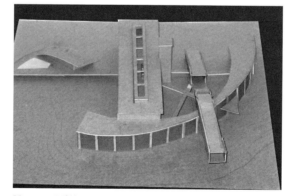

Newry Mill—Development model stage 2
The design was developed at a larger scale in an attempt to refine the program and the model diagrams. At this stage, the translation was awkward and out of scale with the existing mill building.

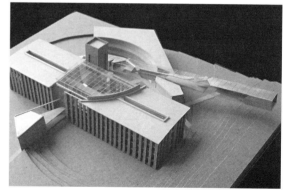

Newry Mill—Final model stage 3
The final version shows another translation of the studies that resolves many of the problems with the preceding explorations. It also can be seen to add a second layer of detail to the development of the individual spaces.

COMMUTER AIRPORT

The project consists of a small, 25,000-sq.-ft. commuter airport hangar/passenger terminal. It is developed directly from models and uses the idea of a cantilevered structure as the driving force behind the architectural language. Design issues such as tension and compression frames, member hierarchy, material, and movement are examined. The design is informed by looking at the body, heavy equipment, bridges, and architects such as Calatrava and Tschumi.

Using this information, a single bay or frame is designed and repeated to produce an 80 ft. × 280 ft. shed. The shed is generic in nature and could be adapted to any number of project programs such as a rail terminal or a pedestrian walkway. A secondary layer of bracing and enclosure is introduced at this point, followed by the insertion of the program in the large space of the shed.

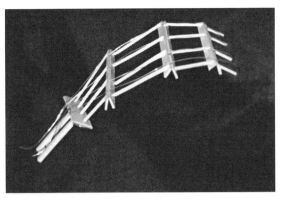

Airport–Concept model stage 1
The initial frame looks at the hand and works to translate it into a mechanical device.

Airport–Development model stage 2
The frame is developed and repeated nine times to establish the armature for the shed.

Airport–Final model stage 3
A layer of skin is applied and each frame is conceived as an operable device capable of opening and closing individually.

FOLK ART MUSEUM

The project consists of an 8,000-sq.-ft. folk art museum with a housing component to be developed on a tight triangular urban site. The focus is on exploring vertical relationships as a guiding means of building form. Two processes are used to explore this. The first uses overlay drawings to produce an interpretive section model. The second process proceeds by establishing a three-dimensional frame, then colliding program elements into this skeletal body.

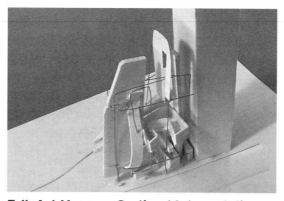

Folk Art Museum–Sectional Interpretation stage 1

An interpretive section model is made. This model includes both the frame and the elements that rely on section interpretation only.

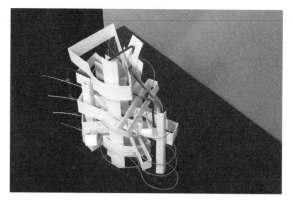

Folk Art Museum–Frame violation stage 2

A frame with intersecting elements is made. The frame is modeled from curved wire and provides a weak reading in comparison to the colliding program elements.

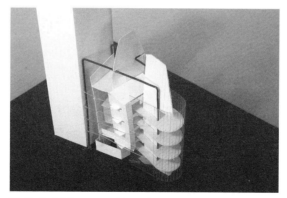

Folk Art Museum–Development model stage 3

A model is made to resolve the conceptual stages. The frame in this case is inverted by interpreting it as glass enclosure, and the stacked elements in the frame are regularized as floor plates.

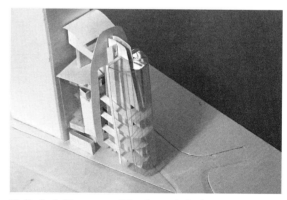

Folk Art Museum–Final model stage 4

The model is further refined to address program fit and recaptures some of the energy of the early model studies.

FOLK ART MUSEUM

The project consists of an 8,000-sq.-ft. folk art museum with a housing component to be developed on a tight triangular urban site. The focus is on exploring vertical relationships as a guiding means of building form. Two different processes are followed to explore alternate approaches. A process using overlay drawings to produce an interpretive section model is selected as the most promising method. Project development proceeds from this information base.

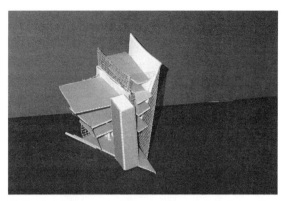

Folk Art Museum–Schematic model stage 2
The next small study reconsiders the sectional relationships by lifting the space off of the site. It also begins to make a rough fit with the project program.

Folk Art Museum–stage 3
The model is increased in size to introduce materials and deal with the interior space in more detail.

Folk Art Museum–sketch/concept model stage 1
This project began by following one of the small models made from the section studies. In some respects, the model relies too heavily on the ground plane for support.

Folk Art Museum–stage 4
The building is reconsidered again, and a new model is built to address issues of enclosure. The design exhibits an overly dense layering of space and a loss of clarity.

Folk Art Museum–Final model stage 5
The final model attempts to refine the organization of the space and brings all the ideas under greater control.

MIXED-USE TOWER

This project consists of a folk art museum
with a 25,000-sq.-ft. high-rise multifamily
housing component. The project is the
product of grafting two different approaches.
The first approach treats the architecture as a
sectional interpretation of a drawing. The
second approach establishes a framework for
the building and then inserts the section
study through that framework. The final
model is a product of working out programmatic issues and negotiating the space
between the frame and enclosures.

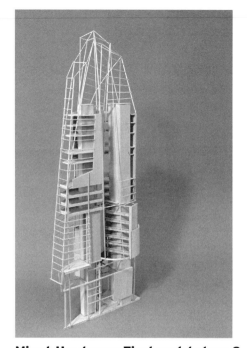

Mixed-Use tower–stage 2
A larger interpretive study of this model incorporates the program and attempts to carry forward the spirit of the initial study.

Mixed-Use tower–Final model stage 3
The final model introduces the structural
frame, accommodates the actual program, and
rationalizes the space. Refinements are in evi-
dence, but some of the energy of the studies
has been lost in the process.

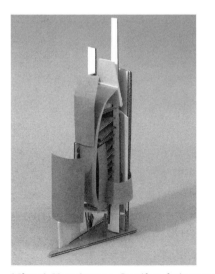

**Mixed-Use tower–Section interpretation
stage 1**
The design is initiated with a study model
derived from section drawings.

MUSIC ANNEX

This project consists of a 15,000-sq.-ft. music annex with a concert hall and rehearsal spaces sited on a college campus. The project uses overlay drawings of music interpretations and site studies to initiate ideas for organization and siting. Folding and the use of the oblique are focused on as a means of translating drawings into three-dimensional studies.

Music Annex—Sketch model stage 1
A small sketch model is made from the drawings. At this point, only the roof carries the idea of the folds. The walls have been extruded from the two-dimensional drawings and require rethinking.

Music Annex—Sketch study stage 2
A slightly larger study is made, and the entire space is folded.

Music Annex—Photo Montage
A photograph of the completed model has been pasted into an image of the site. People have been inserted to convey the scale of the building.

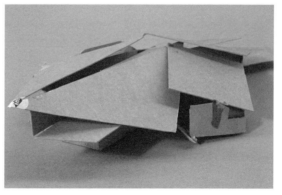

Music Annex—Development model stage 3
A development model is made to reconcile program elements and the folded space.

Music Annex—Final model stage 4
The final model benefits from the introduction of the oblique; however, the presence of the oblique is found primarily in the roofs and not as an integral part of the building.

ENTRY/ARRIVAL SEQUENCE

This introductory architecture project is a good example of a focused, abstract architectural investigation, driven by the design process. The project proceeds through a series of design phases. Each phase looks at a basic problem from different perspectives. In the course of the investigation, the project engages additional considerations such as materials, structure, and site.

The initial design response is based on developing an entry/path/arrival sequence. After several stages of development, the project language is explored through other "modes of making." The translations range from an assembly of planes and surfaces to forming, stacking, and connections. The impact of materials on the scheme and forms is considered through each mode.

As a final phase, the ideas explored through the various studies are anchored into a specific site using a combination of the various material modes.

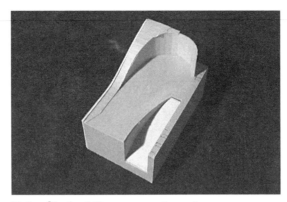

Entry/Arrival Sequence–stage 1
The initial idea for a path and place of arrival is carried out in a simple chipboard study model.

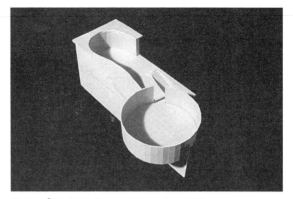

Entry/Arrival Sequence–stage 2
The initial idea is studied and refined into a series of events that develop the idea of path and arrival space.

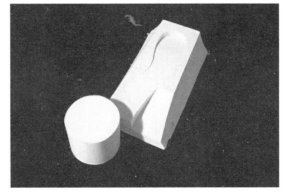

Entry/Arrival Sequence–stage 3
The scheme is translated into a cast-plaster model. Elements read as mass and impressions in a solid.

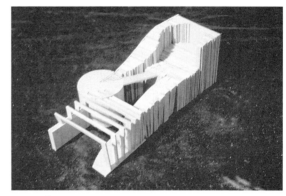

Entry/Arrival Sequence–stage 4
The model is translated once again into a construction made by layering material. This translation engenders the idea of successive frames as well as an engagement of the arrival space into the body of the model.

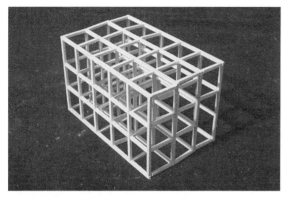

Entry/Arrival Sequence–stage 5

The project exploration shifts again to find ground in the space of a generic grid structure. This "connection mode" is the final form of making used to consider the problem.

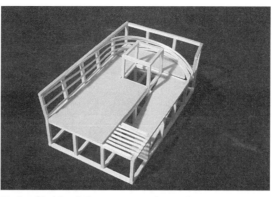

Entry/Arrival Sequence–stage 6

Engagement with the grid begins by working with the internal space of the structure to invest the ideas of path and arrival derived from the previous exercises.

Entry/Arrival Sequence–stage 7

Once the space was invested, the complete enclosure was reestablished and architectural refinements such as screening and modulation were introduced.

Entry/Arrival Sequence–stage 8

The investigation was further refined to introduce the sweeping language of the initial studies, develop the arrival space, and redesign the reading of the screen and frames.

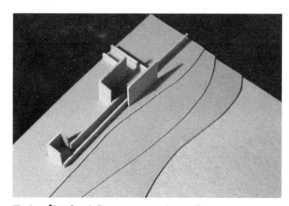

Entry/Arrival Sequence–stage 9

Finally, a specific site is introduced and a small diagram model is made to establish a scheme for anchoring the previous investigations.

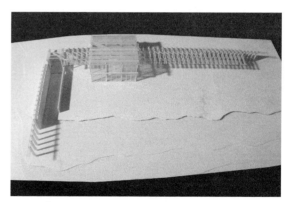

Entry/Arrival Sequence–stage 10

This "siting" is developed in response to the new context. The language of connections becomes the dominate means of expression with the arrival sequence extending out into the surrounding territory.

APPLY

Step-by-Step Case Studies
of Concepts and Techniques

The following projects trace the evolution of
five designs from early conceptual stages to
finish models. Many assembly techniques and
strategies presented in Chapters 2 and 3 are
shown to convey possible applications in the
context of evolving designs.

Case Study A: Residence
Stage 1—Initial Sketch Studies

Strategy

With the project parameters in mind, the designer makes alternative sketch models from small, schematic scaled drawings and pencil sketches. After exploring different approaches to generate ideas, an individual or hybrid model is selected for further development.

Assembly

Rapid construction techniques use knife, scissors, and hot glue.

Project

A 2,000-sq.-ft. house on a narrow infill lot.

Scale: ¹⁄₁₆″ = 1′0″

Models measure approximately 2 in. × 3 in. (actual size) and are kept small for initial studies. *Note:* Even at this scale, the model is not built as a pure massing model but is treated as a solid/void model to understand the contribution of openings to the overall composition of forms.

Materials

■ Poster board

■ ¹⁄₁₆-in. foam core

Illustration

Five alternative approaches are made to generate ideas and explore a range of directions. Work is begun using small, measured schematic drawings, with each model employing a basic formal strategy to organize its moves.

Alternative 1

This scheme is organized as a linear grouping. It becomes readily apparent that the program will need a second story to preserve any yard space.

Alternative 2

This scheme concentrates the program on the second level in another linear side-loaded organization (based on alternative 1).

Alternative 3

This scheme uses a central drum as the focal point for its organization and covers the entire buildable area with a single-story solution.

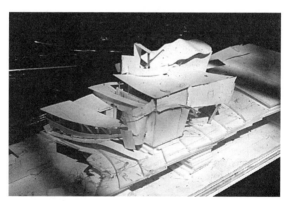

Alternative 4

This scheme engages two volumes with all other spaces expanding from them. With modifications, this scheme is selected for further study with a development model. See Case Study A, Stage 2, in Chapter 4.

Alternative 5

This scheme employs a courtyard defined by a second-story bridge.

Stage 2—Manipulation and Focusing

Strategy

The general direction of the sketch is increased in scale for further study and development. Alternative solutions for different sections of the model are also considered.

Assembly

The model is assembled with relative speed but more accurately than the sketch model. Parts are lightly adhered using white glue, with the intent of cutting and changing the components as the model progresses. A number of building and editing techniques are illustrated during the construction of this model.

Project

A 2,000-sq.-ft. house on a narrow infill lot.

Scale: ⅛″ = 1′0″

The scale of the sketch model is doubled in size for this study. The increase allows for more detail and refinement but is still small enough to lend itself to quick alterations and visualization.

Materials

■ Two-ply museum board paper

Illustration

Alternative 3 is selected from the initial studies and rebuilt for further study. The raised section at the rear of the initial model is immediately lowered to the ground plane. This "tail" is then modified several times to explore different readings.

At this level of study, the development model must show all solid/void relationships to provide the next level of information.

1. The plan is transferred with a knife to the base sheet. *Note:* Although scaled plans should yield accurate parts, adjustments must be made to compensate for the thickness of materials and to conform to small variations that occur in the actual model.

2. Walls are erected and small parts put in place with the aid of the knife point.

3. The shape of the conical stair tower roof is templated directly off of the model. Because this shape varies in its rate of curvature, direct templating is one of the most dependable ways to achieve an accurate fit.

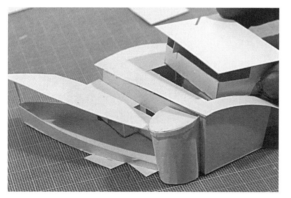

4. The second story is held in place to make a rough template for the curving roof plane.

5. A finished roof is made by adjusting the rough template and recutting the part until an exact fit can be achieved. *Note:* For forms that change geometry in three dimensions, it is difficult to cut shapes that will fit perfectly the first time.

6. An initial "tail" wing is tacked together with the glue gun.

7. The tail is edited by cutting with scissors.

8. Openings are cut directly on the model. *Note:* If needed, these can be cut accurately by using a small triangle to guide the knife edge. See Case Study B in Chapter 4.

9. The resultant openings with small shading additions.

10. A wedge is cut out of the box to try out another angle on the tail.

11. The move is rejected, and the wedge is re-attached to the box. *Note:* It helps to save all parts that are cut off for replacement if the modifications are not satisfactory.

12. The walls of the tail are broken open to study the potential for other arrangements.

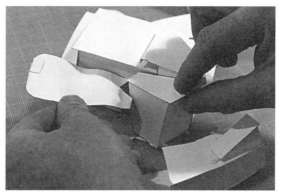

13. Using scissors to cut out small pieces directly on the model, attention is directed to developing the front of the building. *Note:* Attention should move around the model so that one area does not become overdeveloped in relation to other sections.

14. The knuckle formed by the stair tower between the main body and the tail is redesigned.

15. Returning to the rear of the model, a third alternative facade is considered, and the tail is rebuilt one more time. The final parts have been recut to match the level of finish on the other sections.

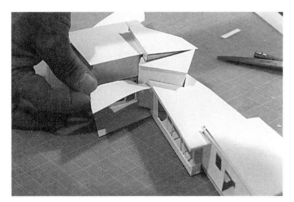

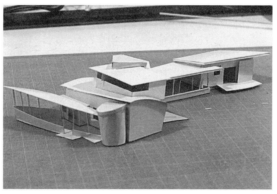

16. An alternative patio covering is considered as the investigation nears completion.

17. The completed development model is shown. *Note:* The site has not been addressed on this model, although it was included at the sketch model stage and has been explored in terms of the way the building will relate to it.

Stage 3—Finish Model and Site

Strategy

With the basic relationships established, the model is again increased in scale and built with greater accuracy.

The presentation/finish model can also be considered an advanced type of study model, as it affords the focus for designing details such as glazing patterns, site elements, interiors, and roof treatments.

Assembly

A number of new techniques and materials applicable to finish models are included in this example.

Project

A 2,000-sq.-ft. house on a narrow infill lot.

Scale: ¼" = 1'0"

This is a typical scale for fully developed house models, as it allows sufficient size for detailing.

Materials

- Three-ply museum board paper
- ³⁄₁₆-in. foam core

Illustration

The model is built as an example of the level of finish appropriate for formal presentations. The abstract detailing relies on implied material simulation. Items that cannot be reproduced accurately at ¼" = 1'0" scale (less than 2 in.) are not included.

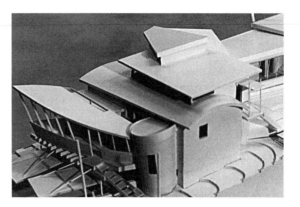

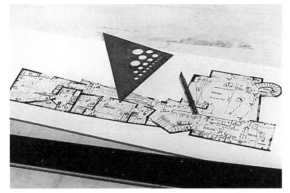

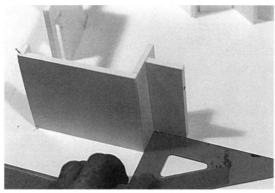

1. The surface of the model base is lightly scored by tracing a set of floor plans with a sharp knife. The plans have been spray mounted and are removed after the wall lines have been transferred. *Note:* Apply spray outdoors.

2. The plans have been removed, and the basement walls are laid out along the scored lines. A triangle is used to ensure accurate corner joints and vertical alignment of walls.

3. Wall connections are held together with straight pins. This speeds construction by allowing successive joints to be made without waiting for glue to dry. *Note:* Corner angles have been cut at 45 degrees to allow paper to meet without exposing the Styrofoam core.

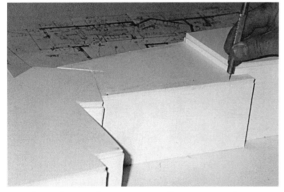

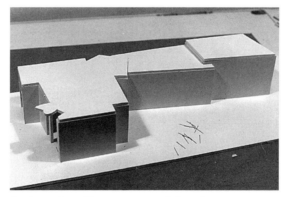

4. After glue is dry, pins can be removed or pushed in if the heads are hidden by other parts of the model.

5. Completed basement and first floor are shown. *Note:* Site contours will be built up around the basement level.

6. Using drawings to template the facade, museum board is cut to include only the dominant mullion details.

7. A thin line of white glue is applied directly to the wall edge.

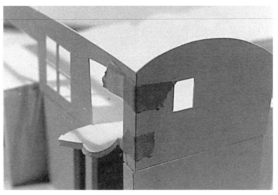

8. A wall joint is held in place with drafting tape until glue can set.

9. Walls continue to be constructed on the main floor of the house.

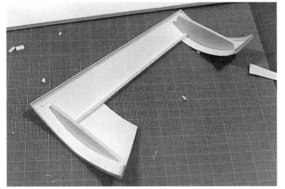

10. A rough curved roof is cut to determine fit, as demonstrated on the development model. The final cut for the roof is reinforced with hidden bracing to maintain radii at each end.

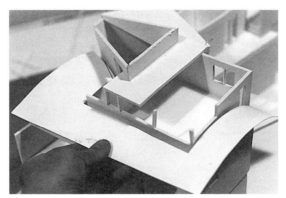

11. The roof is placed on the second floor. Supports allow the roof and the second floor to be taken off for interior model viewing.

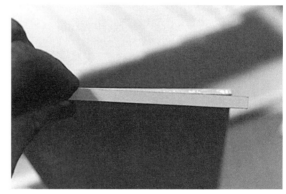

12. Exposed foam core roof edges are covered with museum board. *Note:* Edges should be scaled to their intended depth rather than letting the given thickness of material remain inaccurately sized. In the example, edges have been cut to read 8 in. and 10 in. at scale.

13. A conical entry tower is made from museum board by rolling with a round marker.

14. Street-face components of the first floor are assembled.

15. A roof for the conical tower is templated directly off the model using discarded model material.

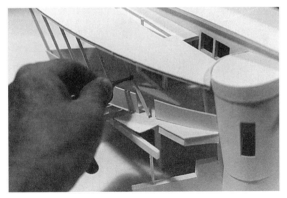

16. Detailing is added, using tweezers to handle the finer elements.

17. The basic body of the model is completed and ready for the site contours. See "Work" in Chapter 2.

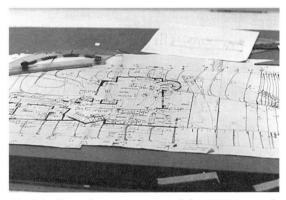

18. A hollow site contour model is constructed directly on the model by using a site drawing with 6-in. contours and ⅛-in. foam core. At ¼" = 1'0" scale, each layer of foam core is equal to a 6-in. change in grade.

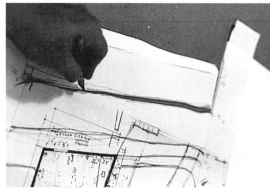

19. Contours are cut between the lines with a 1-in. projection beyond the contour to allow a tab for gluing the successive layers together.

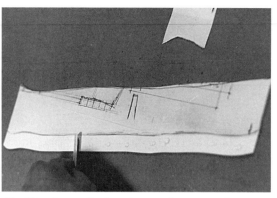

20. Glue is applied and spread out evenly. *Note:* The line of the contour above should be marked so that glue will not get on the material past this point and be exposed. The paper template can also be left on to protect this area until it is in place.

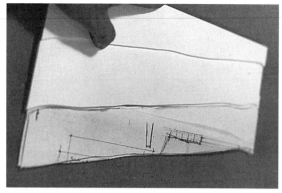

21. The overlapping contours are glued to the 1-in. projection on successive contours. *Note:* This type of site model can be built from the top down instead of from the base up as in the solid contour model.

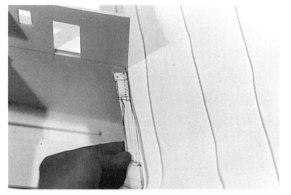

22. After several contours have been connected together, the section is supported from below and attached to the body of the building.

23. Individual contours are continued down the side of the house.

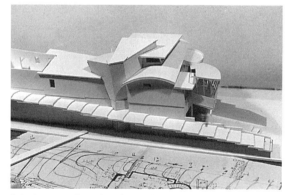

24. A completed side is shown.

25. The opposite side is completed and a notch is cut for the location of site stairs.

26. Site details and ancillary components such as the entry stairs can now be assembled.

27. A pilot hole is drilled in the foam core using the knife tip.

28. White plastic rods are cut and glued in the resulting sockets for canopy columns.

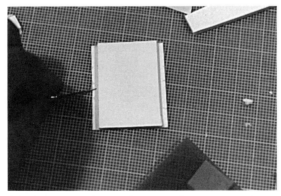

29. Foam core is cut down to the paper and scraped clean to hide the foam at the corner joints. *Note:* This can also be done by cutting joints at 45 degrees, but this technique becomes difficult to control when joints do not meet at 45 degrees.

30. The completed piece is installed over foam core wing walls and effectively covers the exposed foam edges with a clean corner connection.

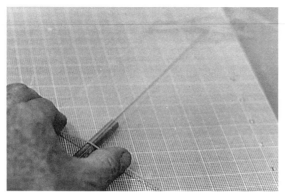

31. Plastic sheeting is cut for the window wall area by scoring with the knife and breaking over the handle.

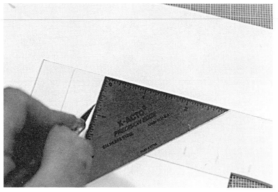

32. Glazing mullion lines can be made by scoring with a knife or marked for the application of adhesive design tape.

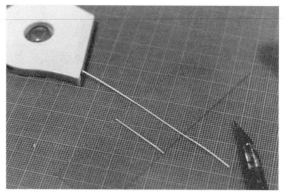

33. White adhesive design tape, 1/32 in. wide, is pulled across lines and trimmed to simulate 1½-in. mullions at ¼" = 1'0" scale.

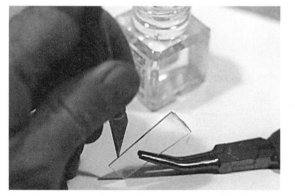

34. A very thin line of liquid acetate Plexiglas adhesive is applied with the knife edge.

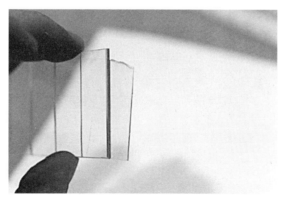

35. The two pieces are pressed together and will set, for handling purposes, in about a minute.

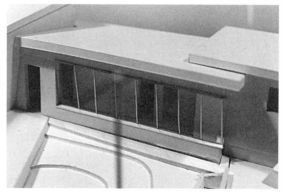

36. The completed window wall is installed in the building face.

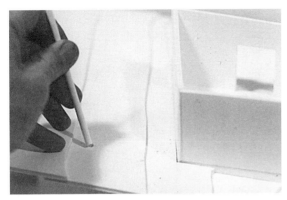

37. Large plastic rods are inserted in the site to serve as abstract trees.

38. The model interior is cleaned out with compressed air.

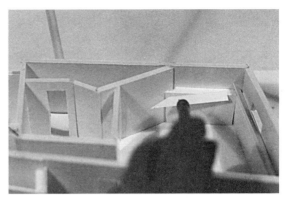

39. Interior components are then built out.

40. A set of scaled stairs is inserted into the circulation tower. *Note:* ⅛-in. stacked foam core serves well as a scaled representation of ¼″ scale tread risers at 6 in. each.

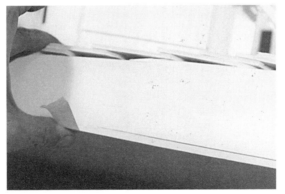

41. Finally, rough interior side supports for the contours are installed. *Note:* Drafting tape is used to draw the materials tightly together until the glue can set.

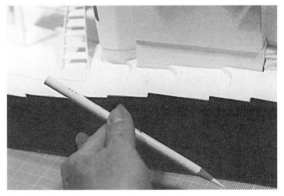

42. Finished museum board side covers are templated directly from the contours.

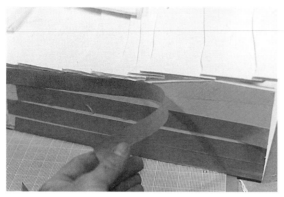

43. The sides are attached with a special adhesive transferred from a paper backing onto the material face. *Note:* Large, flat expanses of water-based glue will warp paper, spoiling the clean surfaces.

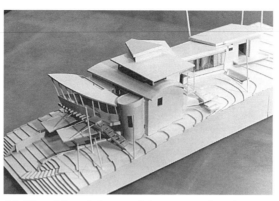

44. The sides of the model are completed. *Note:* Facing over rough cuts can convert studies to finished versions without rebuilding. See "Converting" in Chapter 3.

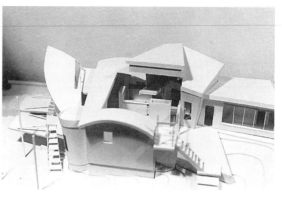

45. The second floor has been built so that it can be removed for a clear view of the kitchen millwork and living space. Keeping the other roofs on helps define the interior spatial qualities.

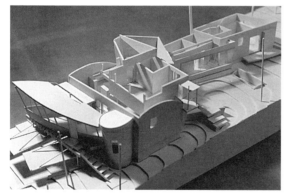

46. The rest of the model can be opened up to display various interior sections as well.

47. Construction proceeds on the project, and a ½" = 1'0" scale framing model is built in two sections (front section shown in the illustration) to work out all of the loading and member detailing. The model is consulted daily during the framing process.

48. The house is completed and modeling projections can be compared.

Stage 4—Further Exploration

Strategy

The continuing possibility to serve as a site for refinement even after the building is constructed underscores the model's usefulness as an evolving site of exploration.

Assembly

The example demonstrates the use of thick, flexible acetate for curved glass surfaces.

Scale: ¼″ = 1′0″

Materials

- Flexible acetate
- Plastic rods
- Museum board
- Foam core

Illustration

The presentation model is used as a further site for exploration. Three alternative approaches for enclosing the back patio area are carried out directly on the model.

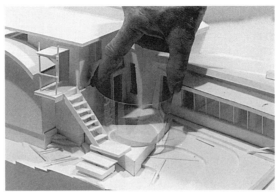

First alternative

The finish model is used to explore porch enclosures by curving glass around slab.
Note: Thick, flexible acrylic has been used, but the actual glass would most likely be made from tangented flat planes.

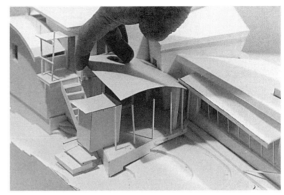

Second alternative

This scheme explores the use of a curved roof plane with a series of columns cut from plastic rods.

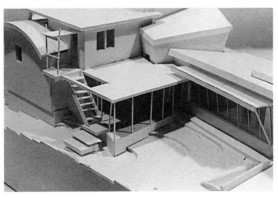

Third alternative

A flat roof solution is tested following the geometry of the slab below and extending out to engage the second-story stairs.

Case Study B: Multifamily Housing
Stage 1—Sketch Model

Strategy

The model is used as a drawing tool to become the prime generator of information.

Assembly

This example demonstrates the use of quick assembly techniques to facilitate spontaneity.

Project

A five-story, multifamily structure.

Scale: Not to Scale

No predetermined scale is used, but the model maintains relatively proportioned relationships between its parts, such as floor-to-floor heights. These heights can be measured and assigned a scale. In this case, actual measurements between the floors is ⅛ in., so a scale of 1″ = 100′0″ would represent about 12 to 14 ft. in height; see "Scale" in Chapter 3.

Materials

- Poster board
- Corrugated cardboard
- Chipboard
- Balsa sticks
- Metal fragments

Illustration

A sketch model is constructed with a specific project program and site in mind.

1. A linear organization is used to begin exploring the project. The model base is then punctured with the knife to provide sockets for a row of balsa stick columns. *Note:* Corrugated cardboard, with the top layer removed, is used for surface texture.

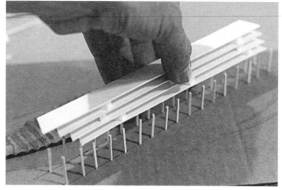

2. Columns are installed, and a stack of floor plates is mounted on top. *Note:* Floor plates have been separated by small pieces of foam core to establish equal floor-to-floor heights.

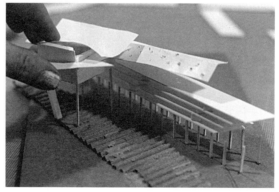

3. Using the initial framework as a focal point to visualize possible moves, roof and building body components are quickly cut with scissors and assembled. The optimum design fit for the unit is found by holding it up to various locations on the framework.

4. A contrasting vertical element is desired. Scrap metal is brought into the ensemble and is programatically folded in as vertical circulation. The entire model took less than an hour to generate and offers many implications for development.

Case Study C: Sculpture Foundry
Stage 2–Development Model

Strategy

The project began with a development model that was then translated into a small, simple finish model and illustrates the evolutionary development process.

Project

A sculpture foundry with classrooms (addition to existing facility).

Assembly

The building of multiple frames is demonstrated, and hot glue is used for attaching balsa sticks to speed the process.

Scale: ⅛" = 1'0"

The scale is relatively large for an initial study but is needed to study framing members as they collide with roof components. Also, it provides sufficient atrium space and wall area for elevation studies. *Note:* This scale is too large in terms of design details at this level of development and makes the model appear ungainly.

Materials

- Corrugated cardboard
- Chipboard
- Balsa sticks

Illustration

The model was initiated from scaled drawings that facilitated a direct move to the development model.

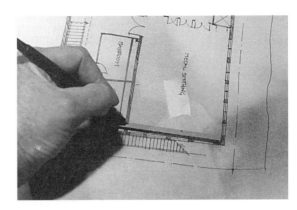

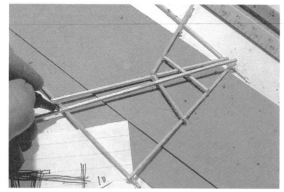

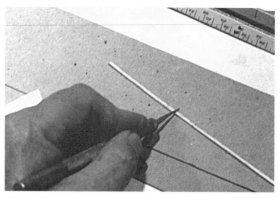

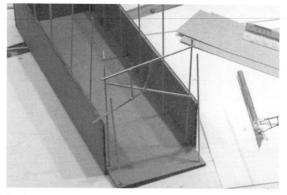

1. Following rough sketches for truss design, sticks are quickly assembled with hot glue. Time-consuming joinery is reserved for the finish model. *Note:* Measurements for additional sticks are templated directly from the model.

2. Thin balsa sticks are quickly cut by bearing down with knife and trimming with scissors. *Note:* The model saw and miter box can be used for thicker sticks, and the ends can be sanded if a higher level of finish is desired.

3. A prototype truss is installed, along with a series of frame uprights on the model base.

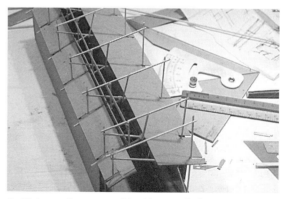

4. Trusses templated off the first construction are added. Uprights are leveled with a small triangle. *Note:* The sides serve as temporary supports and will be cut away from uprights to try alternative facades.

5. Other components, such as walls and roofs, can be templated directly off the drawings in a similar manner to the trusses.

6. Using scissors and knife, roof planes are rough-cut and fitted around the truss system.

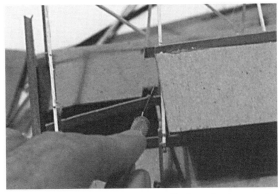

7. Smaller elements are installed and trimmed as desired once their effect has been evaluated.

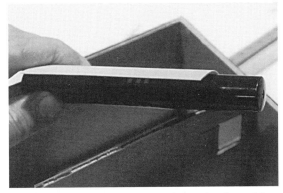

8. A curved canopy is made from chipboard by rolling the board over a felt marker.

9. Changes to openings are cut directly on the model by drafting guidelines and using a small triangle to keep knife cuts straight. *Note:* When using plastic straightedges, angle the knife slightly away from the edge to avoid cuts in the plastic.

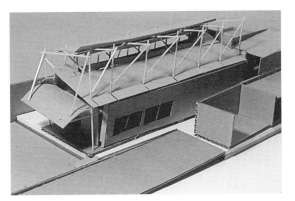

10. An initial facade is designed and evaluated in place.

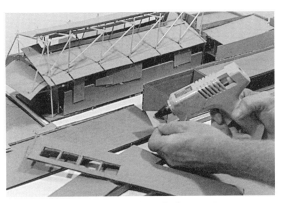

11. The wall is removed and alternative treatments are quickly cut and glued in place.

12. To complete the investigation, a third alternative facade using overlapping planes is tested and work on the finish model is begun. See Case Study C, Stage 2.

Stage 3—Finish Model

Project

A sculpture foundry and classrooms (addition to existing facility).

Assembly

The model demonstrates assembly techniques for small plastic rods as well as the building of context and site.

Scale: $\frac{1}{16}'' = 1'0''$

A small scale is selected to accommodate the site context and the minimal detailing of the larger model. *Note:* Typically, models increase in scale as more is known. In this case, by reducing the scale, the abbreviated resolution of components becomes more convincing.

Materials

- White two-ply museum board
- White plastic sticks

Illustration

The finish model is constructed both to confirm design decisions and to present to clients without the distractions of the rough assemblage.

1. Drawing information is transferred with the knife to the model base, and additional lines are drafted directly on it, as required.

2. Lines are checked for squareness as the model proceeds and adjusted to fit the emerging construction. *Note:* Bluelines become slightly stretched when printed, and, if not checked, transferred construction lines may result in poorly fitting details.

3. A gluing ledger is installed on the interior wall of the building. *Note:* The roof beyond is already showing signs of sagging due to the thin, overspanned material. The installation of reinforcing strips under the roof could have avoided this problem.

4. The knife is used to handle delicate parts.

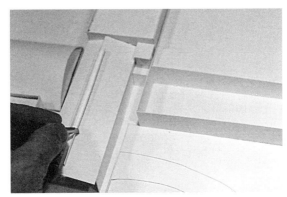

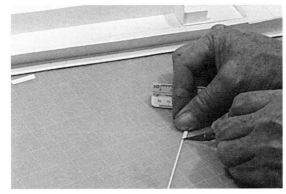

5. The flat rooftops are placed below the wall edges. *Note:* Tweezers can help when handling small pieces.

6. The initial mass model is completed, and the truss frame is detailed using thin, white plastic modeling sticks. *Note:* The accepted convention is to locate flat roofs below wall edges so the resulting parapets can be read on the model.

7. Small plastic sticks can be cut by pressing down on the knife. Larger sticks and rods must be scored and broken or sawed. Ends can be sanded to a clean, square finish.

8. Plastic is joined by placing a small drop of solvent on the joint with the knife tip. *Note:* It is helpful to apply glue over a surface, such as plastic food wrap, that will not adhere to the material.

9. Truss components are glued to the paper with white glue.

10. Subsequent components are installed.

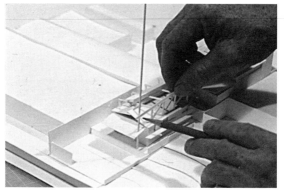

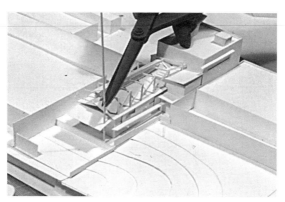

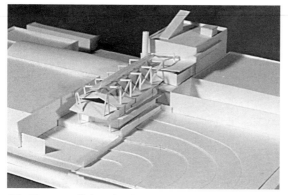

11. The exact lengths of additional components are measured directly from the model.

12. Scissors are useful for trimming pieces, as their pincer motion can be less disruptive to delicate constructions.

13. The small finished model, when side-lit for contrasting shadows, can convey a surprisingly rich level of information.

Case Study D: Office Building
Stage 1 and 2—Sketch and Development Model

Strategy

The sketch model can be used in concert with basic scaled drawings to visualize a general design direction. Once the basic building begins to emerge, the model can be used as a focal point to help visualize additional moves.

Assembly

The example demonstrates techniques for constructing multiple floors and glass walls.

Project

A five-story office building.

Materials

- Poster board
- Plastic sheet for glass

Note: For small models, thick acetate can be used, but it is not ridged enough to be convincing at larger scales.

Scale: ¹⁄₃₂″ = 1′0″

A small scale is selected to reduce the building size for initial sketch studies.

Illustration

The model was generated using scaled schematic plans and sketches, and the basic construction was then used to visualize refinements to the design.

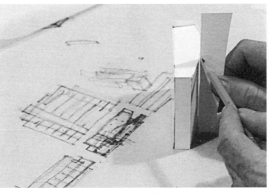

1. Scaled plan and section sketches are measured to produce initial model information. Curved pieces and other components are measured directly from the model to fit the construction. *Note:* Hot glue has been used in places for speed.

2. A drafted floor plate is attached to cardboard using a light coating of Spray Mount, and lines are transferred with a knife. The paper plans are then removed. *Note:* Spray Mount should be applied in a ventilated area.

3. Additional plates are traced from the original plate to keep cuts uniform.

4. Column centers are marked on stacked floor plates and gang-drilled. *Note:* Two columns have been pierced through all four floors to hold them in place. Straight pins can be used for the same purpose.

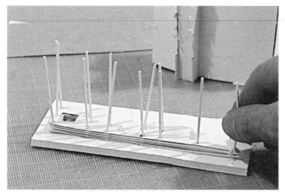

5. Columns are passed through the floor plates. *Note:* Notches in the circulation shaft have been cut to receive the floor lines.

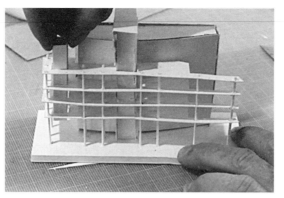

6. Plates are raised to their respective levels and inserted into the shaft slots. *Note:* Connection points are premarked on the columns. The completed unit is attached to the building body and additional shaft elements are inserted through the floors.

7. Thin Plexiglas sheets are cut for atrium glass and covered with white art tape for mullion designs. A small steel triangle is used for scoring acetate with the knife. Plastic sheeting can be broken along scored lines. *Note:* Avoid thin acetate.

8. Plexiglas is assembled using an applicator brush.

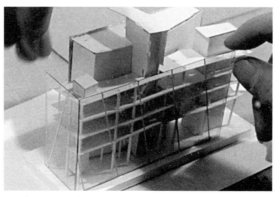

9. The partial Plexiglas construction is fitted to the body of the building.

10. The model is used to visualize terminating roof elements.

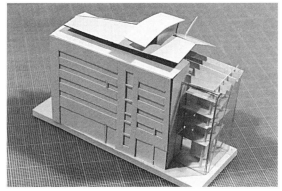

11. The Plexiglas construction is completed, and areas about to be enclosed are refaced with museum board to give the model a finished appearance. Selective parts can be recut as needed; however, refacing is generally less disruptive.

12. Window openings are cut in an overlay sheet and applied to the building face. This method is more practical than attempting to cut holes through the existing model.

13. Understated shadow lines generally read better on small models. *Note:* Additional facings can be cut and applied over all the original cuts to continue elevating the model's finish. See "Converting" in Chapter 3.

Case Study E: Urban Park
Stage 2 and 3—Development and Finish Model

Strategy

Starting with a schematic drawing to determine general plan relationships, the model is used to develop the design. At each phase, areas to be developed are based on reactions to the emerging structure.

Assembly

The project demonstrates the speed that can be attained using wood sticks, even with a dense forest of members. It also illustrates the building of base and context models.

Project

Proposal for an urban park construction.

Scale: 1/32″ = 1′0″

The scale is relatively small to accommodate the large size of the site.

Materials

- Balsa modeling sticks
- Foam core and chipboard

Illustration

The model of an urban park structure, occupying a city block in length, is used simultaneously as a sketch, development, and finish model to develop the project.

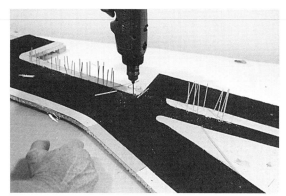

1. As in previous examples, the model is started by drilling a series of holes in the base to install column lines.

2. The base is made from an acoustical ceiling tile. Streets are painted flat black, and concrete islands and walks are made from chipboard.

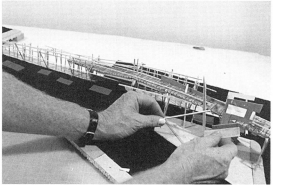

3. Balsa sticks are quickly assembled with hot glue. A concrete tower made from chipboard is integrated into this milieu.

4. Hot glue and pins are employed to keep the explorative aspects of the model moving at a steady pace.

5. Additional components are brought into the evolving design and sized in response to the other elements. Interaction between the model and the components suggested by it illustrates the idea of ongoing discovery in the design process.

6. A ramp, kiosks, benches, and other program components are installed. Roof shards are cut from balsa sheets and pinned to the column/ beam structure.

7. Final roof elements are added to complete the installation, and context buildings are built for the base. *Note:* Context models are built from foam core and painted flat gray with auto primer.

8. The model has been photographed at street level to convey the experience of inhabiting the space. *Note:* Curving roof forms have been made from Mylar drafting film.

9. A comparison of this bird's-eye view to the previous vantage point illustrates the range of readings that can be extracted from the model with the aid of a camera. See "Model Photography" in Chapter 8.

ADVANCE

Creating Curvilinear Forms and Special Techniques

The majority of modeling materials, such as boards and sticks, are conducive to building orthogonal planar shapes. Designs may often be steered by the propensity of these materials toward planar solutions when something more sculptural is desired.

In response to some of the limitations of these materials, the following section presents a range of techniques for making sculptural shapes. Because sculptural elements are more often needed as components of a model, many of the examples present ideas for creating individual shapes. These can be expanded to entire models if desired.

Equipment and Materials

Equipment

Most of the equipment used for making sculptural shapes is similar to that used for other types of model making; however, there are several specialized tools that can be helpful when working with alternative materials like wood, wire, metal sheets, and clay.

Aside from the power tools needed for woodworking, most of these tools are relatively inexpensive. For more information on woodworking and metal equipment, see "Alternative Media" in Chapter 8.

Materials

Sculptural forms can be crafted from a variety of materials. In the case of Platonic solids such as cones and spheres, conventional cardboard materials or metal sheets work well. For irregular and curvilinear forms, materials such as wood, foam, clay, wire, and plaster are more suited to the task. For additional information on working with wood, metal, and plastic, see "Alternative Media" in Chapter 8.

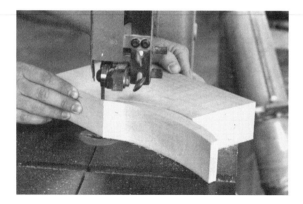

Cutting Thin Metal Sheets

- Wire side cutters
- Tin snips
- Scissors
- Matte knife

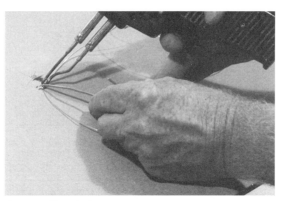

Connecting Wire

- Soldering irons (see "Basic Equipment" in Chapter 1 for soldering instruction)
- Hot glue gun
- Thread

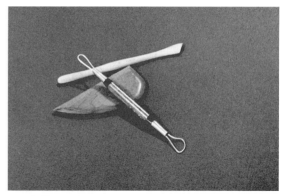

Sculpting Clays

- Cutting wires
- Shaping stick
- Smoothing board

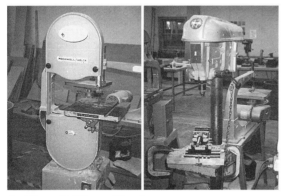

Cutting, Drilling, Shaping

- Band saw
- Table saw
- Jigsaw
- Belt sander

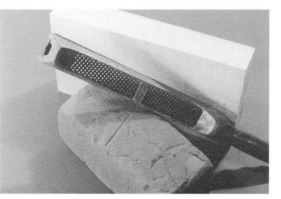

Carving Wood and Styrofoam

- Surform
- Hot wire

Carving Wood

- Carving knives
- Sandpaper

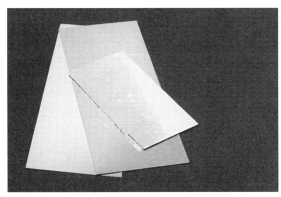

Sheet Materials

- Cardboard and paperboard
- Chipboard
- Bronze and aluminum modeling sheets

Wood Modeling Sheets

- Balsa
- Plywood
- Basswood

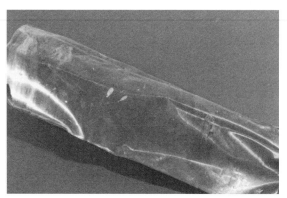

Special Metal

- Galvanized metal sheets and ducts
- Aluminum flashing
- Malleable copper sheets

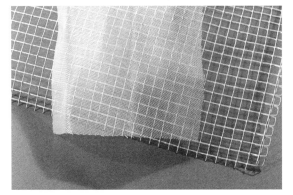

Metal Screens

- Screen wire
- Hardware cloth

Metal Rods

- Copper wire
- Aluminum wire
- Coat hangers
- Wood and plastic modeling sticks

Poured and Spread Liquids

- Molding plaster
- Papier-mâché (made from white glue and newspaper)
- PermaScene (a mâché material used by model railroad builders)

Modeling Clays

- Lizella clay
- Plasticine (plastic modeling clay)
- Sculpey (can be hard-fired in a conventional cooking oven)

Cut and Carved and Shapes

- Wood blocks
- Styrofoam blocks and shapes

Found Objects

- Styrofoam and rubber balls
- Cones, drinking cups, and bowls
- Cardboard tubes
- Plastic and foam packaging forms

Found Objects

- Old tools and utensils
- Household items
- Electronic parts
- Acrylic domes

Found Objects

Modifying Objects

Many shapes such as cones, spheres, and other complex forms can be found in a variety of everyday objects and provide quick, accurate solutions. To match the qualities of other materials, such as paper, they may be painted or plastered. The problem in employing these materials is finding a match at the scale of the model.

Generally, found objects are not exactly the right size or shape, but by altering shapes such as cones and spheres, a large variety of secondary shapes can be generated.

Found objects can also be manipulated to integrate conventional modeling components. This may involve cutting, breaking, melting, unraveling, distorting, penetrating, and so forth, to achieve the desired integration.

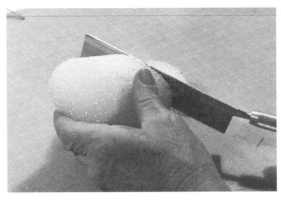

Modifying Objects
Styrofoam cones can be sawed at an angle to alter their shape.

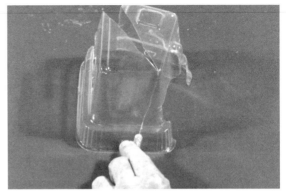

Modifying Objects
Plastic packaging can be cut with a knife to produce secondary forms.

Modifying Objects
This pasteboard cone has been truncated to change its form.

Modifying Objects
A small fragment from a lightbulb is used to create a curved wall surface.

Assemblages

This model type is made with found objects and other fragments to generate ideas.

By reading ordinary objects at another scale, the objects may be used as architectural elements. The resultant combinations can suggest forms not readily achieved with conventional materials.

Objects are most effective when used in combination with conventional model components and manipulated to yield secondary forms.

Found Cardboard Assemblage

A model using found chipboard elements. The body of the model has been cut from a cardboard dome. Sectional frames create the spherical crowning element. See "Transparent Forms" in Chapter 5.

Found-Object Assemblage

Found objects and common modeling materials such as plastic rods have been combined to produce this quick assembly. *Note:* Forms such as the spray paint cap have been cut to integrate elements.

Stone Assemblage

By assembling several configurations from fragments, interesting relationships can be uncovered that other materials may not suggest.

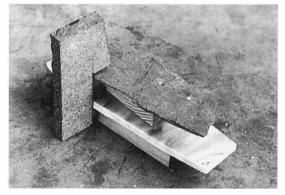

Stone Assemblage

Not only can the fragments provide a ready collection of forms, but the material qualities convey a sense of weight not found in paperboard constructions.

Metal and Plaster Assemblage

A variety of objects, including metal balls, rods, and a cast-plaster site, have been used to create this assemblage.

Planar Forms

Curved Planes

Many curved shapes can be made using common paperboard materials as well as wood and metal; see "Alternative Media" in Chapter 8. These can be assembled as complex planar forms or used to cut patterns for curvilinear solids.

The projects on the right employ simple curved planes. Cardboard planes can be curved by rolling them over curved objects, as discussed in Chapter 2. Techniques for curving metal sheets are shown on the following page.

Curving Chipboard

The components of this sculptural model have been made from chipboard sheets.

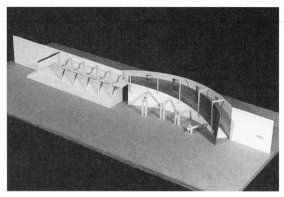

Curving Thin Wood

Balsa sheets can be used for curved sections on small models. Gluing the sheet to a base or intersecting edge can help hold the curve. *Note:* For thick wood, cutting a series of lines on the back side will allow it to curve.

Curved Metal Plane and Sphere

A curved sheet of thin metal forms the large wall. The metal sphere on top was built from pattern-cut segments. *Note:* Tape covers the joints between the segments. See "Curvilinear Solids" and "Pattern-Cut Geometric Solids" in Chapter 5.

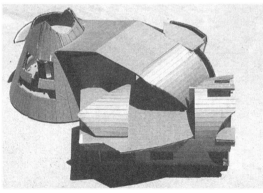

Curving Corrugated Board

To achieve a smooth curve, board should be cut at about ⅛-in. intervals through the top layer. *Note:* The lines on the cone shape radiate from a center.

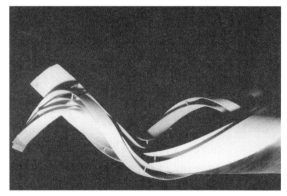

Bending Thin Wood Sheets

Thin basswood sheets can be soaked in hot water and curved, then held in place to dry.

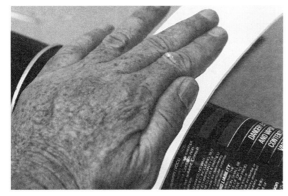

Curving Foam Core

Foam core can be rolled like thinner materials, or a number of lines can be cut through the top layer of paper. *Note:* With Artcore, a layer of paper can be removed from one side.

Working with Thin Metal Sheets

Thin metal sheets can be cut and bent easily. Bolt patterns can be embossed on the surface by hammering lightly with a pointed metal object such as a nail or punch.

Cutting Metal

Sheet metal can be cut with tin snips or metal stud shears. It can be cut from a variety of materials, including metal ducts (shown), aluminum flashing, and copper and bronze sheets.

Bending Metal Sheets

Small pieces of thin, flat metal can be curved by holding the edges and pressing with the thumbs. The sheet will need to be overbent slightly to hold the desired curve when released.

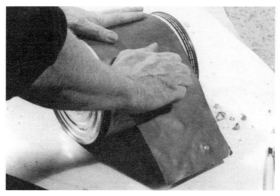

Bending Metal Sheets

Sheets can be rolled over large objects such as this gallon paint can to introduce curves in the same way cardboard is curved.

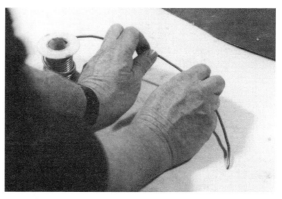

Bending Soft Metal Rods

Small copper rods and lead solder can be bent to smooth radii by using the thumbs and pushing outward. For longer pieces, sections can be bent incrementally by moving down the wire one section at a time.

Planar Solids

Platonic Planar Solids

Rectangles/Pyramids

Simple Platonic volumes can be cut from solid blocks of wood (shown below) or made by joining flat planes. One of the most common shaped volumes in architectural modeling is found in the hip roof.

The following steps detail some of the points to be noted in constructing a simple hip roof form.

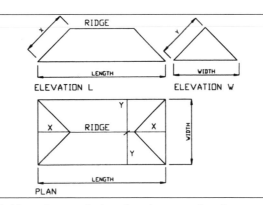

1. Elevation and plan drawings need to be made to obtain true plan dimensions for the four face components. To determine plan dimension X, use X dimension on elevation L. To determine plan dimension Y, use Y dimension on elevation W.

2. Cuts should be angled inward to achieve a mitered edge. If this is not done, the material thickness of all but the thinnest sheets will collide at the joints.

Wood Massing Model

The volumes for this model have been cut on a table saw. This method can be much faster than forming the volumes with cardboard planes. The blocks can be sanded to upgrade the finish when desired.

3. The small triangular face on the right (being put in place) has not been undercut with an angle. In comparison to the tight fit of the same element on the opposite side, this joint illustrates the potential for rough, unresolved edges.

4. Pins are used to hold the balsa sheets for assembly.

Complex Planar Solids

A large variety of planar forms can be made by attaching flat planes to define a space. Several examples are shown using planes in a variety of ways.

Planar Solids

An endless variety of volumes and forms can be made using the relatively low technology of chipboard planes.

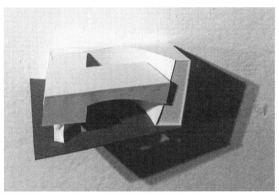

Planar Solids

Chipboard planes have been used to model these forms. *Note:* The planes have been made to warp as they follow curved surfaces.

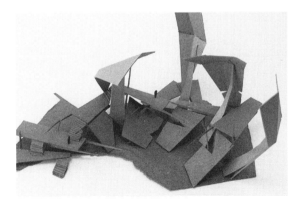

A Sketch Assemblage

Complex forms can be sketched with chipboard planes to imply volume.

Faceted Mylar Forms

Curved and faceted planes can be used to define complex curvilinear spaces.

Basswood Mass Model

Shapes have been cut on the table and band saw to produce multifaceted volumes.

Transparent Forms
Exterior Skeletal Frames

These models are similar to wire frame drawings; however, whereas the *wire frame* employs a minimum amount of members to describe only the edge conditions, the *skeletal frame* incorporates a sufficient quantity of members to describe the surface of the form. These models can describe complex forms with relative ease and have the advantage of allowing the viewer to see through to interior space.

Two approaches to frames:

1. Create a series of frames or lines using individual members.

2. Bend and warp hardware cloth, screen wire, or other malleable sheet material.

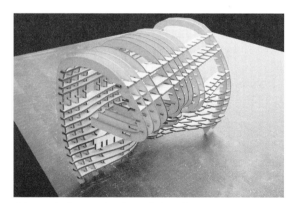

Shape Using a Series of Sections

A complex volume can be described by cutting sections at regular intervals and attaching the frames with members cut in the opposite direction. Frames for this model were cut by a laser cutter (see Chapter 8).

Chipboard Frames

By cutting successive frame segments from chipboard, a curving form can be described through the visual connection of their repetitive outlines.

Frames and Planes

A solid/void model that uses repetitive frames to describe its surfaces in combination with solid planes.

Warped Hardware Cloth

The model has been constructed using layers of hardware cloth bent in various configurations to define spatial volumes.

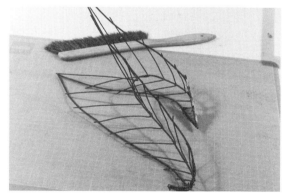

Warped Plane

Wire has been soldered in a series of ribs to describe the surface of this form.

Covering Frames

Skeletal frames can be covered with different materials to achieve the appearance of solid forms. This technique often offers the most controlled method for modeling complex curved shapes. Techniques related to this idea can be seen in the following section on working with plaster in regard to covering malleable screen wire.

Covering Chipboard Frames
A variety of shapes can be made from strips of chipboard and covered with lightweight tracing paper.

Screen Wire Volumes
Screen wire is dense enough to read as a surface and malleable enough so that it can be folded to create volumes. Screen wire may require a heavier-gauge wire frame to keep it in place.

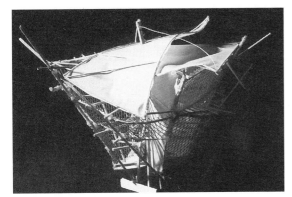

Covering Frames
By covering a frame with material that can follow its curving surface, such as cloth, drawing trace, or Mylar, solid surfaces can be created to contrast with open components.

Covering Chipboard Frames
The form has been covered with a premixed papier-mâché material sold at craft stores as PermaScene. Tracing paper is used as a base surface. Papier-mâché can also be used over screen wire and hardware cloth.

Covering Frames
Elastic stocking material was stretched over a series of frames and varnished to produce this form.

Interior Skeletal Frames

Transparent wire frames, which outline the edges of space like three-dimensional drawings, may be built to understand interior relationships between intersecting geometries. The spaces at collision points would normally be obscured by exterior wall surfaces, but because only the edges can be built, overlapping spaces can be seen and developed.

To give definition to the space, it is helpful to build out all solid surfaces, such as the floor plates, that will not obscure the area of study.

Inexpensive and easily manipulated plastic drinking straws are used for this study. The straws work well, as they can span large distances and can be cut with scissors and connected with Scotch tape. Other inexpensive materials to be considered are cardboard strips for curved lines and balsa sticks for large spans.

½″ Scale House Entry Study
This ½″ = 1′0″ scale drinking straw model was built to develop overlapping interior spaces at the entry.

Transparent Mixed Media
Materials such as hardware cloth and screen wire may also be used to allow visual access for interior development.

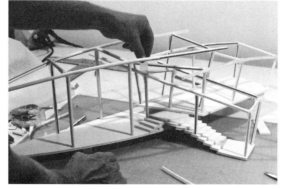

½″ Scale House Entry Study
By looking through the model and focusing on the edges of the three-dimensional "drawing," it is possible to visualize the relationship between the intersecting planes of the interior projection at the entry stairs.

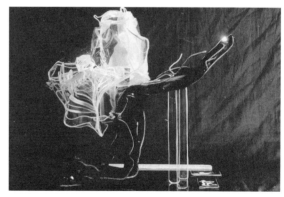

Transparent Media
An ambiguous reading can be achieved using layers of wire, melted Plexiglas, and other clear acrylic materials.

Transparent Plastic

It is sometimes desirable to incorporate thicker pieces of plastic in models for transparent layers and bases. These materials offer similar advantages to skeletal frames in allowing the viewer the ability to see through to interior spaces and can also be used to build visually interactive layers.

In all but the thinnest sheets, plastic usually means the use of Plexiglas. Plastic and acetate sheets for glazing (addressed in earlier chapters) are related to these thicker sheets but do not require special equipment to fabricate.

Material

Plexiglas is available in clear and colored 4 ft. × 8 ft. sheets. Thickness can start as small as ⅟₁₆ in. and progress to ⅛ in., ¼ in., and ½ in. Many suppliers sell scrap sheets that can be used if smaller pieces are required.

Equipment

Plexiglas sheets of approximately ⅟₁₆ in. can be cut with scoring knives or tools and broken similarly to thin plastic sheets. Thicker sheets require power tools like those used in working with wood. For more information, see "Plastic and Foam" in Chapter 8.

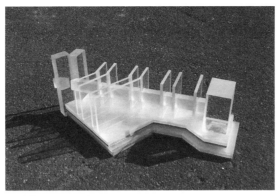

Plexiglas Walls
This model for a site space employs ¼-in. Plexiglas. The model provides a layered reading of the building diagram.

Transparent Plastic Model
The roof form and walls employ transparent layers of plastic in order to reveal inner spaces and create visual interaction between the layers.

Translucent Plastic Models
The two models on the left achieve an ephemeral quality by using thin acrylic sheets and sanded Plexiglas. The material quality of these sheets yields a reading that is crystalline and flowing. *Note:* Plastic can be bent by placing in an oven on very low heat for a few minutes, then rolling the sheet over forms such as paint cans or twisting them.

Curvilinear Solids

Pattern-Cut Geometric Solids

Geometric, or Platonic, solids such as the sphere and cone can be made from assembled sheet patterns. The advantage to constructing them this way is that, unlike found objects, they can be made to fit exact scales.

The resulting spherical forms will be slightly flattened, as true spherical segments are curved in two directions; however, the results will be acceptable for spheres with diameters up to about 4 in.

Sphere Pattern

The sphere is made by dividing the desired volume into a series of segments similar to those described by longitude and latitude lines on a globe. About 24 segments are needed to create an acceptably even pattern. More segments can be used, but at some point they may become too small to handle. If fewer segments are used, the sphere will start to appear flattened at the sides.

Techniques used to assemble the segments are shown on the following page. *Note:* Computer models use the unfold feature to resolve volumes into flat patterns, similar to the example. After edges are joined together, almost any shape imaginable can be produced from them. See "Computer Modeling" in Chapter 8.

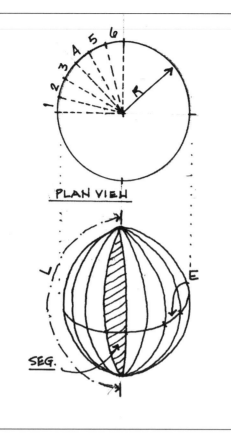

Conceptual View of Segment (Seg.)

Dimension E = circumference (2π R) ÷ the number of segments

Dimension L = half the circumference (Length along one segment line from axis pole to axis pole.) The plan view at the top shows the layout of six segments in one-quarter of the circle.

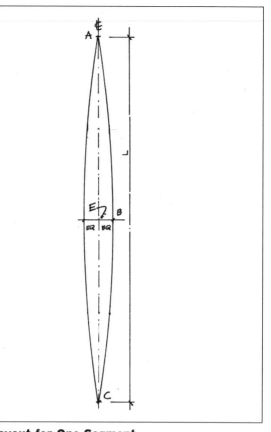

Layout for One Segment

1. Draw a centerline equal to dimension L.

2. Cross the centerline with marks equal to dimension E.

3. Draw a three-point arc through points A, B, C.

Note: The sides of the segments must be curved as shown to fill space at the edges. Simple triangular shapes will not work.

Sphere Model

With the drawings used as a guide, a sphere is built from a series of curved planar segments. The second drawing is used to determine the correct size and edge radius for each segment, which depend on the desired scale of the sphere.

The process begins by cutting a series of flat segments and then proceeds by gluing the edges together to form a sphere.

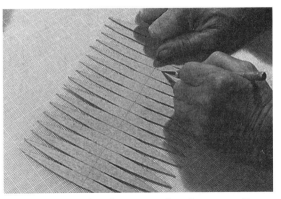

1. The pattern has been cut, leaving a small section attached but scored at the middle to facilitate assembly.

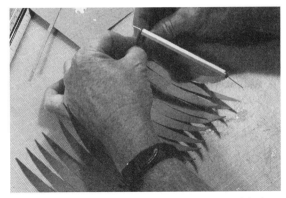

2. A stick is pinned in the middle to establish the correct diameter of the sphere.

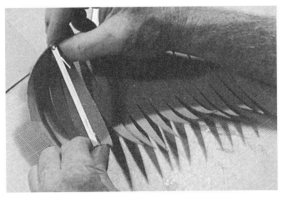

3. Each segment is glued to the edge of the segment next to it. It is helpful to add reinforcing glue to the inside of these joints once they have set.

4. The completed sphere can be painted or covered in plaster and sanded smooth for a finished appearance.

5. The shape can also be distorted to create other related forms, such as elongated football shapes.

Cone Pattern

Cones can be constructed as a measured pattern or rolled from paper to quickly approximate the desired size and shape.

The construction of a measured cone is shown on the right. A rough cone assembly is demonstrated at the far right.

To produce a measured cone shape, the pattern shown below should be followed.

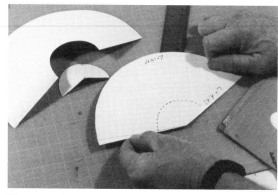

Measured Cone Pattern

A pattern cut from poster board to form a cone with a 2-in. radius (dimension L) and 4-in. height (dimension H). The angle between L radius legs is 158 degrees. *Note:* An extra tab has been glued to the edge to join the seams.

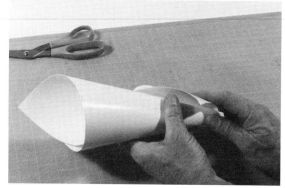

Rough Cone

To make a rough cone, material can be rolled tightly at one end and glued together.

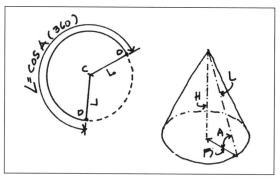

Measured Cone Pattern

L = square root of dimension H2 + R2.
To find angle A, use H/R = tan A.
The pattern will be the smaller part of the pie with the dashed line along the curve.

To Build the Cone

1. Draw two lines (L and L) from a single point joining at the angle shown [cos A (360)].

2. Measure out on lines to find L and draw a circle from this radius.

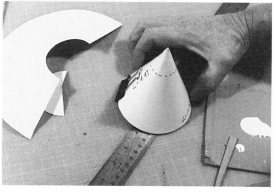

Measured Cone Pattern

The cone has been joined at the seam using a clamp until the glue dries. A second cone may be cut from the top to truncate the form, as shown by the dashed line around the top of the cone.

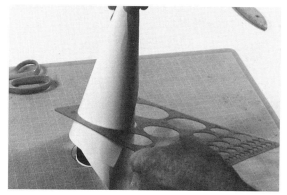

Rough Cone

To trim, a circle template can be passed over the cone, traced, and cut as desired. For angle cuts, slant the template and trace around the cone.

Cut and Carved Forms

For quick assemblages, wood blocks and Styrofoam can be cut on a table or a band saw to provide a large range of shapes. Polystyrene foam can also be cut using a hot wire cutter.

Scrap lumber from construction sites works well for this type of assemblage and is relatively inexpensive.

For more on equipment and wood types, see "Alternative Media" in Chapter 5.

Shapes Cut on the Band Saw
Shaped forms can be easily cut on a band saw from blocks of wood. The saw can be used to do rough carving, as done by a knife but much more quickly.

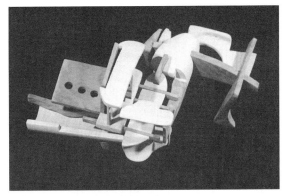

Carved and Sanded Wood
Given time, wood can be cut, sanded, and carved to make any shape imaginable.

High-Rise Assemblage
A model for a high-rise tower built from band-sawed wood, balsa sticks, and chipboard.

Styrofoam
Blocks can be carved with saws or Surforms and sanded into shapes. They can also be covered with plaster. *Note:* Use fine, even-celled blocks such as those sold for modeling or flower-arrangement bases.

Carved Styrofoam Shapes
This Styrofoam massing model has been carved from polystyrene foam with a hot wire cutter, then sanded smooth for a high level of finish.

Cutting and Carving Wood

A variety of affordable hand and power tools can be used to cut and finish wood model parts. The following illustrations give some suggestions as to how each can be used to shape and cut wood blocks. *Note:* Although power drills are not shown, they are useful for a variety of tasks and can be used in a manner similar to the examples shown in "Cutting Materials" Chapter 2, and "Case Study D" Chapter 4, for cutting/drilling holes.

Carving Wood

Shapes can be carved from blocks before or after shapes have been rough-cut with power tools. Small hobby chisels can be used, but professional wood-carving chisels will make the job go much faster.

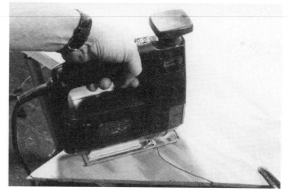

Cutting Curves

Curves can be cut in plywood and boards with an inexpensive jigsaw. These saws are limited to wood about ¾ in. thick. Thin metal can also be cut by using metal-cutting blades.

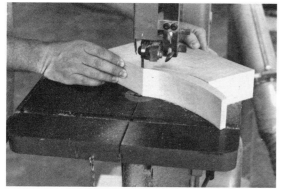

Cutting Curves

Using a band saw is the quickest way to produce rough shapes before carving and sanding. The bed can be angled for compound curves.

Sanding Blocks

Wood blocks may be smoothed with the belt sander using 100-grit belts. Shapes can be carved using coarse belts. In many applications, shaping wood on the sander may be more effective than using carving chisels.

Cutting Blocks

Wood blocks can be quickly ripped from larger pieces of wood on the table saw. *Note:* Always use a push stick, as shown, instead of your hand when working close to the blade.

Building with Plaster

Molding plaster is a versatile material that can be used to make a variety of shapes. It is inexpensive, sets rapidly, and can be sanded to a smooth finish.

Several methods are available:

- Making forms and covering them
- Covering existing shapes
- Pouring into molds

See "Alternative Media" in Chapter 8 for mixing information. *Note:* Building with plaster can be extremely messy and is best done over a disposable surface.

The following examples demonstrate the making of curvilinear forms by covering screen wire shapes with plaster and a precoated casting gauze.

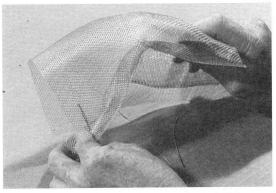

1. Screen wire is cut with scissors, molded into the desired form, and held in place with pieces of wire and string. *Note:* Materials such as hardware cloth can be used for armatures, but it is helpful to cover them in screen for plaster application.

2. The wire is then stuffed with newspaper to help prevent the plaster from falling directly through the screen. *Note:* This step may be omitted if falling plaster is not a problem.

3. A thin mix of plaster is made, and newspaper strips are dipped into the plaster and draped over the form. The plaster usually must be applied to one side at a time, allowing it to set before rolling the form over and coating the opposite side.

4. After the paper layer is finished and has set, a thicker batch is mixed and the paper is coated with a layer of pure plaster. When cured, this layer can be sanded smooth. Any remaining pockets or gaps can be filled with additional plaster and sanded smooth.

Building with Precoated Plaster Cloth (Rigid Wrap)

Typically, precoated plaster cloth is used to make casts for broken bones. This product, which can usually be found at craft or medical supply stores, is much easier to control than conventional plaster. A common brand of this cloth is sold in craft stores as Rigid Wrap.

The initial smoothness of this product and lack of waste, as compared to traditional plaster, should be evident from the example.

1. Plaster-coated gauze is used to cover a screen form by cutting strips from the roll and dipping them in water.

2. The gauze backing eliminates the need to back up the screen with paper. By crossing directions with additional layers of material, the form can achieve much greater strength.

3. After the finished form is allowed to set, a final layer of pure plaster can be smoothed over the surface to fill rough areas. When fully cured, this coating can be sanded to an even finish.

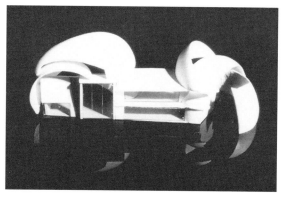

Plaster Model
This model was made using techniques similar to those used for covering. A series of warped and twisted shell components have been individually crafted, sanded, and assembled into one model.

Covering Styrofoam

Styrofoam is often coated with plaster to disguise its porous surface and match paper modeling materials such as museum board. Once plaster has set, it can be sanded smooth.

A Styrofoam ball is covered with plaster and sanded smooth.

Plaster-Covered Ball

1. A layer of plaster is spread over the ball. Often, this must be done on one side first. After this side has set, the other side can be coated.

Plaster-Covered Bowl

This half-oval shape has been covered with a thin coat of plaster. *Note:* The shape was carved from a block of Styrofoam.

Plaster-Covered Ball

2. The ball is sanded smooth. Plaster tends to clog up sandpaper and will require the use of several fresh sheets for final smoothing.

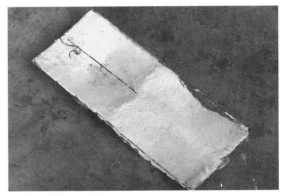

A Plaster Surface

This warped plane was made by stretching screen wire over a wire frame and covering it with plaster. *Note:* Gauze was used instead of newspaper to carry the plaster.

Coating Chipboard

Existing shapes can be covered with a layer of plaster for texture or to match white paper. Spackling or premixed Sheetrock finishing compound can be used for this as well. Integral color can be achieved by mixing a small amount of powdered dye in with the plaster or spackling. Chipboard is used as a base because it allows the plaster to grip its relatively porous surface. Although it offers the simplest form of backing surface, this material is not ideal. The water content inherent to plaster can cause it to lose its form, and the surface grip is such that plaster may flake off after it has dried. These problems can be partially solved by using heavier material and reinforcement and gluing cloth to the surface to provide extra gripping power.

Spreading Plaster on Chipboard
Plaster can be spread directly onto chipboard and sanded smooth. Several layers may be required to achieve the desired consistency.

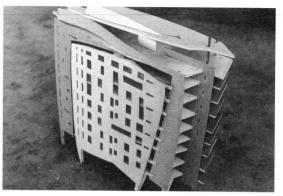

A Plastered Model Facade
The surface of this building facade has been covered with spackling to produce a textured finish. *Note:* Integral color has been used on one of the layers to provide contrast.

Plaster Contours
Although contours can be covered with plaster, a negative mold of the site can also be made and cast in plaster. See "Molding with Plaster and Resins" in this chapter.

Plaster Contours
Contours of this site model have been built up by applying spackling over chipboard and sanding it smooth.

Molding with Plaster and Resins

Plaster can be poured into molds to form a variety of shapes. Pouring plaster is particularly advantageous when making multiples of the same form and for pouring monolithic (solid) curved shapes.

The molds are constructed as the negative of the desired form. This method is similar to forming techniques for cast concrete, and concrete formwork manuals are full of ideas.

The processes that have been discussed to this point have been additive in nature; that is, the shapes and forms were built up by attaching pieces. The molding process is different from this, because before an object can be formed, its opposite, or "negative," must be constructed.

Plaster must then be poured into the form or negative to yield a "positive" shape. Forms can be poured as solids or backed with cloth to create "thin shell" forms.

The following projects were made using casting techniques. Basic casting and mold-making techniques are illustrated in more detail on the following pages.

Multiple Forms
The multiple forms for this multistory study were made using a wire frame mold. Successive pours were popped from the mold and strung together on the three columns.

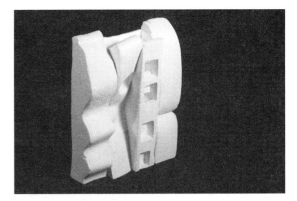

Plaster Cast Model
A form was made first as a negative of the model. Shapes were then carved and sanded out of the rough casting.

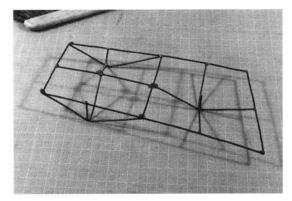

Molding Frame
This frame was covered in tape and used to create the plaster mold for the example above. *Note:* The mold was greased with petroleum jelly to keep the plaster from sticking. Pam (cooking spray) can also be used.

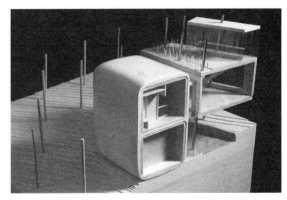

Fiberglass Model
This model has been made from fiberglass sheeting and resin layered over a mold, similar to boat construction. Several sheets are needed as well as a final coat of urethane before sanding smooth and painting.

Basic Casting

Casting plaster and other materials involves the use of a mold or negative. This form will be the reverse volume, or "negative," of the form you are trying to make. For example, if the desired form is a half of a sphere, the mold will be a bowl. To remove the casting, the mold must be flexible or slightly conical. If sides are "undercut" or have a lot of texture, the casting may be caught in the mold. Undercuts can be employed if the mold can be peeled away or broken off. A release agent is needed to help keep the material from sticking to the mold. A thin coat of petroleum jelly can be wiped on the form or an aerosol cooking oil can be lightly sprayed on the form.

Project A–Pouring Resin

Following product mixing directions, polyester resin has been combined with a catalyst and poured into a plastic mold that can be peeled off. Common release agents cannot be used, as they will react with the resin.

Project A–Cast Resin and Mold

The mold is peeled from the hard resin casting. Resin offers a very smooth surface finish. It can also be bought as a clear casting resin at craft stores. *Note:* Dyes of various colors can be added to clear resin, as desired.

Project B–Pouring the Mold

Plaster has been poured into a muffin pan sprayed with a release agent. This mold is ideal, as the sides are slightly conical. If the sides sloped in the opposite direction, the casting could not be extracted.

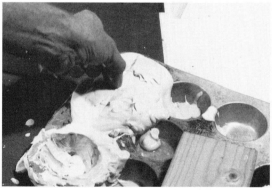

Project B–Reinforcing the Casting

Wires or sticks can be pushed into the wet plaster to reinforce the casting. These act like reinforced concrete, supplying tensile strength to the material.

Project B–Casting and Negative Mold

After about 30 minutes, the plaster can be pulled from the mold. *Note:* The "positive" form of the plaster is the opposite of the "negative" form of the mold.

Casting Molds

Casting molds, or "negatives," can be made from a variety of materials. They do not need to be elaborate constructions. All that is required is that they hold the plaster until it is set in the desired shapes.

The examples on this page show some of the possibilities.

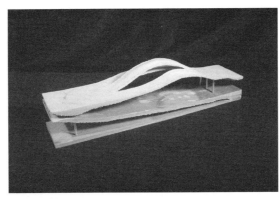

Sand Casting

A box mold can be filled with sand. The sand can be shaped and a layer of anchoring cement poured on top. When finished, the sand is shaken out. Successive layers can be built up to create multilevel structures. See Chapter 8.

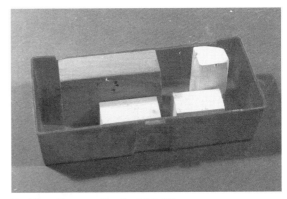

Rubber Box or Bucket Mold

Rubber boxes and buckets work well because they are flexible and can be expanded to release the casting. *Note:* Objects have been placed in the box and will leave spaces in the casting wherever they displace material.

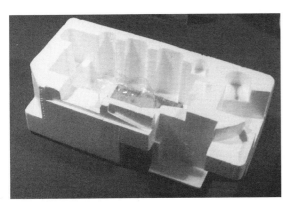

Found-Object Mold

Interesting mold shapes or "negatives" can be found in packing spacers and other found objects. The shapes that would result from pouring this mold must be visualized by reversing the image of the negative volume.

Plastic Mold

Clear plastic molding material can be bought or found as a variety of packaging items. This molding material can be peeled away from the casting, allowing the use of limited "undercuts."

Casting in a Wood Box Mold

A wood box may be built by nailing sides to a baseboard or holding the sides with weights, as shown. All of the objects higher than the sides of the box will become holes through the casting. *Note:* A release agent was sprayed on.

Augmented Casting Methods

Postcasting Techniques

After the initial pour, operations such as the casting of additional layers or pushing objects into wet plaster can be used to further manipulate the casting.

Form Removal

Several techniques may be used to break the casting from the mold and extract objects from the plaster.

The casting of additional layers is illustrated at the top of the page. Problems of form removal are demonstrated below.

Building Up Casting
Using the casting on the previous page, another set of forms is built on top to add layers to the pour.

Imprinting Forms
The formwork has been removed to reveal the built-up section as well as depressions made by pressing blocks into the wet surface of the casting.

Removing Objects
Cardboard and plastic forms can be pulled away easily from the dry casting. Other objects can be extracted only after the plaster is trimmed back with a knife. Gluing objects to the base will help stop plaster leaks.

Removing Objects
The use of clay or Plasticine allows some undercutting to be employed, but these objects must be dug out of the casting. If wood blocks are used, they should be sanded and slightly tapered or they will not come out.

Negative Cavities
The holes were created where plastic film containers were taken out of the casting. *Note:* The casting will be fragile for some time after it is set and is easily broken with the stress of removing objects even after curing.

Multimedia

Although the models presented in earlier chapters have generally been made using one type of material, various materials can be combined to make the model. This has already been seen to some degree in contrasting site materials as well as glazing and screen wall applications. Further use of multimedia can help establish the coding of elements, as discussed in Chapter 3, "Development: Coding and Hierarchy of Materials," and also helps convey a sense of materials as they relate to the project's meaning and finishes.

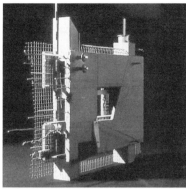

Multimedia
A simple two-part combination of heavy wood planes and light, wire hardware cloth helps to reinforce the binary dialogue of the project.

Multimedia
A collection of materials including foam core, chipboard, wood, and cork sheeting helps code each section of the model to create a readily understood ensemble.

Multimedia
A large model measuring 4 ft in height, this construct employs Plexiglas, steel, and plaster to convey the dynamics of the space and materiality of the primary elements.

Multimedia
A combination of wire, hardware cloth, paper, foam core, and wood sticks has been used; these materials readily lend themselves to modeling elements such as columns, planes, and open grids.

Multimedia
A concept model using wood shards and sticks with foam core and Plasticine (curving lines in center). Materials have been selected based on contrasting color and the ability to form shapes and planes.

Malleable Materials

Malleable materials such as Lizella clay and Plasticine can be easily formed to take on complex sculptural shapes. Of the two materials, Plasticine is generally used because it does not dry out and crack. In addition, because it is not water based, it can be used in combination with paper materials.

It can be difficult to achieve hard edges with malleable material, and they often require internal wire and wood supports to maintain their shape. However, there is no need to build a negative form (as required in casting plaster models), and subtracting parts is relatively easy.

Clay is worked using sculpting tools such as cutting loops, shaping sticks, kitchen knives, and smoothing boards; see "Equipment" earlier in this chapter.

For forms that will set hard after molding by hand, materials such as Sculpey, a ceramic hybrid available at craft stores, can be molded and fired in an ordinary kitchen oven.

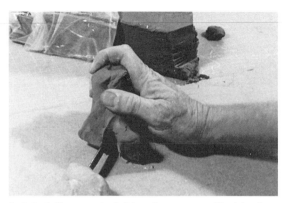

1. Modeling material has been cut off a block of Plasticine and formed by hand. Material can be removed as desired with a kitchen knife and sculpting tools. *Note:* The material is easier to work when it is warm. Hand molding will help transfer body heat.

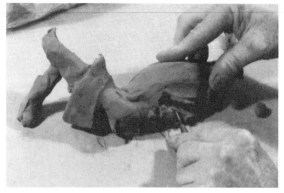

2. Wire loops like those used for working with clay can also be helpful for carving out recesses in the material.

3. Cantilever projections can be supported by inserting wire or wood rods through these sections into the body of the model.

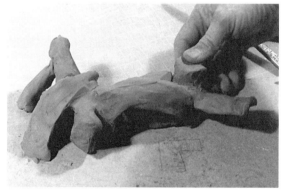

4. The completed form can be smoothed out by hand or with sculpting tools. *Note:* Removal of all hand marks can involve an inordinate amount of time.

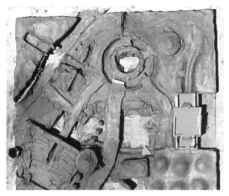

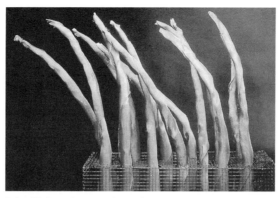

Malleable Site Model

A Plasticine site model can be molded in a similar manner to the actual site soil and used for quick studies. *Note:* It can be difficult to transfer final grade elevations from this type of site model.

Plasticine Concept Model

This spatial interpretation of the book *Everglades: River of Grass* by Marjory Stoneman Douglas is facilitated by the plastic qualities of clay materials.

BUILD

Implementing Model
Exploration as Built Work

Examples of model usage can be found in every level of the design environment, ranging from sole practitioners to firms with international reputations. In practice, modeling offers one of the strongest ways to understand the impact of design decisions on the built work and is of particular value when working with complex geometries.

The following projects present examples of models from several types of practices. Many of the strategies discussed in Chapters 3 and 4 can be seen at work, as well as the connection between built work and the model history that helped form it.

Mack Scogin Merrill Elam Architects

(Formerly Scogin Elam and Bray)

This office makes extensive use of the model in the development of every project. A cross section of work reveals many of the strategies in Chapter 3 applied in response to a particular need or situation. Whereas the structure of one project may be difficult to understand without the aid of a detailed model, another may require a scaled-up section to study the spatial experience.

The role of the model is also seen to vary depending on the design evolved. In some cases, a combination of models and drawings has been used, and in others, multiple alternates or exclusive reliance on the model formed the rule.

Examples drawn from six different projects are used to illustrate the diverse role of the model in the daily course of this firm's practice.

Buckhead Library

Atlanta, Georgia

The models from the project demonstrate two primary ways they are treated. First, because the project was initially developed with the drawings, a small ⅛" = 1'0" scale model was built to confirm decisions. In the second instance, in order to develop the entry sequence and canopy elements, the front section was increased in size to a ¼" to 1'0" scale. At this scale, the model was large

enough to convey the experience of the space. The image of the completed building confirms the ability of the scaled-up model to predict a reality.

Buckhead Library–⅛" scale
This small development/finish model was made after the overall design relationships were established. It depicts a three-dimensional sketch of the entry canopies at the front of the building.

Buckhead Library–¼" = 1'0" Elevation
The front section of the building has been doubled in scale in order to develop the design of the entry canopies. The model and elevation drawings were used in concert to compose its elements.

Buckhead Library–Completed Building
The completed building, in a view similar to that taken of the ¼" scale model, reflects the quality of space projected in the design studies.

BIS Competition
Berne, Switzerland

Laban Dance Centre Competition
Deptfrod Creek, London, England

Reston Museum
Reston, Virginia

Models played a central role in the development of these three projects. The models used for the Reston Museum demonstrate a strong reliance on alternatives. In the BIS competition, the idea of alternatives was expanded to the production of numerous parts, combined to create dozens of schemes. The Laban Dance Centre models were generated in an extensive progression.

BIS Addition–Scheme 1

This project required three schemes for an addition to the central conical tower. A small context model of the urban area was used to test relationships with the urban context.

Laban Dance Centre–Full Model Array

The full evolutionary array of models used to develop the Laban Dance Centre design is shown, including every possible stage of development with many alternative explorations.

Reston Museum–Alternative Schemes

Five alternatives were developed for this project. After using drawings to help develop the program on the first model, small two-dimensional sketches were used to initiate the other schemes.

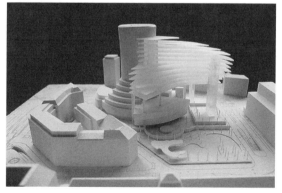

BIS Addition–Scheme 2

In the course of the developing schemes, numbers of alternative variations were generated. In this view, the addition takes the form of a series of shifted layers rotating off the tower's axis.

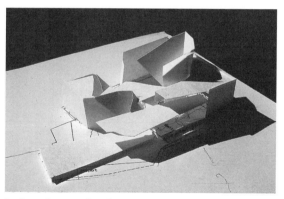

Laban Dance Centre–Sketch Model

A small sketch model extracted from the model progression above at the point where early conceptual models were translated into program space.

Morrow Library

Morrow, Georgia

Beginning with a small concept drawing, the majority of design work was carried out directly in model form. Three clear stages of model progression were used, along with a scaled-up model of the central tower.

Unique to the project was the construction of an adjustable model to test roof relationships, as well as the production of construction drawings from measurements taken from the models. To produce drawings of the tower shown below, the model was not only measured but photocopied and traced to create elevations; see "Transferring Model Data" in Chapter 8.

Morrow Library—Adjustable Model
The model was constructed to operate like a puppet and used to adjust relationships between the roof planes. The corner points of each roof could be moved by pulling sticks protruding below the baseline.

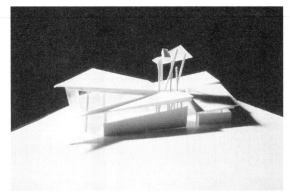

Morrow Library—Development Model
Once basic relationships were established, a small study model was made to refine the general relationships. The tower model shown on the bottom left was made to develop its components.

Morrow Library—Finish Model
At this point, the design was generally complete and drawings were made to refine the elevations. Exposed structure was used in the building, and the final model included all of it to study its visual effect.

Morrow Library—Completed Building
When implemented, the building confirmed many of the decisions the model helped resolve.

Turner Center Chapel
Atlanta, Georgia

Although several of the previous examples included scaled-up sections used to work out ideas, the Turner Chapel project approached the need for closer study by employing a combination detailing/framing model. Owing to the close proximity of interwoven truss members, the lower half of the finish model was scaled up to a ½" = 1'0" model and used to work out (or resolve) the detailing relationships for the glazing connections.

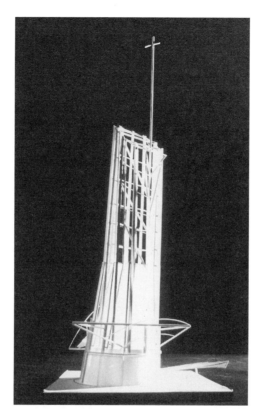

Turner Chapel—Finish Model

This model was preceded by several small studies, and the entire structural system was drawn on the computer to locate dimensions and angles. Although the 80-ft steel building to the left attests to the eventual success of the design, what could not be understood at this point was the three-dimensional interaction between steel members in the lower half of the building.

Turner Chapel—½" = 1'0" Model

The lower section of the tower was glazed and a framing system that would ensure against warped surfaces was required. To work out the detailing, the lower section was scaled up and each member modeled within the inch. Although computer modeling may have been a viable alternative, two-dimensional computer drawings did not provide enough information to control the complexity of relationships.

Callas, Shortridge Associates

Seagrove House

Santa Rosa Beach, Florida

Among other projects, this firm has designed many outstanding houses and uses the study model as a site for exploration throughout the process.

The model is a key element in understanding the dynamic space of the Seagrove House. Of special interest is the evolution of model refinement, particularly in the development stage, and the use of the model on the site as a tool for construction visualization. The images on this page compare views of the on-site model and the project as it nears completion. All roofs are constructed so that they can be removed from the models to reveal interior spaces and framing systems.

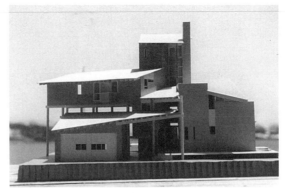

Seagrove House–Finish Model
North elevation of the final model was used during construction to understand overall relationships and framing. The model has been increased in scale from the last development model on the following page and detailed.

Seagrove House–Finish Model
South elevation of the final model. When compared with a similar view of the built work, it becomes clear that the model space carries strong predictive powers.

Seagrove House–Built Work
As it nears completion, the active space of the built work reflects the model's ability to orchestrate the composition. On entering, the space exceeds the promise of the model.

Seagrove House–Built Work
The built work offers two different readings from front to back. Whereas the north elevation breaks apart to perform a dance in space, this elevation engages the southern horizon.

Seagrove House

Study/Development Models

These models represent explorations used to define various sections of the building. At this point, a rough general scheme has been established and study begins by orchestrating the overall building. As sections are generally resolved, focus can be seen to shift to alternate solutions for individual elements.

The study culminates in a development model with relationships similar to the finish model but less detailed.

Seagrove House–Stage 1

At this point the house appears related to its final form, but the walls have yet to be defined. Individual elements are only suggested, and other forms of expression are explored.

Seagrove House–Stage 2, Front

The major elements on the north elevation appear to be formed at this stage, and alternative elements such as the angled box (with taped corners on the second story) are experimented with.

Seagrove House–Stage 3, Lakeside

The south elevation of the development model appears generally formed. Study has been focused on the tower and the spaces directly below it.

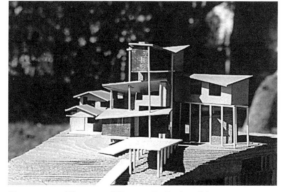

Seagrove House–Stage 4, Lakeside

At this point, most of the spaces on the south elevation have been established, and final refinement can take place.

Seagrove House–Stage 5, Front

This development model is similar to the final model, except less attention has been given to detailing openings and intersections.

MC2 Architects Inc.

Hemphill House

Atlanta, Georgia

Dekalb Avenue House

Atlanta, Georgia

This design-build firm uses the model on every project, which underlines the point that modeling can benefit every form of practice.

Models for the projects on the right were used in concert with drawings to develop the houses. The projects were built as speculative in-town developments and focused on aspects of the site to direct the model study.

The models are from the development state of the projects, and although sketch model studies were made early on, many of the important issues of expression and detailing were resolved directly on these models.

The model for the Hemphill House was used in several ways, but one important aspect, illustrated above, was the framing detailing for the roof structure. The model for the Dekalb Avenue House illustrates the development of the long, sweeping granite wall in relation to the built work below.

Hemphill House Model
The roof structure describes a hyperbolic curve. Every member has been creatively engineered to shape the design and control its weight as it floats over a glass clerestory.

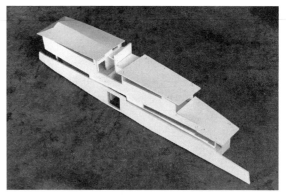

Dekalb Avenue House
The model is a good example of a solid/void study at the development stage; ultimately, it helps guide the detailing to make the building appear to rise out of the linear granite wall.

Hemphill House
While the shallow curve is difficult to see in this small image, the flying roof form reads well as it hovers over the house below. Careful study with the model ensured that detailing of the roof supports maintain this reading.

Dekalb Avenue House
Relationships established by the model can be seen to have carried through in the built work as the house nears completion.

Venning, Attwood and Kean Architects

Harvey Law Offices

Atlanta, Georgia

The nature of interior space is such that dynamic planes and elements can be extremely difficult to understand in drawing form. Although these designers typically work in model form, it was particularly important for this project that decisions be made with study models. Views of the built space are paired with model views and reveal the way the model allows the viewer to "walk through" the space.

View Up Central Stairs/Law Library

The model view above shows the screen panels and hyperspace described by the stair structure. The image at the top right was taken looking into this area. The screen panels, stairway, and bookshelves can be seen moving up through the space.

View Along Entry Wall

The view of the model space to the right is taken in the hallway as one enters the space along the curving wall. The model face has been cut away to allow vision into this area. The image on the far right of the built work was taken in the same space on the opposite side of the curving wall.

Roto Architects Inc.

This firm employs a flexible improvisational working style that adapts itself to the inevitable and unique aspects of each project. Much of the work has been designed and built through collaborative relationships with clients. In the course of this collaboration, various design methods have been explored, with modeling playing a key role in the development of new systems.

Sinte Gleska University (SGU)

Antelope, South Dakota

Sinte Gleska University is the first and oldest tribal university in the Americas. Roto Architects was asked to plan and build an entirely new campus for the university. The project used models to develop highly refined readings of the spatial and diagrammatic structures of the Lakota traditional systems of movement and rest. The detailed model of the multipurpose building displays many of the aspects in respect to focusing and hierarchy.

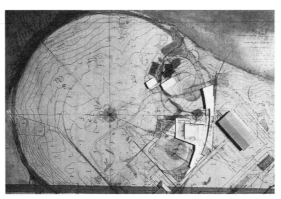

SGU Master Plan

Models and drawings have been used in concert to map out site relationships that reflect traditional Lakota spatial systems.

SGU Multipurpose Building

Modeling elements were used to develop and detail every structural member and incorporate traditional Lakota beliefs and a layering of ordering systems.

SGU Technology Building and Student Center

The ribbed roof structure, moving from left to right, employs modeling to describe the form of mythological star formation bridging between the two buildings.

SGU Multipurpose Building

A highly developed detail of the Kapemni, or universal model (center), considers every structural element in relation to scale and hierarchy, extending attention down to the 27 symbolic ribs of the buffalo, as shown in the center of the roof structure.

Teiger House

Bernardsville, New Jersey

The project sought to express concepts of dynamic human organizations in three-dimensional diagrams. The models and drawings were used to develop linear, incremental ordering systems with frequencies and phasing that worked simultaneously in plan and section.

The finish model reads as a series of units that reflect this system, and the framing models reveal the incremental aspect and simultaneity of layers. This ability to see through the layers of the framing model makes it a valuable site for exploration of internal relationships, as discussed in "Transparent Forms" in Chapter 5.

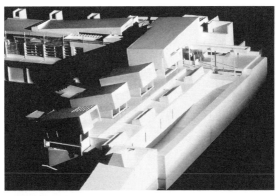

Teiger Finish Model
Although the built work employs a variety of color and materials, the model relies on abstraction to allow materials to be imagined and convey the overall pattern of formal relationships.

Teiger Framing Model
The transparent nature of the framing model is not only used to develop sectional relationships but also plays off the conventions of repetitive framing members to establish an incremental ordering system.

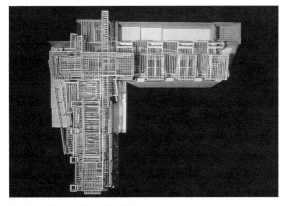

Teiger Framing Model
The overlapping rectangular frames set up multiple ordering relationships when apprehended as a stack of superimposed images.

Dorland Mountain Arts Colony

Temecula, California

The project replaces a small retreat building for an arts colony. The building reflects the way that indigenous structures form unique volumes based on the constraints of time and materials. The models are an exercise in three-dimensional drawing. By placing key members to shape the volume, a structural frame is developed, which springs from unique construction and bracing systems.

Carlson-Reges Residence

Los Angeles, California

This residence was built as a series of additions grafted onto an existing industrial building. Materials were primarily brought into the project from a scrap yard adjacent to the building. As much of the work was developed as an ongoing work in progress, models were used to direct overall moves on each section and evolve expression during construction.

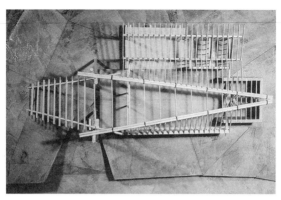

Dorland Mountain Arts Colony
The diagram of the triangulated frame and its subsystems can be clearly read in the plan view.

Dorland Mountain Arts Colony
The volume generated by filling in the spaces demonstrates the effectiveness of using a three-dimensional diagram to establish the skeletal outline. The model also facilitates the rethinking of triangulated bracing systems.

Carlson-Reges Residence
The quality of the existing space is reflected in this interior model, and the effects of the new light monitor can be experienced just as it might read in the space. See "Interior Models" in Chapter 1.

INTERFACE

Combining Digital and Physical Model Information

Until recently, the use of digital modeling programs and the use of physical models have traveled along divided paths. However, over the last five years, there has been a growing shift toward combining the two. On one hand, the complete exclusion of the physical model has been recognized as a limitation from a perceptual standpoint. Conversely, the ability to manipulate form and generate controlled drawing information from digital programs, particularly curvilinear forms, has spawned the adoption of digital modeling methods. This chapter explores the digital/physical modeling relationships found in current design firms and the emergence of the *rapid prototyping model* (referred to as RP). Co-opted from the industrial and engineering design industry, this tool allows three-dimensional models to be generated directly from computer models. While there remains discussion concerning the secondary role these models play in contributing to design exploration, there is no doubt that this process bridges the gap between digital and physical models. See Chapter 8 for information concerning rapid prototyping processes and equipment.

Morphosis

From conversation with architect Ben Damon

Morphosis has traditionally designed with drawings and physical models. With the shift to computer modeling, there was a desire to see virtual space rendered in physical space at regular intervals. Rapid prototyping provided this capability and led the firm to become one of the first architectural practices to purchase rapid prototyping equipment.

The way that Morphosis works between the computer and rapid prototype models is probably exemplary of the way this relationship will develop for many firms. For Morphosis, the computer is perceived as the best way to speed up exploration, so concept and massing models are initiated with the computer. From this stage, they engage in a period of back-and-forth dialogue between a number of small rapid prototype models and the computer models. Each generation of rapid prototype models is changed and explored in the computer. Then large paper models are built to study interior spatial relationships. The computer also is felt to be important during the design development stage, as all changes to the computer model keep the drawings automatically updated and provide a high degree of accuracy.

Typically, firms that do not own rapid prototyping printers send files out and have models made at an interim design point and on completion. Having the model printer in-house has changed all this and facilitates an ongoing dialogue between physical and virtual models. Also, difficult forms and complex curves can now be explored with confidence and control. The printer can also be used to make full-scale details.

RP models at Morphosis are used in the form in which they are printed with limited attempts made to improve their slightly rough appearance. Their primary concern is to learn something from the model, and they accordingly regard all of their models as study models.

When asked about the eventual shift to all-digital information that many consider inevitable, Mr. Damon responded emphatically, "Physical models will never go away. . . . We will never be able to completely shift over." His feelings were based on the removal imposed by the computer, whereby the depiction of space is divorced from the tactile process. For Morphosis, physical models offer a way to understand space that cannot be seen or experienced in the computer. Also, physical models are viewed as the most powerful and accurate vehicle for communicating with clients.

Morphosis has relied on Form Z for computer modeling in the past but has shifted their model work into TriForma to take advantage of the seamless interface with MicroStation.

Rensselaer Polytechnic Institute's Electronic Media and Performing Arts Competition

The RPI project serves as a good example of rapid prototyping capabilities. Because of the ability to transfer modeling information directly to the powder printer, the designers were free to explore form beyond what was previously possible (without using clay or other plastic media). The project proceeded by fitting the program to a fixed configuration then draping the enclosure around it. Earlier interest in the egg form was used as a starting point, then pushed and pulled in a Boolean approach to arrive at the refined shell. Due to the relatively small size of the 8-in. cubic printer bed, the model was tiled and made up of six or seven separate pieces.

Rensselaer Polytechnic Institute's Electronic Media and Performing Arts Competition
This model is one of a series made to design the performing arts building. It was developed using Form Z and a 310 powder printer from Z Corp. It is made of several pieces in order to overcome the size limitations of the printing bed.

Rensselaer Polytechnic Institute's Electronic Media and Performing Arts Competition
This section model of the building illustrates the advantages of being able to output different cross-section and scale studies. Once the computer model is in place, this can be done with very little additional time or expense.

Mack Scogin Merrill Elam Architects

Mack Scogin and Merrill Elam have a long tradition of designing and developing projects through physical study models. Some of these can be seen in Chapter 6. Like many firms, the way they work has evolved to include computer modeling. It is probably accurate to say that most of their projects are currently developed on parallel tracks. One track uses physical models to develop the project and the other track uses computer modeling images to communicate and study aspects of the project. This has not led to the kind of reliance many have come to place on the computer model as the primary generator of form. Rather, the computer is used to control and generate those things that it is best suited for, such as complex organic forms, while physical models are used extensively for all other studies. Large-scale physical interior models are felt to be particularly valuable in understanding space.

The firm uses Form Z and AutoCAD as their primary digital programs. Rapid prototyping has played a role in their model making as well, but like computer modeling, it is generally limited to organic forms. This typically results in a hybrid construction, with the majority of the model made in-house and special parts being sent out to be made with stereolithography.

Illustration

The following examples are from two projects that illustrate both ends of the spectrum. The Children's Museum is modeled almost entirely with rapid prototyping; however, it is instructive to see that the generative and explorative studies are made with traditional sketches and physical models.

Conversely, the Fine Arts Center has been made mostly by hand with special sections made as rapid prototype components.

The Children's Museum

This project uses a combination of methods to explore and develop the design. The initial move is started with a hand drawing; then a foam model is made to capture the dimensional suggestions of the drawing. Computer models are drawn to give precise definition to the space. Finally, an RP stereolithography model is output to produce physical confirmation of the space.

The Pittsburgh Children's Museum
The hand sketch of the project is ambiguous and suggestive in the way clearly defined computer drawings typically are not.

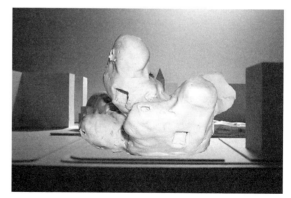

The Pittsburgh Children's Museum
A foam sketch model attempts to interpret the space implied by the drawing.

The Pittsburgh Children's Museum
A computer model of the space is made to refine the space and program fit.

Fine Arts Center–University of Connecticut at Storrs

This project uses a hybrid approach. Stereo-lithography models are made only of parts that are thought to be too complex for hand-modeling techniques. These parts are first assembled with each other (to overcome size limitations of the modeling equipment) and then assembled with the hand-cut components of the entire building model.

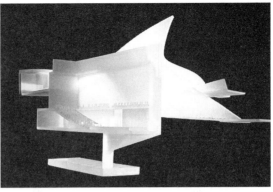

Fine Arts Center–University of Connecticut at Storrs
The flowing curvilinear parts on the rear section of the building have been RP-modeled as a collection of several parts and attached to the hand-cut parts.

The Pittsburgh Children's Museum
A stereolithography model output from computer modeling information.

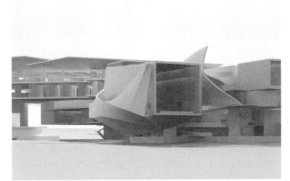

Fine Arts Center–University of Connecticut at Storrs
A computer rendering of the building shows the section of the building where rapid proto-typing has been employed.

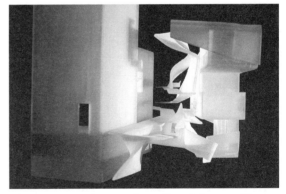

Fine Arts Center–University of Connecticut at Storrs
The stair components are made from several RP pieces and incorporated into the hand-built model.

Eisenman Architects

From conversations with Larissa Babij and Peter Eisenman

Peter Eisenman's office has a long history of exploring space with the extensive use of physical models. Over the past 15 years, the computer has come to play a large role in the design process, but it has not replaced physical models. The primary advantages of the computer are the ways in which it can handle complex space and extend conceptual possibilities. At the same time, the physical model plays an important role in understanding what has been created and developing large-scale studies. In response to these methods, Mr. Eisenman comments, "I develop in the computer because you can do things in the computer you cannot do in the 3D model, but you model them to understand what they are really like. There is always a conscious dialogue between the computer model and the three-dimensional model. . . . We work back and forth between computer models. . . . I make all my spatial corrections on three-dimensional models. . . . With the computer you can just jerk anything around. . . . With three-dimensional models, I can see what is really happening . . . what the space is going to be like because you know it is an analog of the space."

Mr. Eisenman's office uses Rhinoceros for many projects as well as 3D Studio MAX. (AutoCAD is used for two-dimensional drawing.) The choice varies depending on the project, but Rhinoceros appears to be the most applicable. Physical models are built, for the most part, in the office. The computer models provide a great degree of control over the work, both in the design process and for the actual building drawings. Sections are cut through the Rhino computer model to get a precise reading of how the building needs to be built. The physical models are also important for checking what has been done in the computer in order to correct things such as spatial conflicts.

The City of Culture, Santiago, Spain

The example shown is from the City of Culture in Santiago, Spain. Over the years, Peter Eisenman has developed a working method as a form of spatial excavation in which he overlays a drawing of the historical map of the city, the city grid, and the topography. This composite is then manipulated to begin making spatial interpretations. For the City of Culture, the first manipulations were made with Rhinoceros to produce a conceptual drawing model. Complex glass facade and soffit elements run through the whole project. Conceptual computer drawings were translated into large-scale detail models to explore these elements. Changes made to the models were measured by hand and conversely applied to the computer drawings. This process was carried back and forth during the entire development phase of the project.

The City of Culture, Santiago, Spain

Biblioteca Soffit Wireframe Drawing
A computer drawing of the soffit is made to begin informing the space.

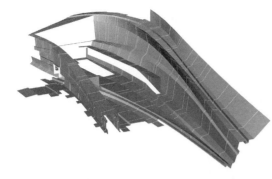

The City of Culture, Santiago, Spain

Computer Rendering of Soffit
The drawing is refined and rendered in the computer.

The City of Culture, Santiago, Spain

Bienale Model
The computer drawings are translated into hand-built physical models to refine and understand the quality of the space.

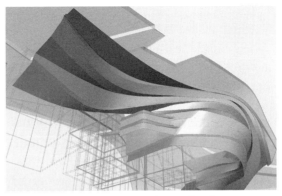

The City of Culture, Santiago, Spain

Music Theater–Computer Rendering
A computer drawing initiates the interior space of the theater.

The City of Culture, Santiago, Spain

Biblioteca Soffit Model
The computer drawings are translated into hand-built physical models to refine and understand the quality of the space.

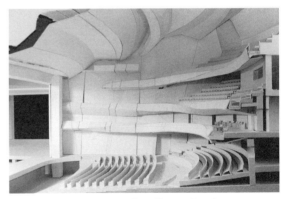

The City of Culture, Santiago, Spain

Music Theater–Physical Model
The computer drawing is translated into a hand-built physical model to refine and understand the space.

Gehry Partners LLP

Frank Gehry's office represents a unique case in which two poles of design methodology coexist. The office probably has developed one of the most sophisticated digital systems for project delivery in the industry, while at the same time adhering to traditional physical modeling methods.

In a recent lecture, James Glymph, head of Gehry Technologies, stated that, although they had tried many approaches to design development using computer modeling, in the end the computer proved to be too slow. The computer is viewed as an additional tool, good at some things, such as refining design, and not particularly good at others. As Mr. Glymph was quick to point out, "It would be a serious mistake to think it could replace models and drawing entirely."

The key program for generating three-dimensional computer models from physical models is CATIA, an aerospace program developed by Boeing aircraft. The models are marked at intersections and grid points. The points are digitized to define XYZ spatial coordinates, then fed into Rhinoceros, and rationalized into curves. This information is transferred to CATIA, where it is hyperrationalized, and the final computer model is completed. Details such as the many varying stone panels and support points are mapped as "accurate plugs of program" with parametric modeling programs. These drawings can be pushed and pulled in the computer model to produce automatically adjusted components.

Once the computer models are finished, three-dimensional drawing models can be transmitted directly to fabricators and contractors. This process has allowed Gehry to gain precise control over production and costing.

Keeping in mind that many of the things computers can draw have little connection with actual material properties, the office is developing a program to model the behavior of planes that can bend and fold using defined rules. The planes will exhibit the properties of gravity and indicate when stress limits have been exceeded.

As shown in the Walt Disney Concert Center project on the following pages, design development makes intensive use of physical models. Physical modeling exploration is typically intensive, with around 30 to 40 physical models produced for each project. Computer modeling rarely comes into play. At some later development stage the physical model may be digitized and output as a rapid prototype for further study.

The Walt Disney Concert Center

The models shown here represent a classic model progression in Gehry's office. Very little of what is explored and developed at this stage involves digital modeling. To fully appreciate the process, it should be noted that the stages shown here represent only 5 out of at least 20 different models.

The Walt Disney Concert Center–Stage 1
The first phase of the project came as a result of a competition entry and defined the space as a ziggurat and pavilion.

The Walt Disney Concert Center–Stage 4

After further refinement of the program, blocks were used to correlate the spaces with building form. At this point, a tower was included in the project.

The Walt Disney Concert Center–Stage 10

The space of the main hall is defined at this point and surrounding components are experimented with. Shown here are the vestiges of the competition pavilion, dome, and ziggurat.

The Walt Disney Concert Center–Stage 15

At some point, the idea of working with flowing theater curtains begins to inform the exterior reading of the building planes.

The Walt Disney Concert Center–Stage 20

The final model shows a rethinking of material and final rendition of the flowing planes. *Note:* The tower has been deleted from the project.

WDC Acoustic Model

A large-scale model (very large) was made of the concert hall to enable consultants to test and adjust acoustic qualities.

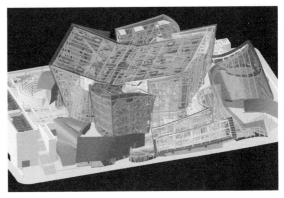

WDC CATIA Model

After inputting and refining the information, a computer model of the entire building, structure, and mechanical systems is generated with CATIA.

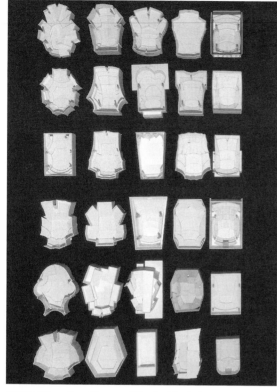

WDC Theater Space Study Models

This image shows the exhaustive array of study models made to develop the concert hall. These are all handmade models and are typical of the kind of three-dimensional rigor the office brings to every project.

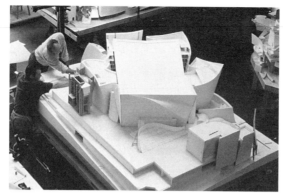

WDC Digitizing

The large final model is being marked in preparation for the digitizer.

Bilbao Guggenheim CNC Milling Model

In many cases, the flowing forms of the project are output to make a large CNC milling model such as this one. The CNC process is better suited for large models (see "Rapid Prototyping," Chapter 8).

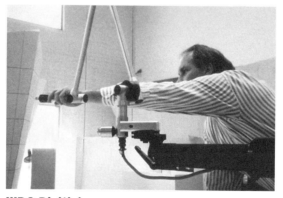

WDC Digitizing

Each of the many intersecting points is recorded by the digitizer to be translated into a CATIA computer model.

The Barcelona Fish

The Barcelona Fish (produced in conjunction with the 1992 Olympics) provided an information base for design methods used in future projects.

In this case, the project was fully developed with hand-built physical models then translated into digital information. Distortions can be made by the computer drawing, so it was important to confirm its accuracy with a rapid prototype model.

The Barcelona Fish—Physical Model
The physical model of the fish has been completely worked out at this stage.

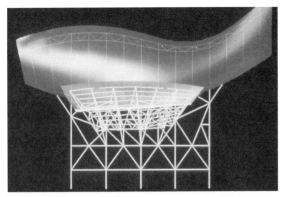

The Barcelona Fish—Computer Model
The model is digitized, and a computer model is drawn and output to make an RP model.

The Barcelona Fish—Built
The built fish carries the intent of the original model and provides an information base for future projects.

Garofalo Architects

From conversation with Doug Garofalo

Doug Garofalo represents the end of the spectrum in pursuing form making beyond Euclidean concepts with sophisticated modeling interfaces. The evolution of computer modeling programs and their integration has had a radical effect on the way he approaches architecture. Unlike the practices of many design firms discussed in these pages, Mr. Garofalo's firm does not employ any physical models during design development. For the flowing, continuous space he is exploring, traditional modeling is thought to offer either too many limits or too little control.

To facilitate the exploration, he uses MAYA, modeling software developed for the animation industry. The program is sophisticated in modeling complex curves and uses spline curves to define space rather than faceted and triangulated surfaces. Mr. Garofalo finds it to be intuitive to operate, allowing objects to be pushed and pulled similar to the way actual plastic objects might react. Form Z and other mainstream modeling programs are thought to be limiting in two ways. Not only do they approximate curved space with triangles, but a traditional architectural attitude concerning the generation of form (through extrusion and Euclidean block building) guides many of the operative commands. In contrast, working with MAYA can open doors to worlds that have yet to be discovered.

Mr. Garofalo's work has been translated using various RP processes, but he finds computer numerical controlled (CNC) milling is best suited to the larger constructions.

The Cloud Project

The production of the Cloud piece is an excellent illustration of how future construction delivery will be handled. In this case, all information is taken from the computer model and seamlessly fabricated by computer-controlled machinery. A large CNC five-axis milling machine can be seen at work at CTEK in Los Angeles. This same company makes many of Gehry Partners' projects using technology developed for the automotive industry. Even with the large-scale capabilities of the CNC equipment, the parts are so large that they must be made in several sections and spliced together.

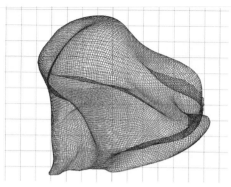

The Cloud
Meteorological information is used to make a three-dimensional digital map of a particular cloud. This computer model is then sent directly to a CNC milling machine to begin cutting the parts.

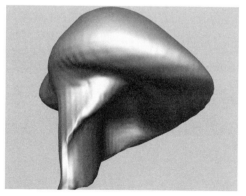

The Cloud
The cloud is refined and rendered in the computer.

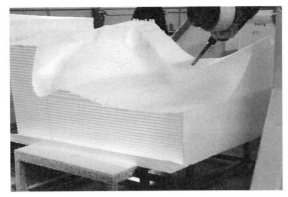

The Cloud

Guided by the computer model, the drill bit of the miller makes many passes over the surface of a foam block to cut away material.

The Cloud

The rough-cut foam mold is then coated with a material like automotive filler, recut, and sanded to refine the surface. The miller arm and frame can be seen in the background.

The Cloud

Each component part is reinforced with steel rods, and attachment edges are embedded.

The Cloud

The parts are taken out of the mold, fitted together, and sanded to transition smoothly into each other.

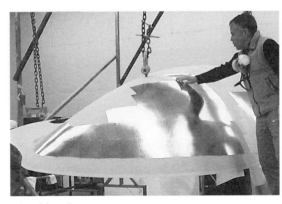

The Cloud

The surface of the parts are laminated with thin sheets of titanium metal.

The Cloud

The completed cloud is hung from the gallery ceiling.

Richard Meier & Partners Architects

From conversation with associate architect Rene Logan

Richard Meier's office has traditionally used the model to confirm design decisions. Before the introduction of the computer, design work proceeded through drawings, a limited number of student models, and a finish model. Models have always been carefully built and are intended to forward the precision of ideas.

With the move to digital methods, drawings remain primal to design development, but the computer model has taken over the role as primary form maker. Massing and form decisions are developed with the computer model, then a physical model may be made (in-house or by a model shop) to study the entire project or sections such as a glass curtain wall. One of the reasons for working primarily with the computer and avoiding rough-study models during the design stage is that the office has a high concern for craft. In most cases, a final presentation model will be built and is valued both as a communication tool and as confirmation of design decisions.

While the office typically does not employ rapid prototyping to make entire formal elements, many styrene and Plexiglas planar parts are laser cut or etched directly from computer information. These parts are made by service companies from drawing files sent online and returned by express mail the following day.

In terms of modeling programs, the office finds Form Z to be "clunky" in its operations, with relatively unsophisticated rendering capabilities. TriForma and 3D Studio MAX are the preferred programs, and they regard them as standards of the industry. At this point, the office uses TriForma but is considering 3D Studio MAX to take advantage of the seamless interface with AutoCAD (their two-dimensional drawing software).

Models

The projects shown here are all hand-built physical models and illustrate the various types of three-dimensional information that are typical of Meier's office. These range from highly refined finish models built by professional model shops to multiple massing studies and large-scale in-house constructions.

Federal Building and U.S. Courthouse, Islip, NY

Section Model
This finish model has been made with many laser-cut parts.

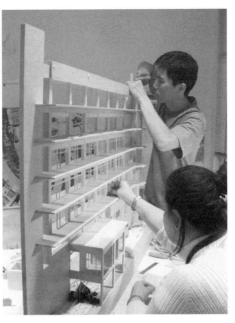

Model Shop
Office design staff are at work building a large-scale facade model. At this scale of study, every mullion can be shown and will provide an extremely accurate reading of the building.

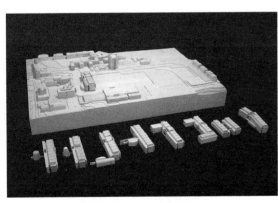

University Building Study Models
Multiple studies have been made in trying to refine a massing scheme for the project.

Antoine Predock

From conversation with architect Peter Arathoon

Antoine Predock's practice represents another office with a strong tradition of studying projects through models. Projects are typically initiated with sketches and clay models. Far from simple concept models, these models include a direct relationship to program and can be used as a guide through the life of the project. In regard to these models, Mr. Predock explains, "When a project is formative or embryonic, the drawings are often terse and immediate, a kind of encoding or DNA that will inform the making of the building. These preliminary or anticipatory drawings lead to three-dimensional clay models, which can be very tiny; three-by-five inches like Cal Poly, or very large, like the one for Agadir, which is five feet long and three feet wide. I am still exploring as I work with the clay, but I am working toward a finality. Compared to a drawing on paper, the models are very real; they are the building. They are not massing models; they rationally address section and plan."

Relatively recently, the office has augmented their three-dimensional approach to design by purchasing a Z Corp powder printer. With this and Form Z, projects have begun to be refined with rapid prototyping methods. Currently all projects are initiated with drawings and clay models, and RP is employed to refine and update the model.

However, other roles are envisioned wherein a project might be initiated with Form Z and RP, then move to the clay models, or eventually, be completely executed in Form Z.

Like many offices based on traditional models and expanding into rapid prototyping, Antoine Predock's office views the RP models as a great help in communicating with large groups but sees them as an added tool rather than a complete replacement for the clay models.

As the model bed of the Z Corp, the RP printer is a relatively small, 8-in. cube. Most of the RP models the office makes are small-scale studies of building and site relationships. However, larger sectional studies are made of single rooms by assembling several RP components. Likewise, RP components are used in conjunction with traditional wood and paper model parts. All model parts are made in-house by the designers and are the focus for Mr. Predock when working with the design staff. The office has also recently purchased a laser cutter that they use to make orthogonal parts.

The office uses VectorWorks, a Macintosh-based CAD program popular on the West Coast, for two-dimensional drawing. This program and Form Z make up their primary digital drawing software.

Clay Models

These are unique to Antoine Predock's office and represent the kind of direct connection that carving and forming spaces by hand offer.

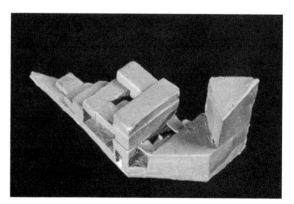

Arizona Science Center, Phoenix, AZ
This study is removed from the site and context to reflect a singular building study.

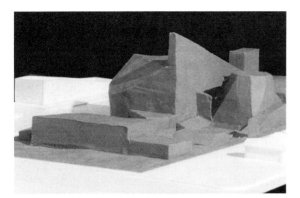

Classroom/Laboratory/Administration Building at California State Polytechnic University, Pomona, CA
One of the small 3- by 5-in. studies placed in context with the campus buildings.

Clarke County Government Center
This model appears to be much larger and operates at the scale of a small urban inhabitation.

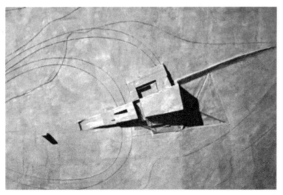

Spencer Theater for the Performing Arts
The clay provides a strong relationship with the site, becoming an extension of what usually are conceived as separate systems.

Borden Partnership llp

Gail Peter Borden takes the kind of hybrid approach of a practitioner who is comfortable with both the representational language of the computer and physical models. Unlike that of many designers who work with computer models for one phase and shift to physical models for another, Mr. Borden's work is explored with the simultaneous use of models and digital information. This results from a desire to exploit the advantages both media have to offer. For Mr. Borden, the physical model is primarily centered around exterior studies that have to do with reading the overall project, while computer models are best suited to interior, sectional, and perspective simulations of the space. Computer models are also used as the most expedient means to generate a virtual community of projects.

Computer Model of the Entire Suburban Block
In his project to develop affordable modern housing prototypes for alternative community design, Mr. Borden studied each prototype using digital and physical modeling. In some cases, the digital model offers the advantage of views inside the space and three-dimensional sections. In contrast to the more abstract computer images, the physical models offer more presence. In the model of the entire block, the computer is well adapted to the production of multiple variations and their insertion into a virtual reality.

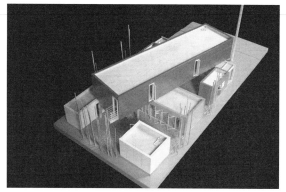

Physical Model
The house can be walked around, touched, and viewed from every perspective to apprehend the space.

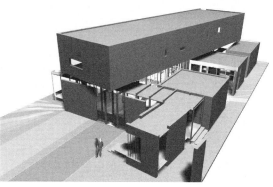

Computer Model
The computer model provides a base of information that can be rendered in various ways to obtain perspective images and make three-dimensional sections.

Physical Model Detail View
Physical models can be photographed to produce views similar to the computer views.

Computer Model Section
The ability to instantly cut the computer
model for section studies at any scale is a dis-
tinct augmentation of traditional modeling
capabilities.

Computer Model Interior Rendering
This interior view would be difficult to obtain
without building a large-scale model.

Coop Himmelb(l)au

Coop Himmelb(l)au has traditionally relied on the generation of sketch models and drawings to initiate projects. Their energetic spaces have always questioned barriers. As a result, the integration of computer modeling into their practice has not engendered a radical shift in their design direction. Rather, its primary impact has been to provide another means of extending the radicalized rigor for which they are known.

An illustration of the continuity of working methods can be seen in the Woflsburg Science Center model. It is unclear if this direction was suggested by the possibilities of rapid prototyping or merely exploited the process as an expedient way to control the work. In any case, it is instructive to see that the initial studies are made with paper models in which intentions are already clear. Only after some period of development is the apparatus for conversion injected into the process.

Because the exacting nature of the digitized model brings about a perceived loss of possibilities, digitizing is avoided until late in the design process. They address the predilection toward an open-ended process with this explanation: "In this predigitized state, the models exhibit a certain fuzziness that allows a layer of interpretation to come into play." This chance to read the model for inference and ambiguity is similar to the richness offered by the layered sketches and drawings.

Aside from the computer's role as an aid in realizing modeled forms, Coop Himmelb(l)au also uses it to generate topological studies such as those shown for the BMW showroom on the following pages.

The Open House, Malibu, California

Their description of the design process for this project is at the core of all the office's work and extends to their attitude toward digital media. "Created from an explosive-like sketch drawn with eyes closed with intense concentration, the hand acts as a seismograph, recording those feelings created by space. It was not the details that were important at that moment, but the rays of light and the shadows, brightness and darkness, height and width, whiteness and vaulting, the view of the air."

The Open House, Malibu, CA

Initial Drawing
The multivalent reading provided by layers, indeterminate lines, and smudges offers a number of readings that are unique to this kind of marking.

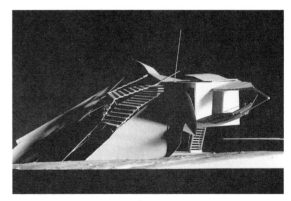

The Open House, Malibu, CA

Interpretive Study Model
The spirit of the drawing finds space in a model made from the drawing above.

The Open House, Malibu, CA

Final Model
The final model translates all the energy of the drawing into a crisp, finely edited set of delineations.

Musée des Confluences, Lyon, France

This museum is a public place providing access to the overlapping and hybridized knowledge of our age. The architecture is characterized by interactions, fusion, and mutation of different entities and combines the typology of a museum with the typology of an urban space.

To do this, the design process is hybridized as well. Along with a genetic section sketch, the topological space of the digital model is pulled and distorted to discover an urban landscape, while surfaces and nodes merge inside and outside into a dynamic sequence of spatial events.

Musée des Confluences, Lyon, France
Initial computer topology.

Musée des Confluences, Lyon, France
Building space emerging from computer topology.

The Open House, Malibu, CA

Computer Rendering
The digital rendering attempts to make a reality of the space, but in some ways domesticates the raw energy of the model.

Musée des Confluences, Lyon, France
Initial sketch section.

Musée des Confluences, Lyon, France
Digital rendering.

Science Center Museum, Wolfsburg, Germany

This project responds architecturally to changes in the scientific worldview such as the logic of "either/or." In this case, a mutating fluid form acts as a metaphor for the infinite scientific process of gaining knowledge. A large, featureless exhibition space provides a neutral body that is transformed by plugging and adding additional bodies. The sculptural, open proposition is typical of the way Coop Himmelb(l)au's office approaches a project. In this case, RP modeling is introduced at the end of the process to gain full control of the space.

Science Center, Wolfsburg, Germany

Initial Sketch/Concept Model
This model captures the feel of the working strategy, but even at this stage is connected with the program.

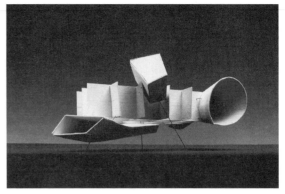

Science Center, Wolfsburg, Germany

Development Paper Model
A refined manipulation of the rough study achieves flowing, continuous space with only paper as material.

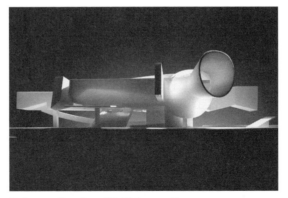

Science Center, Wolfsburg, Germany

Rapid Prototype Final Model
The model space has been fully refined and yet retains the enigmatic nature of the studies.

BMW Welt, Munich, Germany

This project consists of a center for brand experience and vehicle delivery, a marketplace for differentiated and changing uses, and a sign for the BMW Group. It consists of a large, permeable hall with a sculptural roof. The small section drawing for the project is typical of the genetic sections that have informed Coop Himmelb(l)au's projects from the beginning. Even with the integration and expansion of ideas enabled by digital possibilities, these small drawings remain relevant to the process. The physical models almost negate the need to rely on digital aids, as they carry all the spatial complexity that one associates with digital production.

BMW Welt, Munich, Germany
Formative section sketch.

BMW Welt, Munich, Germany
Interior view of model.

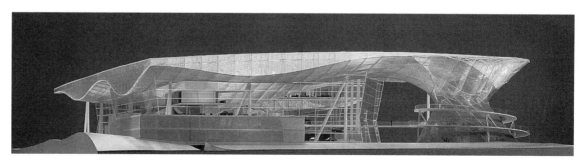

BMW Welt, Munich, Germany
Physical model.

EXPAND

Topics for Continuing Exploration

This chapter provides further information concerning alternative media, related models, transferring model dimensions, photography, digital media, computer modeling, rapid proto-typing, and detailed presentation models.

Alternative Media

Most of the models in this book have been made with paperboard materials. These materials are valued for being inexpensive, quick to assemble, and easy to modify. As such, they are ideal for the majority of study models; however, there are situations in which it is advantageous to use wood, metal, plastic, and plaster in model making.

These media can be combined as an expedient way to construct components or they can be employed for expressive purpose. Although they may not completely reflect the behavior of full-scale components, they may provide a better understanding of material properties.

The use of these materials has been touched on in the previous chapter, and although a detailed treatment is beyond the scope of this book, the following sections augment earlier information on material choices and equipment used to work with them.

Plastic and Foam

For plastic materials such as Plexiglas, the tools applicable to working with wood can be used effectively. Plexiglas can be cut with a table or band saw, and a belt sander can be used to smooth and shape edges. If clear, polished edges are desired, a strong electric wheel is required. Grit compounds for buffing can be purchased in graduated degrees of coarseness and applied to the wheel in three applications. Starting with coarse grit compound and moving from medium to fine, edges can be buffed to a clear smooth finish.

Polystyrene is a dense foam suited to cutting and shaping to make quick sculptural forms. Blocks or sheets can be laminated together with contact cement or construction glue to create larger pieces. Although the material can be cut with a hand or power saw and shaped with a Surform tool, a hot wire cutter can make shaping more accurate. The wire cutter uses a tightly strung, heated wire to slice through the foam. The pieces can be guided by hand or held steady by mechanical guides similar to those found on a table saw. Foam can then be sanded to even out surface variations.

Polystyrene Model
The blocks of foam that make up this model have been cut with a hot wire and sanded smooth.

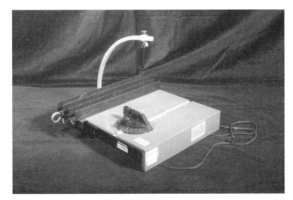

Hot Cutting Wire
Equipment heats a thin wire so foam can be pushed through it to cut like a band saw.

Wood

Constructions made from wood are often built as finely crafted presentation models. For this level of finish, books listed at the end of this chapter are good sources of information. However, for study models and simple presentation constructions, there are many uses for wood. For massing models and sculptural shapes, wood blocks can be cut quickly with a band saw and sanded smooth with a belt sander; see "Cut and Carved Forms" in Chapter 5. Balsa sheets and sticks also can be used to produce finish constructions with simple equipment, as shown to the right.

Materials

For simple models, wood sticks and soft wood scraps work well. Woods with an even grain structure and a degree of softness such as mahogany or basswood (ironically, classed as hardwoods) are the preferred materials for high-level finish models. Many of these materials can be found at hobby or modeling supply stores; however, for larger blocks of mahogany and basswood, a hardwood lumber supplier is the most likely source. Large blocks can also be made by glue-laminating smaller ones together.

DIMENSIONAL MODELING STICKS

- Balsa—inexpensive and cuts easily
- Basswood—more expensive, but holds form better than balsa, and ends can be sanded with accuracy
- Mahogany—often used for rich color, with similar qualities to basswood
- Oak dowels—must be sawn for clean cuts

SHEETS

- Balsawood sheets—finished appearance, cut easily, span well, and reflect material thickness of smaller to midsized models
- Modeling plywood—similar properties to balsa, can be cut with a power saw or can be rough-cut with a matte knife and sanded smooth

WOOD BLOCKS

- Balsa
- Basswood
- Mahogany
- Pine, spruce, cedar, fir—common soft-woods used in residential construction and entirely adequate for study models

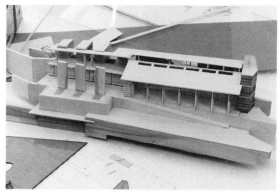

Wood Model
The planes for these models are typical of what can be made from thin basswood sheets and modeling plywood.

Wood Model

Woodworking Equipment

For balsa sheets and all sticks, simple X-Acto knives and modeling hand saws can be used. All other wood materials (especially blocks) will require power tools or carving knives.

The basic power equipment needed to work with wood includes a table saw, a band saw, and some form of belt sander. These can be inexpensive tools, as the wood is relatively soft and cuts will probably be small.

Power tools can be used to rough sculptural shapes. Carving tools and power sanders can be used to finish the shapes.

Table Saw

An inexpensive table saw with an 8-in. blade. On low-end saws such as this, the rip fence is inaccurate and must be checked with a square. *Note:* Avoid small modeling table saws, as they are very underpowered.

Belt Sander

Handheld home construction types or pre-mounted units can be used for model sanding work. Shown is a handheld type. It can be mounted with homemade clamps or with an aftermarket bracket.

Drill Press and Hand Drill

In making inexpensive models, a drill press can be useful. Alternatively, a hand drill can be mounted on an aftermarket stand and used as a substitute until use of a drill press is warranted.

Handheld Jigsaw

This type of saw can be used for rough cuts and limited curved cuts. It is wise to compare the power ratings on jigsaws, as many inexpensive saws can cut only the thinnest of materials.

Band Saw

Shown is a minimal-size, two-wheel saw. *Note:* Avoid inexpensive three-wheel band saws; because of tight wheel radii, they break blades regularly.

Metal

Models are rarely constructed entirely from metal; however, rods, wire, and shaped planes can be very useful as component pieces.

Materials

Many of these materials can be found as common items in hardware stores. Small rods and tubes, as well as sheets of aluminum and bronze, are available at most hobby and modeling shops. Heavy-gauge metal can be purchased at a metal supply yard.

THIN SHEETS

- Aluminum and galvanized flashing
- Galvanized metal
- Copper, bronze, and aluminum modeling sheets
- Screen wire aluminum, bronze, and fiberglass
- Hardware cloth with holes from ⅛ in. to ½ in.

WIRE, RODS, AND TUBES

- Copper, brass, and steel wire
- White plastic-coated wire
- Copper, brass rods and tubes
- Coat hangers
- Heavy-gauge steel and aluminum wire
- Reinforcing bars

ALUMINUM SHAPES

- Rods
- Round and square tubes
- Angles

HEAVIER-GAUGE METAL

- Rods
- Square stock
- Plate steel
- Angles

Fabrication Equipment

Cutting, connecting, and bending heavier metal parts can be involved.

Connecting

For small rods and plates, joints can be soldered or, in some cases, hot-glued. For larger pieces, bolted or welded connections are required.

Welding on thin metal with arc welding equipment tends to burn holes in the metal very quickly. For best results use a small MIG welding unit (recently available at reasonable prices). These units feed a thin wire from a spool to serve as a constant welding rod and are easy to use. They are also surprisingly portable and have low power requirements. Thin metal can also be brazed with oxyacetylene torches and spot-welded.

Note: Without more specialized equipment, aluminum cannot be welded.

Cutting

For small rods and plates, hacksaws and tin snips can be used. Cutting of thicker metals, other than those for which tin snips are applicable, can sometimes be accomplished with metal-cutting abrasive wheels used in a circular saw or in an electric miter box. Metal blades in a powerful jigsaw or Sawzall can be effective for cutting sheet metal up to 1/16 in.

For heavy cutting, equipment beyond what is common to most model shops is required. These included oxyacetylene torches, power hacksaws, nibblers, metal-cutting band saws, plasma torches, and shears.

Bending

Thin sheets and wire rods can easily be curved and bent by hand. Some pieces can be held in a vise and bent with pliers or a hammer. Anything thicker will require special equipment and is usually not used.

However, for those interested in bending thick metal:

- It is necessary to heat large solid rods with an oxyacetelyne torch before bending.
- Thick metal sheets require the use of a bending brake.
- Structural shapes such as tubes and angles must be passed through a rolling mill.

Plaster

Material

Molding plaster, also referred to as Hydrocal, is available in small cartons at hardware stores or in 100-lb. bags at Sheetrock supply stores. Be sure to specify "molding" plaster, as other varieties are prone to shrink excessively when drying.

Tools

Once plaster has cured, it can be sanded, cut, and carved similarly to wood, with many of the same tools, such as Surforms, sandpaper, carving knives, chisels, and band saws.

Mixing Plaster

For small batches, one-gallon plastic buckets, plastic containers, and cut-down milk jugs make excellent mixing bowls. For larger batches, five-gallon paint and Sheetrock buckets serve well.

Plaster is mixed in a ratio of about two parts plaster to one part water. This means that any container should start just about one-third full of water. It is also helpful to leave some room in the container for adjusting the mix. Plaster is then shaken into the water in a sifting manner until an island of plaster begins to form on top of the water. At this point, the solution is mixed by hand until all lumps are smoothed out. The mix should be about the consistency of pudding, or thinner for coating tasks. For papier-mâché-like applications, the mix should be runny. With practice, you will be able to get the proportions right, but until then the mix can be thickened by adding plaster or thinned with more water.

The working time until plaster begins to set is about 10 to 20 minutes, so it is best to mix quickly to allow time for application. If you work fast enough, successive batches of plaster can be mixed in the same container without cleaning it. However, once a batch has begun to harden in the container, it can no longer be used, as lumps will be carried into the new mix.

Using cold water can retard the setting time, and warm water will speed it up. Plaster will set hard, if the mix is made correctly, in a matter of 30 to 40 minutes. Additional layers can be built on top of a first layer of plaster right away but must sit for a number of hours before water has evaporated sufficiently to allow sanding.

Clean Up

Containers must be cleaned of residual plaster before reusing. If left to dry in a flexible plastic container, plaster can be popped out. To wash containers, use a bucket of water so waste plaster can settle to the bottom and be thrown out later. All plaster should be put in trash cans and never down the sink, as it will settle and block plumbing drains.

Anchoring Cement

Anchoring cement is a good alternative to plaster and is commonly available. It is much stronger than plaster and in many cases will not require models to be internally reinforced with wire.

Conventional Molding Plaster

Very flexible, affordable, and readily available.

Precoated Plaster Cloth

Best suited for covering wire forms.

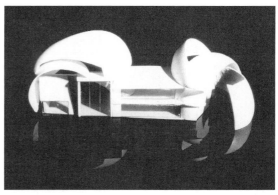

Plaster Model

This building model was made using techniques similar to those used for covering. A series of warped and twisted shell components have been made individually, sanded, and assembled into one model.

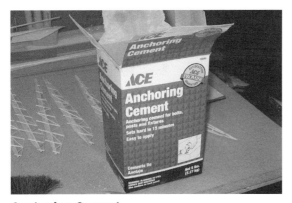

Anchoring Cement

A much stronger alternative to plaster and conveys the qualities of concrete at model scale.

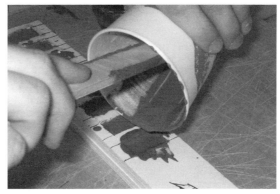

Placing Molding Material in Forms

Material is mixed in a manner similar to that of plaster. A stiff mix is needed for sloped pours.

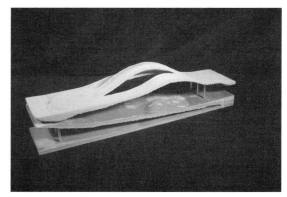

Anchoring Cement Model

A model made using a sand-casting technique. A box is filled with alternate layers of sculpted sand and cement. When finished, the sand can be shaken out of each layer.

Related Models

Urban Models

Urban models are used as design tools in the same way as other design models. The shift in perception is primarily one of scale. These models move from studies that show the context of adjacent blocks to neighborhoods, districts, and entire cities. Unlike context models that depict only existing buildings, they are made to design sections of a city. While these models could be made with computer programs and often are, the large size of real estate they represent is much easier to comprehend with large physical models than with relatively small computer screens.

The two models in the top illustrations come from Clemson University's Daniels Center, Charleston, SC. The two models on the bottom are from the Charleston Civic Design Center (UDC). The models are under active consideration in the planning of different redevelopment efforts within the city. They provide valuable illustrations of how models can convey a three-dimensional understanding of urban proposals.

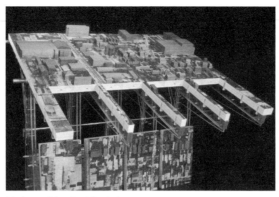

Urban Study Model
This model was built to reconsider the conventions of representing urban fabric. The table can be swiveled to provide abstract plan or perspective views, and context buildings are treated in the same manner as proposed structures.

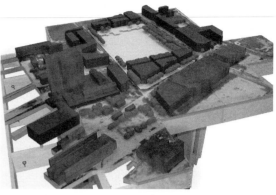

Upper Concord Street Neighborhood
The model was made to develop proposals for public space and adaptive reuse as part of a vibrant new mixed-use neighborhood plan for the area. Edges extended to talk about the way the area knits into the urban fabric.

Cooper River Bridge Neighborhood
This model was made to study the area around the old and new bridge locations in order to reconnect the neighborhood. Revitalization goals look at ways to provide places for new homes, public spaces, and businesses.

Charleston Gateway
Arrival into Charleston is via three ragged traffic interchanges. This model is an active-study model used to explore design options to recast this approach and create a considered gateway experience.

Industrial Design Models

Another area where models are widely used is industrial design. Physical models play several roles and work in concert with computer models. Traditionally, models were used to develop rough ideas, create prototypes, and test ergonomic properties (the way in which the body interfaces with the object). Today, models still play an active role, but computers and rapid prototyping are used extensively to test versions of the actual product.

The examples provided by Ryobi Tools show several important aspects of industrial design modeling studies.

Band Saw Mock-up

The three models at the right were made to develop a design for a band saw. They show the various ways a product can be studied and presented.

Appearance Model
The model was made using foam, body filler, and paint. It was used to develop the design of the casing and visually accessible working components.

Rapid Prototype Model
A stereolithography model shows all the working parts through a translucent cover material. This allows the actual parts to be tested for fit and operation. Rapid prototyping was first developed for the engineering and industrial design industry to make these kinds of modeling research tests.

Computer Model Rendering
The computer rendering studies the finished image of the saw in detail.

Ergonomic Models

Ergonomics is the study of how the body engages material objects ranging from tools to car seats. The fit between the body and an object can be tested effectively only with physical materials at full scale so that comfort or strain can be registered directly. Computer models may be well versed in rendering products but can only give some indication of how it might feel, for example, to push a pill cart across the floor and access lower drawers. While it is probable that computer models will be programmed at some point to simulate the reaction of bodies, it is doubtful that companies will fully trust products to feel as predicted.

The tools shown to the right were developed by Ryobi and show various alternate components used to test the dynamic fit with the hand and arms when in action.

Model Maker at Work

The model-makers craft involves traditional methods and, above all, the production of various ideas for testing. Whether these are done on the computer or hand built, the thinking behind them is similar.

Planar Models

Various planar models with different handle configurations have been made to study the comfort and effectiveness of user interface.

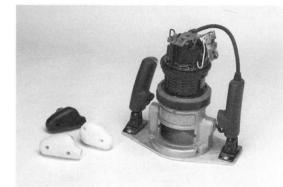

Buck with Eggs

Several alternative handle "eggs" are shown with slightly different contours.

Router Handle

The fit between the hand and the operation of switches is tested on the router handle.

Artwork

Models can be used for large-scale design projects, such as site or gallery installations, in the same way they are used for building design. The strategies and techniques for three-dimensional exploration are completely applicable and can serve to work out ideas that otherwise may remain only partially developed.

Illustration

The examples for the two gallery installations on the right were approached in a similar manner to interior models, with all design work being conceived directly on the models.

In each case, the study model for the project is shown at the top, with the actual full-scale construction displayed below.

Without the ability to test model elements in relation to each other, full-scale visualization would be difficult.

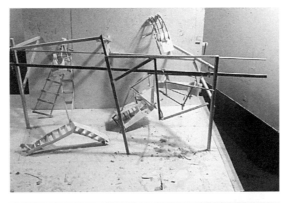

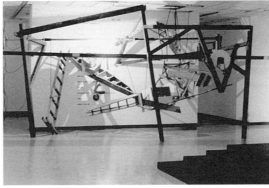

Gallery Installation

This sketch model was used to develop the frame and suspended characters for the full-scale construction below. The model was built to 1″ = 1′0″ scale because of the small amount of space it represented and the need for large-scale details. Balsa sticks, museum board, and wire make up the parts.

Sculptural Machine

The design for the "Painting Machine" shown below was worked out with the ½″ scale model. Although many of the details were developed on the full-scale construction, all the major relationships were investigated on the model and provided a clear map for the full-scale construction.

Transferring Model Data
Measuring Models to Locate 2-D Drawing Dimensions

Projects that have been executed completely in model form can be measured and translated into two-dimensional drawings by the following methods.

How to Measure

Points of intersection in space are measured with the scale rule as X, Y, and Z dimensions from a base plane and two 90-degree reference lines. It is helpful to buy or construct a small scale rule suited to the delicacy of the work. Make sure that the base of the ruler begins at 0', 0".

The triangle is used to mark the height of the intersection above the table plane. The triangle also helps locate the correct point on the measuring rod directly over (normal to) the edge of the reference grid below; see the section on the Morrow Library in Chapter 6.

In complex cases (and with much larger budgets), architects may employ digital equipment similar to that used for aerospace design. A digitizer is placed at the desired points on the model, and X, Y, Z coordinate readings are automatically recorded to generate drawings; see Chapter 7.

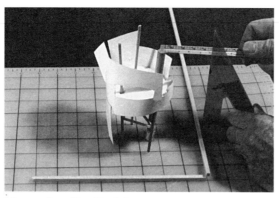

Measuring the Model
The ruler is extended out 90 degrees from the reference grid to mark the X dimension of a point. The height is marked on the triangle, then the ruler is swung 90 degrees to record the Y dimension.

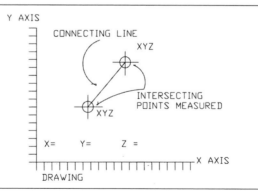

Drawing
The X, Y, Z coordinates are located on the plan drawing. Lines between the points are connected to describe the form in plan. *Note:* Z coordinates can be shown only on elevations and sections but should be noted on plans.

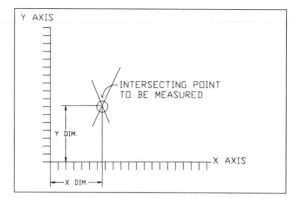

Plan View
This view is looking down on the point to be measured. The X and Y axis correspond to the sticks at the edge of the grid. The resulting X and Y dimensions would be transferred to paper and noted for their height above the plane of the measuring surface (the gridded tabletop shown to the left).

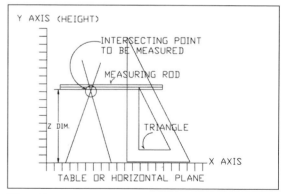

Elevation
The height (Z axis) of the point to be measured should be marked on the triangle. *Note:* The triangle also helps maintain a 90-degree relationship between the reference grid and the measuring rod.

Drawing the Model in 2-D Views

When modeling information precedes drawn information, models must be measured and converted to two-dimensional plan, section, and elevation drawings. Although this must be done in a way that will ensure accurate building dimensions, only key intersecting points are actually needed for construction.

Plotting every point needed to draw complex geometries can be a time-consuming process. Accurate numbers must be used for intersections, but shortcuts can be employed to draw reasonably accurate images of the model for visualization purposes and to show elevation details.

Two common methods for converting models to plan and sectional drawings are shown on the right. Both of these methods involve taking 90-degree views, "normal" to the plans and elevations, with either a camera or a photocopier. See "Model Photography."

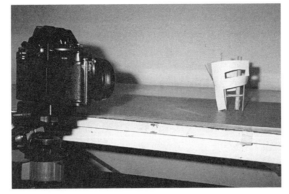

Photographing
Models can be photographed "face on" and traced from enlarged prints.

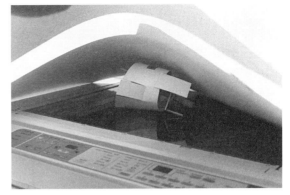

Copying
Models can be placed directly on the glass of a copy machine to make elevation images. See the Morrow Library in Chapter 6.

Photographed Plan View
The warped planes of this model are difficult to fully measure. By reducing them to a plan view, they can be drawn with a degree of accuracy and ease.

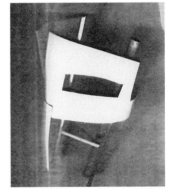

Photocopied Image
The resultant images can be traced and scaled. They will be somewhat distorted, but the directly measured X, Y, Z coordinates will ensure construction accuracy.

Model Photography
Photography Techniques

Although detailed information on film types, shutter speeds, and lens openings is limited, the following guidelines can produce acceptable results using a 35mm camera. It is highly advisable to photograph models as soon as they are finished, as time quickly takes its toll on these constructions; see "Digital Media" in this chapter for information on digital cameras and imaging techniques.

Film

Whether you are shooting indoors or outdoors, daylight print film is the most flexible and forgiving type of film. You can also use Ektachrome slide film, but the exposure tolerances will be tighter. Film speeds range from 100ASA to 400ASA. The lower the number, the more light you will need; however, the resolution is much better with 100 or 200 speed film.

Exposure

Images tend to remain focused in foreground and background areas (depth of field) at smaller lens openings, about F8 to F16. White models can bounce so much light off of their surfaces that light meters often call for openings smaller than required. It is wise to test the meter reading with a neutral gray surface. Moreover, for the best insurance against the variables of artificial light sources, it is important to bracket your shots (take exposures above and below the meter readings).

Outdoor Lighting

Shooting outdoors is the easiest solution to lighting. The camera will tend to read lighting conditions correctly, low-speed film can be used, and automatic cameras are effective. A calm, sunny day with the sun at a lower angle in the sky (early or late in the day) produces the best modeling shadows. Experiment by turning the model around and watching through the lens as different shadows are cast.

Daylighting
High-contrast lighting effects can be captured on very clear days with lower afternoon or morning sun angles.

Shaded Daylighting
Even light can be obtained in outdoor settings on overcast days or in large shaded areas.

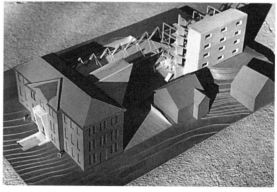

Daylighting
The sun can be used for medium contrast as well, by avoiding extremely clear conditions and working closer to midday. Models should be turned in the sun to find optimum shadow angles.

Indoor Lighting

Lighting can be accomplished by using a single blue Photoflood (compatible with daylight film color characteristics). The use of a single source of light will allow you to simulate the shadow-casting effects of the sun. Light can also be bounced off a whiteboard to soften its effects and control the way it hits the model. For even lighting, two lights can be placed on opposite sides of the model. The light source must be out of the camera eye, preferably behind it to avoid hot spots. To help with this, a hood can be used on the lens to shield side light from the lamp.

You can also photograph the model indoors, using daylight from a north-facing bank of windows, with a tripod and very slow shutter speeds. The camera can be hand-held down to shutter speeds of about ⅛ of a second using a steady hand or something to brace against. Shutter speeds cannot usually be controlled on automatic cameras.

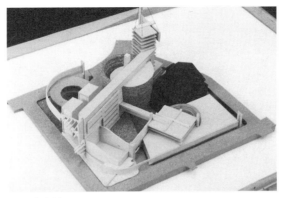

Daylighting

Models can be photographed indoors with sufficient daylight. North-facing clerestory windows work well to avoid unwanted mullion shadows and provide plenty of light. Slow shutter speeds are recommended.

Grazing Light on the Model

A single-source lamp can be used from below to graze light across the model. The light can be bounced off of white sheets or covered with cloth to soften harsh effects.

Even Lighting

Using two light sources placed slightly in front and to either side of the model provides an evenly lighted surface.

Single-Source Light

Strong shadow patterns that make the forms read as sculptural objects can be created by using a single light. For best results, turn the model and move the light to experiment with shadow angles.

Views

Models can be photographed from many angles depending on what one wishes to communicate. Overall or bird's-eye views can convey a sense of the total building. Low views, shot up into the model, can give the effect of being on the site looking up at the building. A model scope (a special device like a small periscope that can be fitted to the camera) can be used to photograph interior views and help capture eye-level views. Special extension tubes and other lens devices can also be made to bring the camera eye down into the model at less expense.

Models can be photographed "straight on" to eliminate as much perspective as possible and to create images similar to elevation drawings. These views can be useful as tracing guides to produce orthographic drawings from models, as discussed in "Transferring Model Data" in the preceding section.

The sculptured or modeled view is probably the most common view used for capturing the overall geometry of a model as a three-dimensional object.

At Eye Level

The eye-level view is taken at a height of a scaled figure to simulate the view of a person moving through the space.

Bird's-eye View

The birds-eye view is taken looking down on the model and provides an overall picture of a complex or object.

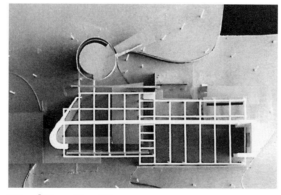

Plan/Elevation View

This view is a frontal shot taken 90 degrees to the model plane. Images of this type simulate orthogonal drawing views and can be used to convert model views to plan drawings by tracing over them.

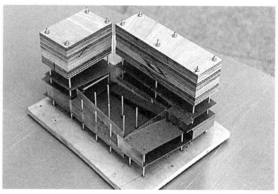

Sculptural View

The sculptural view is similar to the bird's-eye view but taken from lower angles to display the three-dimensional quality of the forms.

Backgrounds

A smooth, regular-textured background with some tonal contrast to the model, such as chipboard, black cloth, or brown kraft paper, can work well. Clean, even surfaces, such as concrete or carpet, can serve as backgrounds out of doors, as long as there is enough area to keep the edges out of the camera frame.

Several ideas are shown to help illustrate how backgrounds can work, ranging from the natural sky to gray backdrop paper.

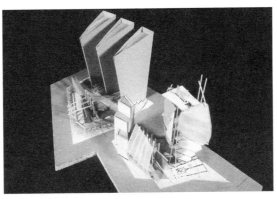

Black Contrasting Backdrop

For light-colored models, dark backdrops such as black cloth or backdrop paper can be used to highlight tones. For dark models, light paper can be used.

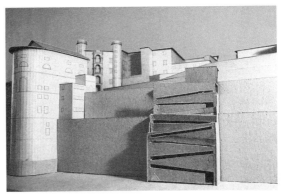

Blue Paper

The outdoor sky can be easily simulated with blue paper placed behind the model.

Curved Backdrop

Although dark backdrop paper or cloth can completely negate the background, gray-and-white paper, placed under the model and rolled up the wall, will create a smooth gradation of tones.

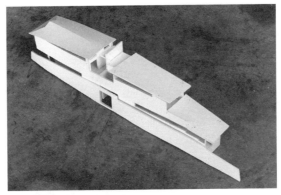

Natural, Even Surface

A concrete floor, sidewalk, carpet, or other even-toned surface can be used as a neutral background. Light surfaces should be sought for dark models and dark ones for light constructions.

Natural Sky

The outdoor sky can be used by placing the model on a ledge and shooting into the model at an angle that will crop out all other background objects. This works best facing north in order to avoid glare from the sun.

Digital Media

Over the last ten years, visual communication has increasingly employed digital media as an integral part of the design process. This shift has produced a quantum expansion in the way drawings, photographs, and graphics can be brought together. Images of the model can be downloaded into programs such as Photoshop and combined with other images with far less work and expense.

It should be noted that with these new tools come drawbacks, but as a rule, the advantages are well worth the limitations. Many of the limitations encountered are the result of the increasing use of home publishing hardware to perform tasks such as photography, scanning, and printing. While nonprofessional equipment provides an affordable production facility, image quality can suffer.

The key components of digital imaging are:

- Digital cameras
- Scanners
- Design software
- Printers
- Storage devices

Digital Cameras

The digital camera is an integral part of digital media. As cameras become increasingly affordable, their integration into the documentation of architectural projects has become commonplace. One of the main reasons for this shift can be attributed to the convenience and economy of moving camera files directly to imaging programs.

Cameras range from snapshot models to high-end professional equipment, with prices starting around $100 and escalating to well over $2,000 for professional cameras and lenses.

Model Documentation

Techniques

As the ideas, backgrounds, and lighting techniques are similar, the information concerning taking model images with film cameras applies directly to digital cameras. The real difference is learning to treat a point-and-shoot digital camera like a 35mm single lens reflex (SLR) camera.

Camera Settings

Resolution

The camera should be set to give the highest-quality image available. Lower-quality settings can save camera memory, but the trade-off will be very poor images when trying to enlarge work. Images for e-mailing and other low-resolution purposes can be reduced in size after downloading and copying.

Compression

Compression removes duplicate information and fills it in with similar information later. This produces a glossing over of the image. The lowest (or least) compression setting possible should be used. Most cameras can be set to take raw files (no compression), but the file will become inordinately large and translation software will have to be used to convert the image.

Manual Settings

Automatic settings may provide acceptable results, but the camera will seldom slow down sufficiently for low-light conditions on automatic. Also, balancing shutter speeds and aperture openings for depth of field cannot be controlled with fully automatic settings. Assuming your camera has the option of manual controls, they should be mastered and used.

Flash/Lighting

Using a direct camera flash as a light source produces poor images. Unless you are taking documentation shots, such as study model records, the flash should be turned off. Day lighting or Photofloods should be used as an alternate source. *Note:* An external flash can be used if it is bounced off the ceiling or a reflector, but this can be difficult to control and usually requires a high-end camera with a flash shoe.

Light Readings

A further refinement can be made by using a gray card when taking light readings. Alternately, the images can be bracketed with the manual control to ensure correct exposure.

Steadying the Camera

Low and artificial lighting conditions require the camera to be mounted on a tripod. Since most midrange models do not have a cable release adapter, care must be taken to depress the camera button with even pressure.

Viewing the Image

Non-SLR cameras suffer from the phenomenon referred to as *parallax*. That is, things seen through the viewfinder shift as you get closer to them, making it necessary to line up shots in the monitor. This technique can work well; however, out of doors, the monitor is hard to see.

Panoramic Features

Many digital cameras contain software for taking panoramic photographs. This can be useful for landscape and other site backgrounds. The process is not perfect, but it can act as a substitute for a true wide-angle lens.

Camera Comparison

Despite their convenience, digital cameras should not be thought of as a substitute for traditional film equipment without considering the advantages and disadvantages.

ADVANTAGES:

Convenience

This is probably one of the main reasons for the popularity of digital cameras. The fact that one or more images can be taken and instantly downloaded saves a significant amount of time.

Economy

The expense of buying and developing film is eliminated.

Assured Results

Rather than waiting for processing results to see if images were correctly exposed, built-in monitors and instant downloads can confirm image quality.

Experimentation

Because of the economy and ability to erase unwanted images, digital cameras encourage exploration of camera angles and lighting techniques.

DISADVANTAGES:

Resolution

Unless you are using professional equipment (6 megapixels or higher), the density of information taken in by digital cameras is well below that of traditional film media. While this may not cause problems with smaller images, it can deliver poor results when trying to enlarge them. Without going into technical explanations, a traditional film image converted to digital format by scanning will contain much greater density than digital camera files.

Hidden Costs

While digital images may appear to be free of cost, a lot of necessary and potentially expensive support software and hardware is required.

Low Light

In artificial lighting conditions, cameras must be operated at slow speeds to take pictures with sufficient depth of field.

Another potential problem in low-speed conditions is that of camera "shake." While cameras can be mounted on a tripod to steady the exposure, many economical cameras do not have cable release adapters or remote controls. Economical models with only automatic mode operate with poor results, while midrange cameras can be operated in manual mode and offer a near equivalent of traditional exposure options.

Lenses

Economical and midrange cameras generally do not have detachable lenses. This means that they try and use a limited zoom lens to meet all needs. In many cases, this can give acceptable results, but conditions that call for true wide angle and zooms must be forgone. In response to this condition, some manufacturers such as Canon do offer interchangeable lenses, and professional-quality SLR cameras are moving down in price.

Image Storage in Camera

Under travel conditions, the quantity of images that can be taken with a traditional film camera is limited only by the amount of film that can be carried or bought at a nearby store. Digital camera owners need either a number of expensive memory chips, a laptop, or an image tank in order to free camera space.

Power Source

Digital cameras require a lot of power to operate, and they typically exhaust batteries in a short time. In low-price models, this can quickly become a hidden expense. The majority of midrange models come with a rechargeable battery. However, uninterrupted operation requires the use of at least two batteries (one on charge and one in use).

Digital Camera Selection Guide

While this is not intended to be an in-depth guide to selecting a digital camera, those unfamiliar with their basic aspects may find the following information useful.

Cameras can be grouped in three price ranges:

- Economical

- Midrange

- Professional

Economical

- Cameras typically have 2-mega pixel capacity (or slightly more).

- Lens quality is more on par with point-and-shoot film cameras and cannot be changed.

- Cameras have automatic controls only.

- Viewing is accomplished through an eyepiece and a small monitor.

- Power source is provided in many cases by short-life AA batteries that cannot be recharged (rechargeable AA batteries are available).

Midrange

- Cameras have at least 3 to 5 megapixels.

- Lenses are made of quality ground glass and can be changed on some models.

- Optional manual controls are available.

- Viewing is accomplished through an eyepiece and a small monitor.

- Some cameras come with remote-control triggering devices.

- Batteries are rechargeable.

Professional

- Cameras have 6 to 11 megapixels and are built with SLR bodies.

- Features and operation are very similar to traditional 35mm film cameras such as cable release controls and a variety of interchangeable lenses.

Camera Brands

Digital cameras are made by many traditional film camera companies, and as a rule quality is equivalent to the kind of reputation these companies have built. A case in point is Canon and Nikon. Manufacturers such as Olympus and Fuji may offer better value than the leading names.

Rating Camera Quality

Camera quality can be reduced to four primary factors:

- Resolution
- Lenses
- Software
- Power supply

Resolution

Resolution determines how sharp an image will be. Camera resolution is generally rated in terms of megapixels. Megapixels are a measure of the amount of information (in this case, pixels) the camera can record. Each megapixel is equal to a million pixels. Generally speaking, the number of megapixels determines how large an image can be printed from the camera file and still maintain acceptable image quality. A 3-megapixel camera can produce a 5 in. × 7 in. image at 300-dpi resolution (300 dots per inch should be the minimum target size for printing quality). As of this writing, 5 megapixel models are commonly available for midrange cameras and should be purchased if possible.

Lenses

Camera lenses range from plastic to quality ground glass. The quality of the lens glass will be a limiting factor in obtaining image sharpness. Better-quality cameras provide zoom lenses and the option of changing lenses.

Zoom Types

Digital cameras employ their own zoom terminology, namely, *optical zoom* and *digital zoom*. Optical zoom is accomplished with traditional lens magnification technology and is really the only type of zoom that can be used without degrading picture quality. Digital zoom is not really a zoom feature at all but merely increases the size of the image with the same amount of information. It should be avoided unless low-quality images are of no concern.

Software

The internal processing software has a notable effect on the image quality. Some models are arguably superior to others in this regard, but at higher quality levels, this debate can be mute.

Memory Disks

Memory disks are not an indicator of camera quality, but they deserve some consideration. Cameras come with two main types of disks: flash cards and memory sticks. Arguments can be made as to the merits of each, but both work reasonably well. What is of more importance is the amount of information they can hold. These chips are like small hard drives and are rated in megabytes. Cameras usually come with an 8- or 16-megabyte disk. At high-resolution camera settings, each image takes about 1.7 megabytes of space. This means that a 16-megabyte disk can hold only about 20 images. For this reason, it is usually necessary to buy a much larger-capacity disk (128 megs or larger).

Power Supplies

Cameras come with either AA batteries or some form of higher-capacity rechargeable battery. Since digital cameras consume power so quickly, high-capacity rechargeable batteries are a priority choice.

Viewing Method

Most digital cameras locate the image to be taken through a view port, similar to point-and-shoot film cameras. Images can also be seen in the monitor (usually on the back of the camera). The viewfinder is acceptable but can cause problems with images at close range, as the captured image is shifted from that seen by the lens. Single lens reflex film cameras (where the image is actually viewed through the lens) came about to combat this problem, and high-end cameras emulate this configuration.

Scanners

A scanner is needed to convert drawings and photographs to digital files.

While professional scanning is usually accomplished on a high-resolution drum scanner, affordable home/office scanners have greatly improved and can serve most needs. The limitation is that home/office scanners are small flat-bed types and force the designer to scan large images in sections for reassembly in imaging software.

Scanning with home units has become highly automated. This makes scanning easier but can degrade quality. A partially automated operation allows you to preview images and make sure the area you wish to scan is all that is being captured. This mode

of operation helps ensure accurate exposure readings and reduced file size. Also, a lot of time can be saved in touch-up work by ensuring that the scanner glass is spotless.

Upon opening the software, you have the opportunity to change or approve the default resolution setting. Selecting the correct scanning file resolution size is important in striking a balance between image quality and the resultant file size. This is a function of how large you plan to print the images and what size files your CPU and hard drive can handle when working with a number of images. Large originals will produce very large files, and higher dpi settings require longer scan times.

Usually scans of 300 dpi are sufficient if image printing sizes stay below 5 in. × 7 in. For photomontages, you may be able to use from 150 to 200 dpi if the originals are large. For the highest-quality images and drawings, 600 dpi should be used (this is more important for drawings than photographs). For small originals such as 35mm slides, 1,200 dpi is necessary.

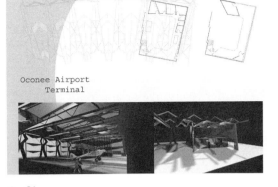

Oconee Airport
Terminal

Software

Imaging Software

Imaging software such as Photoshop from Adobe is needed to open and manipulate the various image files produced from drawings and photographs.

Graphic Design Software

Design software such as InDesign from Adobe and QuarkXpress is used by graphic designers to produce complete compositions made up of photography, graphics, and text. The real strength of these programs lies in handling large amounts of text and assembling compositional elements. However, companion programs like Photoshop and Illustrator are needed to accomplish this.

Photoshop

While there are many other imaging software packages available, Photoshop is the predominant program used by designers. For limited page presentations, its graphics and text capabilities can eliminate the need for any other type of program. (What can be said about Photoshop also pertains in a general way to other imaging programs.)

Features

The following information is not intended to provide instructions for the operation of the program but should serve as an overview of its general use and features.

Photoshop provides multiple functions (photography, graphics, and text handling), but its true domain is working with image files. This includes the ability to crop, resize, splice, and touch up a variety of aspects such as color, contrast, and opacity.

Image Size

One of the first things to be checked when opening an image is its size in pixels per inch. This will determine the resolution of the image as you proceed with other operations. Digital cameras often download at 72 and 180 pixels per inch and create image sizes too large to print on home printers. Increasing the pixels to 300 will reduce the image dimensions while maintaining all of the information (or original file size). File size can be reduced by resampling the image at smaller pixel and dimension sizes, but information (and thus resolution) will be lost.

Files produced from scans can become so large that the entire program is slowed down to the point of frustration. If image quality can be maintained, this situation can call for the reduction of file size. On the other hand, if you desire the sharpest image possible, as much as 600 pixels per inch may be required (especially when dealing with drawings).

Cropping and Cutting

Images can be cropped in a variety of ways that provide flexible image manipulation. Tools such as the lasso and magic wand allow you to cut out specific sections of images. These features can be used to cut model images out of backgrounds and overlay them on images such as site photographs. Another common use is to cut out the background around the model and fill it with color.

Adjusting Image Quality

Photoshop provides several tools to adjust contrast, brightness, color balance, and sharpness such as the level and curves controls. While they cannot correct every type of problem, they can be very effective in rehabilitating poor images.

Controls can also be used to change the way images read in compositions. Typical of this type of operation is the use of the hue and saturation command to remove color and opacity.

Touch-up and Painting

Photoshop provides a variety of tools such as the rubber stamp and paintbrush for tasks ranging from touch-up and filling color to painting with samples taken from other images.

Image Mode

Image Mode changes the way the image is read. Grayscale and Bit-map are two types of modes.

Grayscale converts images to black and white and is normally used for photographic images, as it can read the gradations of tones. Also, this mode dramatically reduces the size of files. (Black-and-white images can also be made by desaturating images with the color controls; however, files will still be large.)

Bit-map reads information as sampled bits and is useful for graphics and high-contrast line drawings. Bit-map information can have a tendency to pixelate images, giving them a jagged appearance. Even though high-contrast (black-and-white) drawings are not technically grayscale images, they may be better rendered in the grayscale mode.

Layers

One of the key features of Photoshop is the use of layers. Using layers is like using an overlay system of drawing to create complete layouts and photomontages. A number of layers can be used to contain separate information such as primary images on layer 1, text on layer 2, background image on layer 3, and graphics on layer 4. Each layer can be adjusted independently for opacity, glow, and gradient (fading of the layer), and images can be moved relative to each other. The final composition can then be "flattened" to produce one composite file (this will reduce file size, but a copy of the original layered file should be saved to disk).

Text

Text can be adjusted for a variety of attributes such as type style, point size, color, and justification type. Photoshop includes a number of sophisticated controls for the management of text appearance such as leading, tracking, and kerning. The resultant text can be incorporated into the layout by placing it on top of images or blocks of color.

Text font styles are bundled with every program but are typically limited. The purchase of additional font packages from a company such as Adobe can enhance text design.

Graphics

Graphics in the form of lines and blocks of color can be added to the design with the marquee tools. This is essentially done by drawing rectangles and other shapes on a layer, then filling them with color or images.

Assembling Images

A common task made manageable by the layers palette is that of splicing multiple images. Typically, this comes about when scanning large drawings in sections. Individual pictures can be opened as separate files and placed on different layers. The images on each layer can then be sized, adjusted, and moved as needed to produce one complete image.

Backing Up Images

On opening files, it is good practice to save them under a new name to ensure that the original is protected when editing.

Illustration

The board below shows a presentation made using layers. The boards on the far right show some of the possibilities of montage techniques.

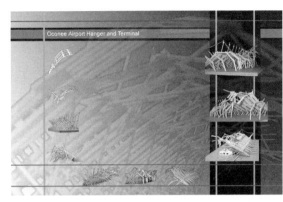

Layered Images

Drawings and photographs can be cut out of backgrounds, imported, and scaled. Each type of information is placed on a different layer—text, graphics, images, and so forth. Each layer can be manipulated for color and transparency. Layered images can be moved on top of each other and large background images can provide visual connections to relate all the elements. When completed, layers can be flattened to make a single file.

Image to be Cut Out

This image was taken in the studio setting and includes distracting background elements. Photoshop or other imaging software can be used to mask or remove the background entirely.

Image with Background Cut

The background of the image above has been replaced with black by cutting out everything around the model base. To produce the image on the right, the background has been removed around the outline of the building image.

Photo Montage

Computer renderings can be enhanced and combined with scanned images of figures and objects to convey a virtual image of space.

Photo Montage

Photographs of the physical models can be combined with photographs of the site to place buildings in their physical settings. Work must be done to make a convincing fit with sloping sites.

Printers

Home/office printers supply the final stage of production needs. Quality ink-jet color printers are increasingly affordable in sizes up to 13 in. × 19 in. However, this size is usually too small for presentation work and relegates their practical use to test prints during the design phase. Test printing is a valuable tool in its own right and can save considerable expense in final print errors. It should be mentioned that size limitations can be circumvented by tiling images and splicing small sheets to produce large-format presentations.

Printer Information

Depending on the type of printer, print quality can be set from as low as 72 to 1200 dpi. Laser printers will run almost as rapidly on 600 dpi and provide the highest quality they are capable of. Ink-jet printers can run at high resolution levels (sometimes referred to only as "best quality" in their menus),

but the printing process will be slowed considerably.

Paper

The use of high resolution settings is also a function of paper type. When using common white-bond, absorbent paper, higher settings will not produce improved results. To take advantage of the higher settings, coated photo papers are needed. Since photo paper is expensive, particularly in large sizes, other types of coated bond paper can be substituted and will help improve clarity.

Storage Devices

The general tasks of file management, transmission, and backup become an issue in their own the right when working with files. The file size of photographic images is such that floppy disk capacity is totally inadequate. While hard drive size has increased to the point that CPUs can now hold many gigabites of information, there still is a need for transportable backup files. The most common hardware devices for creating these are CD, DVD burners, and Zip drives. In terms of capacity, DVDs can hold 1 gigabyte, CDs 700 megabytes, and Zip drives 250 megabytes. While CDs are inexpensive and can be read by almost every computer (with DVDs soon to follow), Zip drives (actually portable hard drive disks) offer speed of operation. Intranets will probably become

the other way this is done, but until high-speed connections become the rule, sending and downloading large files can present many problems.

Digital File Types

Image files typically appear as two primary types: JPEG or TIFF files. Graphic files with monochromatic information utilize GIF file types. JPEG files are good for continuous tone images such as photographs and allow for compression (a consideration for intranet sites). TIFF files retain all the file information and are commonly used by graphic designers to ensure picture quality. To change file type, merely save the file under another name and select TIFF or JPEG when saving.

Computer Modeling
Modeling Programs

The ultimate aim of any design tool is to provide valuable information in an efficient manner. Although a case has been made for the advantages of building physical models, computer modeling can also provide very useful information and should be investigated for its potential advantages.

The speed and sophistication of computer modeling have increased rapidly over the last decade, but debate persists over its ability to match the intuitive nature of physical modeling. Moreover, because of the extrusional logic used by most programs, XYZ coordinate points must be used to create diagonals and warped planes. Inputting these coordinates can be cumbersome compared to the directness of angling cardboard planes. This limitation is compensated for by the ease with which forms can be manipulated. In addition, inherently common operations for the computer such as duplication, distortion, and overlay can be powerful tools for discovery.

Although facility can be developed to the point where drawing speed will compare favorably with physical modeling, one of the clear advantages of these programs lies in their ability to render the model and produce construction documents after the model has been developed.

To implement construction documents and rendering effects, a different set of software is required in addition to the modeling program. To make production drawings from the three-dimensional model, a graphics software is required. To render the model, rendering software or a "rendering engine" is needed. Most of the widely used programs come with two-dimensional graphics software and three-dimensional modeling software bundled together. Usually, compatible rendering software comes with or is available for these programs.

Any modeling program under consideration should employ what is referred to as *solid modeling*. This means that the forms it generates will appear as solids instead of only "wire frames" and when cut or manipulated will present solid surfaces. By simulating the way physical models behave, solid modeling allows computer-generated models to be manipulated with greater intuitive ease.

Modeling programs can form surfaces by creating polygons or by using *nurbs* (nonuniform rational B-splines). The polygon method works by defining planes with three points and combining them to define forms. The results are angular and not very pliable, as stretching, bending, and folding change the smoothness of objects. The only way this can be overcome is by increasing the number of planes, which in turn increases the data load and slows processing significantly. The polygon method is the easiest way to define surfaces, and since buildings are traditionally made up of planes, most architecture software uses this method.

Nurbs, on the other hand, use curve (spline) equations to define surfaces so that objects can be zoomed in on without any loss in geometrical detail. The nurbs are very pliable, like virtual dough, and are excellent for stretching and folding operations. Advanced animation programs like MAYA support nurbs. MAYA was initially developed to model the organic flowing forms found in nature. Advanced animation programs can define force fields of gravity and wind to affect object behavior and simulate real conditions.

Greg Lynn and Doug Garofalo are two architects who have led the way in exploring the possibilities of architecture conceived through MAYA. Greg Lynn has develop a vocabulary to define modeling elements that includes terms like *blep, blob, flower, shred, skin, teeth, branch/strand,* and *lattice.* He uses this language to talk about the specific operations and forms used in virtual modeling.

One convenient advantage of modeling programs is being able to generate and control complex curvilinear solids. While it can take considerable time to make physical patterns for these forms using traditional methods, the unfold operation found in most modeling programs instantly resolves any form into planar components. These patterns can be printed out and joined at the seams to create almost any form imaginable. The drawback to this capability is that the patterns can become so complex that it is difficult to understand where to join the seams.

Form Z Lofted Nurbs Shape

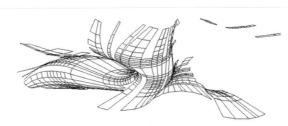

Unfolded Pattern of Nurbs Shape

An important aspect to consider in shopping for software is the ability to translate modeling information between different software packages. Although many companies claim compatibility with other software, even the smallest problems with translation can render this capability useless. For this reason, many designers prefer to use software with all three drawing components from a single source (modeling, two-dimensional graphics, and rendering applications). However, there are programs that are stronger in certain areas of application than others, and it may make sense to use some of these individually, provided they can be successfully integrated into your other software. To allow the user to make an initial test for compatibility, many companies offer sample software that can be downloaded from the World Wide Web.

Although the operation of these programs is beyond the scope of this book, information regarding some of the most popular software is offered in the following section. Most, if not all, of these programs are available for PCs (Windows) and Macintosh platforms, and all employ solid modeling.

See Chapter 7 for a discussion of the use of programs in select design offices.

Software Guide

Over the last five years, digital modeling programs have gained widespread use, with physical models produced directly from digital information on the rise. Although programs such as Rhinoceros and MAYA (developed for the animation industry) have been co-opted by architects, 3D Studio MAX and TriForma remain dominant. Next to these two programs, Form Z enjoys widespread use. While there are a number of lesser-known programs used, most are similar in operation and contribute little that is new to the field of digital modeling. However, one niche program known as Sketch Up is noted for its unique approach to modeling.

Form Z
Company: Autodyssys

This program is easy to learn, relatively intuitive, and inexpensive to purchase. The program models primarily using polygons, but later versions support some nurbs capability. Its rendering capabilities are not very sophisticated, so it is not highly thought of by those wishing to exploit this mode to the fullest. However, many use the program for its modeling properties alone and have no desire to make realistic renderings.

3D Studio Max
Company: Autodesk
(associated with AutoCAD)

This is considered to be a sophisticated program with good rendering capabilities. It is more complicated and takes longer to learn than Form Z, but once learned it can be as easy to run. Professional practices stress the use of the program as completely compatible with AutoCAD and find this to be the most trouble-free method of working between modeling and orthographic drawings.

TriForma
Company: Bentley
(associated with MicroStation)

The same things that can be said about 3-D Studio MAX apply to TriForma. TriForma is a powerful, sophisticated program, and for those who use MicroStation, it provides a seamless program application.

Rhinoceros
Company: RSI 3D Systems and Software

MAYA
Company: Alias

Both Rhinocerous and MAYA are true curve-based programs that support nurbs. Rhino and MAYA were developed to model human forms and are extremely sophisticated in this respect. There is an intuitive connection with these programs that architects appreciate whereby volumes can be directly manipulated. Many find a new perspective in working with programs that were not made by and for architects or engineers.

For animation purposes, gravity and wind can be defined to make objects behave as they would in real space. Architects generally have yet to advance to this level; however, efforts are under way to develop modeling programs that can react to gravity; see Chapter 7.

SketchUp
Company: @Last Software, Inc.

This program is limited in application but is an interesting attempt to reconnect designers with the intuitive operation of the sketching pencil. The main program feature is that of inferring design moves. That is, when the mouse is moved in a particular direction, volumes begin to gain height or width accordingly. This is similar to the way MicroStation and AutoCAD work and eliminates the need to enter coordinates. The process comes close to actual hand sketching but is limited by the program's assumption that all forms are intended to be orthogonal volumes. To deviate from this is cumbersome and can defeat the purpose of the program.

Rapid Prototyping

Over the last ten years, a bridge has been created between physical model building and digital modeling. This bridge is referred to as *rapid prototyping,* or RP. With RP technology, physical models can be made directly from three-dimensional computer models. Although the use of digital modeling programs has become widespread, the direct comprehension offered by the physical model has been missed. To fill this gap, rapid prototype models developed for industrial prototypes have been adopted by architectural design firms.

There are several key reasons RP modeling has made a valuable contribution to the design process.

Interface

One of the main reasons to use RP is in a case where design work is already being developed with digital media (i.e., a modeling program). If this database did not exist, the process could be considerably slower than building paper working models.

Speed

Given that digital information is available, RP models can be made automatically without involving much of the designers' time. Small models take around 12 hours and are usually made at a stopping point in the design process.

Complexity

One of the most common RP modeling tasks is that of making complex curvilinear shapes. This type of form could be made from plastic material such as clay, but conversion into dimensioning systems presents barriers.

Cost

Cost has been an issue with RP models. Typically, information is sent to a company that owns the RP equipment, and for $200 (plus shipping), a small model can be made. Compared to employee costs of a day or two of work, this is a relatively small sum. Compared to an hour of work producing a paper sketch model, it can seem expensive. If multiple RP study models are needed, costs can mount up quickly. The answer to this seems to be in owning RP equipment. The most popular in-house equipment is a powder-based printer made by Z Corporation. Compared to other process and larger equipment, the $30,000 price tag is currently far below that of the nearest competitor. While this cost does not allow every office to purchase, many practices such as Morphosis and Antoine Predock do own their own equipment.

Staging

RP models can be made at any stage, but a typical way of working might be to create a computer-generated massing model, then output a physical model. Next, return to the computer and develop an architectural language, then output a model again. As the project is developed, there might be a switch to paper models to look at larger-scale issues. Due to cost and time, there may be a tendency to produce a limited amount of study models. However, because of the potential for efficiency, models of completed designs are easily justified.

Modification

While it may be possible to modify or edit RP models in some way, they do not lend themselves to this type of direct exploration. Each model stands on its own, and adjustments must be made to the computer model. This is a significant difference from working with paper models.

Hybrid Models

Since RP machinery can make forms that may be difficult to render by hand, many models are made up of a combination of hand-cut parts and RP components.

Finish

Computer-controlled model building is an accurate process; however, due to the way in which the processes works, tooling marks tend to produce a rough appearance. This does not present a problem for study models but requires a finishing treatment if clean, tight surfaces are desired. Sanding, cutting off stems, filling, and painting are common finishing tasks.

Types of Modeling Processes

There are many processes and variations on the basic equipment used to make RP models. A full explanation of each tends to make the field a bit confusing; however, there are really only two basic methods: *additive* and *subtractive*.

Additive

Additive processes build up models by laying down very thin layers or sections of the model. They can do this by spraying melted wax (FMD), spraying glue on powder (powder printers), or producing a chemical reaction that hardens liquid (stereolithography). Additive equipment can be very expensive as the model size becomes larger. To work around this limitation, models can be made in several parts.

There are special uses for each type of process (some are stronger than others); however, the two used most often by archi-tects and other visual designers are stereolithography and powder printers.

Stereolithography

Stereolithography uses a laser to trace a section of the model in liquid. The area traced hardens when hit by the light, then the model bed lowers into the vat of liquid to the depth of the next section (each section is .22 mm thick). In 12 hours or so, the model is complete. Suspended elements and the base of the model are supported by stems made as part of the process. These have to be cut off after the model is complete.

Powder Printers

Powder printers use a vat of powder (commonly plaster) and an ink-jet printer head to spray glue or binder on the powder in thin layers. After a section is sprayed, it hardens and the bed lowers so another section can be added. The models do not need stems to support suspended parts, as the loose powder supports the hardened parts. On completion, models are blown off, and the unused powder is put back in the vat.

Subtractive

Subtractive equipment takes away material by cutting or milling it in sections. To understand the process, picture a spinning drill bit. If the bit is moved sideways after contacting material (commonly foam in architectural models), it can cut a line in the surface. By moving the bit slightly in and out and making many passes, any contour can be cut.

Five-Axis Computer Numerically Controlled (CNC) Milling

To cut away material, the bit needs to be able to approach the model from all sides (five different axes). To accomplish this, the drill head is mounted on a rotating arm, and the work bed is turned automatically to access the underside. The process is often employed when larger models are needed. In some cases, full-scale details and building components are made.

Laser Cutting

While RP modeling is evolving as a complete modeling system, computer-guided laser cutters still have a place in producing components. They can be used to cut flat sheet goods such as styrene and produce a kit of parts for hand assembly. Laser cutters can also be used to etch mullion patterns on plastic, creating highly detailed glazing systems. This type of process lends itself to more finished model building. It is expected that cutting equipment will become more common in-house.

Translation of Files

Before modeling programs can be converted into RP models, the files must be converted to STL files. Drawing programs such as 3-D Studio MAX can convert drawing files to STL as part of their built-in commands. Other programs may need to use a stand-alone program to make the conversion. These files resolve all forms into small triangular facets and then slice them into sections to direct the buildup or cutting of layers.

See Chapter 7 for a discussion of the use of RP in select design offices.

Powder Printer and Laser Cutter

Two of the most popular machines found in architectural offices, due to simple technology and affordability, are shown. Large-capacity equipment is available, but purchasing costs are considerably higher.

The 310 Power Printer from Z Corp
This machine has a bed capacity of an 8-in. cube. If larger models are desired, they must be made in several parts and pieced together. Models take 4 to 12 hours to print depending on size.

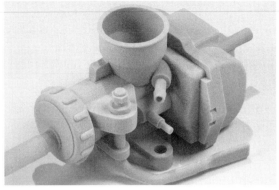

Power-Printed Model
A carburetor printed from the Z Corp printer. Powder comes in different colors, and more expensive models can print parts with several different colors.

Laser Cutter
The cutter traces the outline of parts and operates at faster speeds if etching is required.

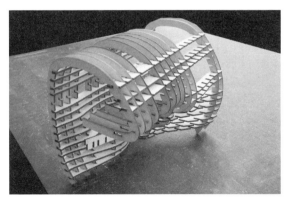

Laser-Cut Model Parts
Model parts can be fed to the laser cutter from modeling programs and divided into discrete sections to cut sheets of cardboard, Plexiglas, or wood.

Resources

Presentation Modeling Books

Highly detailed presentation models are usually built after design work is completed and can make only limited contributions to the design process. However, there are times, such as for elaborate client or marketing presentations, when detailed material simulation is called for. The following books offer information concerning these types of presentation models.

Scale Models: Houses of the 20th Century, Friedrich Kurrent, ed. Translated from German into English, Gail Schamberger. Basel, Boston, Berlin: Birkhauser, 1999.

Architectural Models: Construction Techniques, Wolfgang Knoll and Martin Hechinger. New York: McGraw-Hill, 1992.

The Art of the Architectural Model, Akiko Busch. New York: Design Press, 1991.

Architectural and Interior Models, second edition, Sanford Hohauser. New York: Van Nostrand Reinhold, 1982, 1993.

Computer Modeling Books

For further research, the books listed below discuss computer modeling and various approaches to it.

Folds, Bodies and Blobs: Collected Essays, Greg Lynn. Brussels: La Lettre Volee, 1998.

Architecture Laboratories, Greg Lynn and Hani Rashid. New York: Distributed Art Publishers, 2002.

Folding in Architecture, Greg Lynn. New York: Wiley, 2004.

The CAD Design Studio: 3D Modeling as Fundamental Design Skill, Stephen Jacobs. New York: McGraw-Hill, 1991.

Computer Modeling Programs

3D Studio MAX (AutoCAD)
www.autodesk.com

TriForma (MicroStation)
www.bentley.com

Form Z
www.autodyssys.com

MAYA
www.alias.com

Rhinoceros
www.rsi.gmbn.de

SketchUp
www.sketchup.com

Design Software

Photoshop and InDesign CS
www.adobe.com
1-800-833-6687

QuarkXPress
www.quark.com
1-800-676-4575

Digital Cameras

Nikon Cameras
www.nikonusa.com

Canon Cameras
www.powershot.com

Rapid Prototyping Services

ProtoCam
www.protocam.com
Services: Stereolithography (SLA)
Selective laser sintering (SLS)

Quickparts
www.quickparts.com
Services: Stereolithography (SLA)
Selective laser sintering (SLS)
Fused deposition modeling (FDM)

CTEK, LLC
1402 Morgan Circle
Tustin, CA 92710
www.ctek.us
Services: 5-axis CNC modeling

Rojac
www.rojac.com
Services: 5-axis CNC modeling

Rapid Prototyping Equipment

Z Corporation
32 Second Avenue
Burlington, MA 01803
www.zcorp.com
Equipment: Powder printers

3D Systems
26081 Avenue Hall
Valencia, CA 91355
www.3dsystems.com
Equipment: Multi-jet modeling (MJM)
    5-axis CNC Modeling

Stratasys Inc.
14950 Martin Dr.
Eden Prairie, MN 55344-2020
www.stratasys.com
Equipment: Fused deposition modeler (FDM)
5-axis CNC modeling

Sanders Prototype Inc.
P.O. Box 540
Pine Valley Mill
Wilton, NH 03086
www.sanders-prototype.com
Equipment: Stereolithography (SLA)

Supply Sources

Most of the basic modeling supplies can be purchased at local art supply stores or campus bookstores. If stores are not available in your area, several chain stores sell through the mail. Two well-known stores are Charrette and Dick Blick.

Charrette
31 Olympia Avenue
Box 4010
Woburn, MA 01888-9820
1-800-367-3729
E-mail: Custserv@charrette.com

Dick Blick Art Materials
P.O. Box 1267
150 East Galesburg, IL 61402
1-800-723-2787
www.dickblick.com

Many of the materials used in model making can be found in hobby shops and hardware stores. These include lichen and model trees, wood and plastic sticks, balsa, basswood sheets, modeling plywood, metal rods, bronze and aluminum modeling sheets, small metal parts, sandpaper, molding plaster, PermaScene, and spray paint.

Plastic sheets for windows can be found at Plexiglas suppliers. Thin plastic cover sheets or inexpensive picture frames carried by variety and drugstores can also be used. For very thin window material, sheets of acetate can be purchased at art supply stores and are usually available in several thicknesses.

Some of the more specialized drafting and cutting equipment, such as Acu-Arcs, can be found at architectural printing companies and through Charrette.

Common wood, such as pine, spruce, and plywood, can be purchased at building supply stores. Blocks of hardwood, such as basswood, poplar, and mahogany, can be found at hardwood building suppliers.

Although a range of metal components such as aluminum tubes and angle iron can be found at well-stocked hardware stores, steel supply yards will be the most likely source for square stock, steel rods, and heavy-gauge sheets.

Sheet metal suppliers that stock metal ductwork, flashing, and gutter materials can be good sources for rolls of copper and galvanized sheets.

Large quantities of molding plaster in 90-lb. bags can be found at drywall supply houses.

The following people have contributed models and built work to the text and are credited for their contribution to the diversity and strength of its contents.

Academic Architecture Programs
The Catholic University, School of Architecture and Planning
Studio Critic: Professor George J. Martin

Ali Menke—page 13, bottom right; page 100, top left, bottom left, top right, bottom right; page 101, top left, bottom left, top middle, bottom middle, top right, bottom right.

Clemson University College of Architecture, Arts and Humanities
Studio Critic: Lynn Craig

World Trade Tower model—page 20, bottom left; page 64, top right.

Studio Critic: Criss Mills

Third-year design: *Gabriella Bumgartner*—page 58, top right, bottom right. *Rene Binder*—page 69, top right, bottom right.

Studio Critics: Criss Mills, Harry Harritos

Third year design: Damz Adams—page 75, top middle, bottom middle. *Allison Ford*—

page 87, top right. *Andrew Norton*—page 87, bottom right. *Robert Thompson*—page 91, top left, bottom left, top right, bottom right; page 96, top left, bottom left, top right, bottom right. *Nathaniel Wood*—page 94, bottom left, top right, bottom right. *Seth McDowell*—page 12, bottom right; page 23, bottom left; page 92, bottom left, top middle, bottom middle, top right, bottom right. *Jenny Schildecker*—page 49, top left; page 97, bottom right, top middle, bottom middle, top right, bottom right. *Betty Prime*—page 10, bottom right; page 141, top middle. *Manson Currence*—page 87, top left. *Kenneth Babinchak*—page 18; bottom left, page 87, middle right.

Studio Critic: Harry Harritos

First-year studio: *Michael Brown*—page 24, bottom left.

Studio Critic: Criss Mills

Second-year studio: *Scott Lagstrom*—page 77, left. *Michael Brown*—page 25, bottom right; page 26, top left. *Joe McCoy*—page 76, top left, bottom left, top right, bottom right; page 77, bottom right, right; page 99, bottom left, top middle, bottom middle, top right, bottom right; page 223, top left; page 225, top right, bottom right. *Frayssee Lyle*—page 67, top right, bottom right. *Luke McDaniel*—

page 16, bottom right; page 18, bottom right; page 87, bottom left.

Studio Critics: Criss Mills, Robert Hogan, Martha Skinner

Third-year studio: *Brenna Costello*—page 95, top left, bottom left, top right. *Glen Timmons*—page 72, top middle, bottom middle. *Liza Lewellan*—page 72, top right, bottom right.

Studio Critic: Harry Harritos

Third-year studio: *Paul Schelechow*—page 98, top left, bottom left, top right. *Kevin Kievit*—page 17, bottom right; page 18, top right.

Studio Critic: Robert Miller

MARCH graduate thesis: *Rob Moehring*—page 81, top left, bottom left; page 203, bottom right. *Sidney Mullins, Robert Lipka*—page 75, top left, bottom left. *David Jones*—page 70, top left. *Joshua Allison, Brian Couch, Nikos Katsibas, Kim Kraft, Thomas Reidy*—page 19, bottom right.

Grad 1: *Kenneth Huggins, Sonia Alvarado, Trifon Dinkov, Bill D'Onofrio, Chris Karpus, Ansely Manuel, Bart Shorack*—page 19, top left. *Sallie Hambright*—page 59, top left.

Studio Critic: Ray Huff

Grad 1: *Shane Knight*—page 18, top left; page 20, top left.

Studio Critics: Robert Miller, Ray Huff

Third-year, Fourth-year, Grad 1: *Bryan Atwood, Michelle Bellon, Emily Cox, Amy Finley, Lindsey Georges, Bridget Gilles, Sallie Hambright, Gregory Huddy, Alicia Reed, Justin Smith, Peter Szczelina, Po Tin, Joel Wenzel*—page 208, top right. *David Pastre, Lou Markovic, Michael Osman, Amy Clement, Kelly Gordon, Brad Brown*—page 208, top left.

Studio Critic: Kemp Mooney

Grad 1 design: *Thad Rhoden, Lindsey Sabo, Yuko Murata*—page 25, top right.

Studio Critic: Ron Real

Second-year design: *Knox Jolly*—page 144, bottom left; page 232, bottom right.

Studio Critic: Robert Hogan (could be Martha Skinner)

Second-year design: *Lauren Holmes*—page 157, top right.

Studio Critic: Keith Green

March Thesis studio design: *Steven Kendall Keutzer*—page 157, bottom right.

Studio Critic: Douglas Hecker

March Thesis studio: *Robert Kline*—page 159, top left; page 207, bottom right.

Studio Critic: Franca Tribiano

Grad 1 design: *Christopher Palkowitsch*—page 78, top right.

Studio Critic: Robert Bruhns

Fourth-year design: *Scott Shaw*—page 89, top left, bottom left, top right.

Florida International University School of Architecture

Studio Critic: Rene Gonzalez

Design 1: *Amparo Vollert*—page 14, top right. *Marcus Centurion*—page 163, top right. *Angel Suarez*—page 59, top right, bottom right. *Desmond Gelman*—page 71, top left, bottom left.

Design 3: *Maria Pellot*—page 14, bottom right. *Mauricio Del Valle*—page 74, top left, bottom left.

Design 7: *Mark Marine*—page 14, top left; page 74, top middle, bottom middle. *David Boira*—page 26, bottom left.

Georgia Institute of Technology College of Architecture

Studio Critic: Bruce Lonnman

First-year design: page 13, top right; page 19, bottom left; *Josh Andrews*—page 56, top right, bottom right. *John Sitton*—page 142, bottom left; page 215, bottom right. *Trent Hunter*—page 61, top left, bottom left.

Studio Critic: Lee Kean

Second-year design: *Greg Sugano*—page 13, bottom right; page 74, top right, bottom right. *Brian Karlowitz*—page 145, top left, bottom middle.

Studio Critic: Tahar Messadi

Third-year design: *Micah Hall*—page 14, bottom left.

Studio Critic: Harris Dimitropoulos

Mike Piper—page 50, bottom left; page 61, top right, bottom right; page 64, bottom left; page 80, top left, bottom left; page 216, bottom right. *Casper Voogt*—page 67, top left. *Bernard Gingras*—page 67, bottom left. *Jason Van Nest*—page 143, bottom left, bottom middle. *Sam Hoang*—page 215, top right.

Studio Critic: Denise Dumais

Fourth-year design: *Cameron Beasley*—page 85, top middle, bottom middle.

Studio Critic: Michael Gamble

Graduate design studio: *Rob Bartlett*—page 15, bottom right; page 143, top right; page 151, bottom right; page 202, top right. *Tim Black*—page 20, top right. *Meridith Colon*—page 64, top left. *Daniel Maas*—page 156, bottom left. *Jason Vetne*—page 203, top right.

Studio Critic: Chris Jarrett

Graduate design studio: *Lyle Woodall*—page 84, top right. *Garvin Smith*—page 64, bottom right. *David Guirdry*—page 85, top right; page 161, top left.

Studio Critic: Charles Rudolph

Graduate design studio: *Troy Stenlez*—page 13, top left; page 61, top middle; page 93, top left, top right, bottom left, bottom middle, bottom right; page 215, top left. *Daniel Maas*—page 23, top left.

Studio Critics: Charles Rudolph, George Epolito

High school career discovery class: page 217, top right.

Iowa State University Architecture Department

Studio Critic: Karen Bermann

Pre-Architecture Studio: *Michelle Swanson*—page 58, top left, bottom left. *Kate Podany*—page 217, bottom left. *Jim Hosek, Mike Grace, Kip Cox, Stephanie Clay*—page 69, bottom middle. *Amy Skinner*—page 73, top middle , bottom left, bottom middle. *Lindsey Bresser, Melissa Myers, Jason Kohler, Nick Senske*—page 73, top left.

The Ohio State University Austin E. Knowlton School of Architecture

Studio Critic: Bruce Lonnman

First-year design: page 13, bottom left; page 71, top right.

Studio Critic: Criss Mills

Third-year design: page 26, bottom right; page 70, bottom right; page 83, bottom right.

Southern California Institute of Architecture

Studio Critics: Tom Buresh, Annie Chu, Perry Kulper

Graduate design studio: *Cameron Beasley*—page 19, top right; page 73, top right, bottom right; page 217, bottom right.

Southern Polytechnic State University School of Architecture

Studio Critic: Frank Venning

Vertical design studio: *Chris Crossman*—page 139, top left; page 140, bottom left. *Clyde Clair*—page 16, bottom left. *Paul Deeley*—page 17, bottom left. *Ruben Aniekwu*—page 10, bottom left; page 145, bottom middle. *Chris Garrett*—page 21, top left; page 48, top right. *Thad Truett*—page 21, bottom left; page 48, bottom left. *Scott Jeffries*—page 139, bottom right; page 144, bottom middle. *Don Son*—page 143, bottom right. *Tyrone Marshall*—page 144, top right. *Karin Keuller*—page 145, top right; page 146, top right AD59; page 161, bottom middle; page 216, top left. *Mike Nash*—page 161, top left. *Bart Stone*—page 155, top right.

Studio Critics: Howard Itzkowitz, Jordan Williams

Second-year design: *Scott Fleming*—page 21, bottom right; page 50, top right; page 86, bottom right. *Steve Damico*—page 61, bottom middle; page 85, bottom right.

Syracuse University School of Architecture

Studio Critic: Bruce Lonnman

First-year design: page 15, top right; page 22, top right; page 23, top right; page 56, top left; page 59, top middle, bottom middle; page 85, top left.

Structures: page 25, top left; page 25, bottom left.

Tuskegee University Department of Architecture

Studio Critics: Criss Mills, Patricia Kerlin, George Epolito

Second-year design: *Danielle Dixon*—page 15, bottom left. *Allen Pickstock*—page 71, bottom middle; page 140, bottom middle; page 69, top middle. *Grant Kolbe*—page 71, bottom right. *Dayton Schroeter*—page 140, top left; page 214, top right. *Terrance Charles*—page 144, top left.

Studio Critic: Criss Mills

Fourth-year design: *Stephen Douglas*—page 70, top right; page 71, top middle; page 216, top right.

Studio Critic: Criss Mills, Jack Ames

Thesis studio: *Leslie Musikavanhu*—foreword. *Joaniticka Whitlow*—page 12, top left. *Robert Comery*—page 12, bottom left; page 80, top right, bottom right. *Emilee Eide, Todd Niemiec*—page 48, top left.

University of the Arab Emirates

Studio Critic: Bechir Kenzari

Salha Suliman Al Hassani—page 147, bottom left. *Hanadi Rashed Al Zaabi*—page 147, bottom right.

University of Arkansas School of Architecture

Studio Critics: Tim DeNoble, Michael Bruno, Tad Gloeckler, Steven Miller

Second-year design: *Arthur Banks*—page 22, bottom right. *Juan Andrad*—page 24, top left.

University of Auckland School of Architecture

Studio Critic: Beshire Kenzari

Design 2 and Design 3: *Kenneth Sin*—page 154, bottom right; page 207, top right. *Melanie Tonkin*—page 140, bottom right. *Lucy Gauntlett*—page 146, bottom right.

Studio Critic: Keith Green

Melinda Trask—page 78, top left. *Biancha Pohio*—page 78, bottom right.

University of North Carolina at Charlotte College of Architecture

Studio Critic: Jose Gamez

Fourth-year design: *Zeb Smith*—page 90, top left, bottom left, top right, bottom right.

University of South Florida School of Architecture and Community Design

Studio Critic: George Epolito

Second-year design: *Mike Dailey, Vanessa Estrada*—page 75, top right, bottom right.

University of Southwestern Louisiana School of Architecture

Studio Critics: Hector Lasala, Ed Gaskin

Basic Design Studio: *Jason Simeneaux*—page 79, top left, top right, bottom left, bottom right.

Architecture Design III: *Randy Damico*—page 12, top right; page 24, bottom right; page 81, top right, bottom right; page 88, top left, top right, bottom left, bottom middle, bottom right; page 217, top left.

Wentworth Institute of Technology

Studio Critic: Professor Dr. Sigrun Prahl

Design V Housing, Fall 2003: *David Noe, Erick Swenson*—page 15, top left; page 147, top left; page 225, top middle, bottom middle.

Design Professionals
Jack Ames, Architect

Page 151, top right.

Borden Partnership llp

Page 194, top left, top right, bottom right; page 195, top left, bottom left, top right.

Robert Bruhns/Jack Ames

Page 140, top right.

Callas, Shortridge Architects— by Steven Shortridge

Page 170, top left, top right, bottom left, bottom right; page 171, top left, top right, bottom left, bottom middle, bottom right.

Charleston Civic Design Center

Page 20, bottom right; page 48, bottom right; page 49, bottom right; page 208, bottom left, bottom right.

Coop Himmelb(l)au

Page 196, top right, bottom right; page 197, top left, bottom left, bottom middle, top right, middle right, bottom right; page 198, top left, bottom left, top right; page 199, top, middle, bottom.

Courtesy of Eisenman Architects

Page 182, bottom right; page 183, top left, bottom left, top middle, top right, bottom right.

All Images Courtesy of Garofalo Architects and Iñigo Manglano-Ovalie

Page 188, top right, bottom right; page 189, top left, bottom left, top middle, bottom middle, top right, bottom right.

Copyright Gehry Partners, LLP

Page 184, bottom right; page 185, top left, bottom left, top middle, bottom middle, top right, bottom right; page 186, top left, top middle, bottom middle, top right; page 187, bottom left, top left, top right.

Bruce Lonnman

Page 21, top right.

MC2 Architects Inc.

Page 16, top left; page 17, top left; page 19, bottom middle; page 50, bottom right; page 63 bottom right; page 144, bottom right; page 155 bottom right; page 156, top right; page 157, bottom left, top left; page 172, top left, top right, bottom left, bottom right; page 217, bottom middle.

Courtesy of Richard Meier and Partners Architects

Page 191, top left, bottom lef, top right.

Morphosis

Rensselaer Electronic Media and Performing Arts Center Competition, 2001, Troy, NY. Team: Principal/Lead Designer: *Thom Mayne;* Project Designers: *Edgar Hatcher, Chris Warren;* Project Assistants: *Hanjo Gelink, Carlos Gomez, Eghard Woeste*—page 179, top left, top right.

Antoine Predock

Page 192, bottom left; page 193, top left, bottom left, top right.

Roto Architects Inc.

Page 174, top left, top right, bottom left, bottom right; page 175, top left, top right, bottom left; page 176, top left, top right, bottom left.

Rowhouse Architects Inc.

Page 23, bottom right; page 24, top right; page 50, bottom middle; page 65, top right, bottom right; page 82, middle bottom.

Ryobi Technologies, Inc.

Page 209, top left, bottom left, top right; page 210, top left, bottom left, top right, bottom right.

Mack Scogin Merrill Elam Architects
(formerly Scogin, Elam and Bray Architects)

Page 166, top right, bottom left, bottom right; page 167, top left, top right, bottom left, bottom middle, bottom right; page 168, top left, top right, bottom left, bottom middle, bottom right; page 169, top left, top right, bottom left.

Fine Arts Center, University of Connecticut at Storrs, Mack Scogin with Merrill Elam; Design Team: *David Yocum, Eulho Suh, Chris Hoxie, Cameron Wu, Cecelia Tham, Barnum Tiller, Brian Bell, Helen Han, Kenneth Cowart, Adam Stillman, Helen Chu, Katherine Bray;* Stereolithography Consultant: *American Precision Prototyping, Jason Dickman;* Theater Planning and Design Consultant: *Fisher Dachs Associates, Joshua Dachs;* Performing and Visual Arts Construction Cost Management: *Donnell Consultants, Sean Ryan;* Landscape Architects: *Michael Van Valkenburgh Associates, Matthew Urbanski;* Engineers: *Arup, Caroline Fitzgerald, Neil Woodger, Raj Patel;* Associate Architect: *Lloyd Taft Architect, Lloyd Taft;* Lighting Consultant: *Lam Partners, Bob Osten, Justin Brown*—page 181, top right, bottom middle, bottom right; page 227, top left.

Pittsburgh Children's Museum, Mack Scogin with Merrill Elam; Design Team: *Cecelia Tham, David Yocum, Brian Bell, Tim Harrison, Barnum Tiller, Ted Paxton, Charlotte Henderson, Hillary Ingram, Penn Ruderman, Angela Pearce;* Special Consultants (3D modeling preparation for translation into stereolithography) Model: *Kimo Griggs Architects, Kimo Griggs*—page 180, top right, bottom right; page 181, top left, bottom left.

Jack Thalinious

Page 64, bottom middle; page 214, bottom right; page 156, bottom right.

Frank Venning Architect

Page 16, top right; page 214, bottom left.

Venning, Attwood and Kean Architects Inc.

Page 173, top left, top right, bottom left, bottom right.

Z Corporation

Page 232, top left, top right.

Photography Credits
Christopher Agosta

page 180, bottom right; page 181, bottom left.

Assassi/Productions

Page 176, top left, bottom left.

Borden Partnership

Page 194, top left, top right, bottom right; page 195, top left, bottom left, top right.

Tom Bonner

Page 197, bottom left.

Lloyd Bray

Page 166, top right, bottom left; page 167, bottom left; page 168, top left, top right, bottom middle, bottom left; page 169, top left, top right.

Benny Chan/Fotoworks

Page 174, top right, bottom left, bottom right.

Coop Himmelb(l)au

Page 196, top right; page 197, top right, middle right; page 199, top.

Susan Desko

Page 167, top right.

Courtesy of Eisenman Architects

Page 182, bottom right; page 183, top left, bottom left, top middle, top right, bottom right.

All Images Courtesy of Garofalo Architects and Iñigo Manglano-Ovalle

Page 188, top right, bottom right; page 189, top left, bottom left, top middle, bottom middle, top right, bottom right.

Copyright Gehry Partners, LLP

Page 184, bottom right; page 185, top left, bottom left, top middle, bottom middle, top right, bottom right; page 186, top left, top middle, bottom middle, top right; page 187, bottom left, top left, top right.

Armin Hess

Page 197, bottom right.

Timothy Hursley

Page 166, bottom right; page 168, bottom right; page 169, bottom left.

Courtesy of Richard Meier and Partners Architects

Page 191, top left, bottom left, top right.

Kelly Mills

Page 220, bottom middle, bottom right; page 221, top left.

Photo Copyright Robert Reck

Page 192, bottom right; page 193, top left, bottom left, top right.

Jeff Roberson

Ali Menke—page 13, bottom left; page 100, top left, bottom left2, top right, bottom right; page 101, top left, bottom left, top middle, bottom middle, top right, bottom right.

Roto Architects Inc.

Page 174, top left; page 175, top left, right, bottom left; page 176, top right.

Steven Shortridge

Page 170, top left, top right; page 171, top left, top right, bottom left, bottom middle, bottom right.

Sigrun Prahl and Erick Swenson

Page 15, top left; page 147, top left; page 225, top middle, bottom middle.

Eulho Suh

Page 181, top right, bottom right.

Frank Venning

Page 173, top left, top right, bottom left, bottom right.

David Yocum

Page 167, top left, bottom right, bottom middle.

Marcel Weber

Page 199, middle, bottom.

Brandon Welling

Page 179, top right, top left.

Copyright by Gerald Zugmann

Page 196, bottom right; page 197, top left; page 198, top left, bottom left, top right.

Z Corporation

Page 232, top left, top right.

INDEX